KNOWLEDGE MANAGEMENT IN ACTION

IFIP – The International Federation for Information Processing

IFIP was founded in 1960 under the auspices of UNESCO, following the First World Computer Congress held in Paris the previous year. An umbrella organization for societies working in information processing, IFIP's aim is two-fold: to support information processing within its member countries and to encourage technology transfer to developing nations. As its mission statement clearly states,

> *IFIP's mission is to be the leading, truly international, apolitical organization which encourages and assists in the development, exploitation and application of information technology for the benefit of all people.*

IFIP is a non-profitmaking organization, run almost solely by 2500 volunteers. It operates through a number of technical committees, which organize events and publications. IFIP's events range from an international congress to local seminars, but the most important are:

- The IFIP World Computer Congress, held every second year;
- Open conferences;
- Working conferences.

The flagship event is the IFIP World Computer Congress, at which both invited and contributed papers are presented. Contributed papers are rigorously refereed and the rejection rate is high.

As with the Congress, participation in the open conferences is open to all and papers may be invited or submitted. Again, submitted papers are stringently refereed.

The working conferences are structured differently. They are usually run by a working group and attendance is small and by invitation only. Their purpose is to create an atmosphere conducive to innovation and development. Refereeing is less rigorous and papers are subjected to extensive group discussion.

Publications arising from IFIP events vary. The papers presented at the IFIP World Computer Congress and at open conferences are published as conference proceedings, while the results of the working conferences are often published as collections of selected and edited papers.

Any national society whose primary activity is in information may apply to become a full member of IFIP, although full membership is restricted to one society per country. Full members are entitled to vote at the annual General Assembly, National societies preferring a less committed involvement may apply for associate or corresponding membership. Associate members enjoy the same benefits as full members, but without voting rights. Corresponding members are not represented in IFIP bodies. Affiliated membership is open to non-national societies, and individual and honorary membership schemes are also offered.

KNOWLEDGE MANAGEMENT IN ACTION

IFIP 20th World Computer Congress, Conference on Knowledge Management in Action, September 7-10, 2008, Milano, Italy

Edited by

Mark Ackerman
University of Michigan
USA

Rose Dieng-Kuntz
INRIA-Sophia Antipolis
France

Carla Simone
University of Milano-Bicocca
Italy

Volker Wulf
University of Siegen
Germany

Springer

Knowledge Management in Action

Edited by Mark Ackerman, Rose Dieng-Kuntz, Carla Simone and Volker Wulf

p. cm. (IFIP International Federation for Information Processing, a Springer Series in Computer Science)

ISSN: 1571-5736 / 1861-2288 (Internet)

ISBN: 978-1-4419-3504-5 eISBN: 978-0-387-09659-9

Printed on acid-free paper

9 8 7 6 5 4 3 2 1

springer.com

IFIP 2008 World Computer Congress (WCC'08)

Message from the Chairs

Every two years, the International Federation for Information Processing hosts a major event which showcases the scientific endeavours of its over one hundred Technical Committees and Working Groups. 2008 sees the 20th World Computer Congress (WCC 2008) take place for the first time in Italy, in Milan from 7-10 September 2008, at the MIC - Milano Convention Centre. The Congress is hosted by the Italian Computer Society, AICA, under the chairmanship of Giulio Occhini.

The Congress runs as a federation of co-located conferences offered by the different IFIP bodies, under the chairmanship of the scientific chair, Judith Bishop. For this Congress, we have a larger than usual number of thirteen conferences, ranging from Theoretical Computer Science, to Open Source Systems, to Entertainment Computing. Some of these are established conferences that run each year and some represent new, breaking areas of computing. Each conference had a call for papers, an International Programme Committee of experts and a thorough peer reviewed process. The Congress received 661 papers for the thirteen conferences, and selected 375 from those representing an acceptance rate of 56% (averaged over all conferences).

An innovative feature of WCC 2008 is the setting aside of two hours each day for cross-sessions relating to the integration of business and research, featuring the use of IT in Italian industry, sport, fashion and so on. This part is organized by Ivo De Lotto. The Congress will be opened by representatives from government bodies and Societies associated with IT in Italy.

This volume is one of fourteen volumes associated with the scientific conferences and the industry sessions. Each covers a specific topic and separately or together they form a valuable record of the state of computing research in the world in 2008. Each volume was prepared for publication in the Springer IFIP Series by the conference's volume editors. The overall Chair for all the volumes published for the Congress is John Impagliazzo.

For full details on the Congress, refer to the webpage http://www.wcc2008.org.

Judith Bishop, South Africa, Co-Chair, International Program Committee
Ivo De Lotto, Italy, Co-Chair, International Program Committee
Giulio Occhini, Italy, Chair, Organizing Committee
John Impagliazzo, United States, Publications Chair

WCC 2008 Scientific Conferences

TC12	**AI**	Artificial Intelligence 2008
TC10	**BICC**	Biologically Inspired Cooperative Computing
WG 5.4	**CAI**	Computer-Aided Innovation (Topical Session)
WG 10.2	**DIPES**	Distributed and Parallel Embedded Systems
TC14	**ECS**	Entertainment Computing Symposium
TC3	**ED_L2L**	Learning to Live in the Knowledge Society
WG 9.7 **TC3**	**HCE3**	History of Computing and Education 3
TC13	**HCI**	Human Computer Interaction
TC8	**ISREP**	Information Systems Research, Education and Practice
WG 12.6	**KMIA**	Knowledge Management in Action
TC2 **WG 2.13**	**OSS**	Open Source Systems
TC11	**IFIP SEC**	Information Security Conference
TC1	**TCS**	Theoretical Computer Science

IFIP

- is the leading multinational, apolitical organization in Information and Communications Technologies and Sciences
- is recognized by United Nations and other world bodies
- represents IT Societies from 56 countries or regions, covering all 5 continents with a total membership of over half a million
- links more than 3500 scientists from Academia and Industry, organized in more than 101 Working Groups reporting to 13 Technical Committees
- sponsors 100 conferences yearly providing unparalleled coverage from theoretical informatics to the relationship between informatics and society including hardware and software technologies, and networked information systems

Details of the IFIP Technical Committees and Working Groups can be found on the website at http://www.ifip.org.

Table of Contents

Preface

Knowledge management (KM) is more and more recognized as a key factor of success for organisations: not only structured companies, but also virtual enterprises, networks of organisations or even virtual communities. These organisations of different kinds, are becoming increasingly aware of the need to collect, organise, mobilise, increase, in sum manage, the knowledge characterising their ability to stay alive, adapt and evolve in a turbulent context. Through various organisational and technological approaches, KM aims at improving knowledge access, sharing and reuse as well as new knowledge creation. KMIA 2008 highlights problems, requirements and solutions that are derived from actual, concrete experiences.

The fourteen papers accepted at KMIA 2008 give various answers to the following questions:

What organisational strategies can enable to enact and promote KM within organisations? How to link these organisational strategies with the ICT technology?

Organisational strategies can be related to the evolution of the organisation itself or to its environment: intra-organisational and inter-organisational strategies can thus be distinguished. Some papers emphasize the importance of collaboration and knowledge transfer for team work and collaborative projects that may be intra-organisational or inter-organisational (e.g. inter-organisational outsourcing relationships).

Strategies for designing and manufacturing innovative products are recognised as crucial for enterprises that operate in competitive sectors.

Networks of organisations can help to improve the competitiveness of these organisations: KM can thus enhance competency management in such networks and help an organisation to find relevant costumers, suppliers, or cooperation partners.

Power relationships in an organisation can also influence the KM practices.

What are the various kinds of knowledge, application domains, organisational structures, and their implication on KM?

Various typologies of knowledge were proposed in literature: tacit knowledge, explicit knowledge, know-how, knowledge mobilised by various types of competencies… These various kinds of knowledge are exploited in some papers.

Some KM solutions rely on profiles of organisation competencies and activities. The importance of competencies for innovative product design strategy in competitive sectors is also stressed.

The KMIA papers present applications in medical domain (clinical pathways, dementia management and support system), in automotive industry (design and manufacturing of complex mechanical products), in software design, in environmental planning and in financial domain. Examples of scenarios studied are: project memory, decision support, participatory planning or inter-organisational competency management.

What methods and approaches can be adopted for the design of KM solutions?

Several papers rely on empirical studies for designing a KM solution: e.g. empirical study on a software enterprise, or empirical study on networking needs in small and medium enterprises (SMEs) in Information Technology (IT) domain, or analysis of an experience inof participatory planning in environmental domain. One paper adopt the business ethnography methodology.

What techniques and technologies can be adopted for sustainable KM solutions?

The technical solutions offered by the papers rely on document management techniques, document retrieval, contact management, decision-support systems, memory support systems, ontology-based systems, or knowledge discovery techniques.

For enhancing cooperation among organisations, some papers offer tools aimed at improving mutual awareness among a network of organisations or suggest the use of reusable patterns for supporting collaborative knowledge transfer and for inter-organisational outsourcing relationships.

What are the critical success factors for KM socio-technical solutions?

Relying on a participatory approach with the stakeholders, and with the involvement of end-users and of management, among others, and taking into account the organisational strategy and the collaboration processes in the organisation seem necessary for a successful KM solution.

In some organisations (such as hospitals), a KM solution must take into account the fact that expertise and experience are distributed over different organisational levels and different professions.

The need to take into account the context and the processes is also emphasized: context in clinical pathways, context-sensitive assistant.

Software enterprises adopting End-User Development need to take into account processes of knowledge diffusion not only in the client organisation, but also in their customer-producer relationships.

How to evaluate KM applications in real situations? What are the lessons-learned in each phase of the KM application life-cycle, from conception up to continuous adaptation?

Several case studies are described in the papers: case study about clinical pathways in medical domain, empirical study on the networking needs among

SME in the IT domain, trials in a financial to evaluate the patterns proposed for supporting collaborative knowledge transfer.

Several authors rely on a participatory approach, they derive the chosen KM solution from the organisational strategy and from the analysis of relevant case studies and they evaluate the KM solution in various contexts.

The proceedings present successively the following papers:

- In "KT" CarePacks - A Collaboration Patterns for Knowledge Transfer. Learning form IS/IT - Outsourcing Case at a Swiss Financial Institution", Malgorzata Bugajska presents the "pattern" approach enabling to describe solutions for recurring problems. Patterns for sustainable knowledge transfer for outsourcing relationships are offered through CarePacks – reusable patterns for supporting act of collaborative knowledge transfer. The paper also presents lessons learned from introducing such patterns in a financial institution.
- In "Core Knowledge Management in a Designer Community of the Automotive Field", Stefania Bandini, Sara Manzoni and Fabio Sartori discuss a conceptual and computational approach to the design of KM systems to support people involved in the design and manufacturing of complex mechanical products. They develop an IDS system for the acquisition, representation and use of knowledge of expert designers working in an enterprise in automotive industry.
- In "Knowledge Artifacts as Bridges between Theory and Practice: The Clinical Pathway case", Federico Cabitza, Carla Simone and Marcello Sarini analyse the definition, use and maintainance of Clinical Pathways in hospitals and their different roles for bridging medical knowledge with the related practices by which physicians deal with a specific care problem. This case stresses the need of an integrated approach towards the computer-based support of information and knowledge management in rapidly evolving cooperative work settings.
- In "Managing Knowledge in Urban Planning: Can Memory Support Systems Help?", Adele Celino, Grazia Concilio and Anna De Liddo analyse an experience of participatory planning in environmental domain. They stress the interest of memory support systems in such planning processes as means to capture the argumentation chains produced along the planned actions and supporting them. They present the first results of a research project aiming at developing such a memory support system.
- In "Building a Framework for Actions and Roles in Organizational Knowledge Transfer", Alexander Hoffmann presents a framework that structures roles and actions relevant in organisational knowledge transfer scenarios and that is useful for identifying and classifying factors which leverage or prevent knowledge transfer.
- In "CoLinK: Cooperative Knowledge Management for Engineering Teams", Michael Klingemann and Juergen Friedrich present CoLinK a prototype for a

process-oriented KM system useful in a participatory design project. CoLinK allows engineers to jointly model projects with generic process descriptions augmented with knowledge annotations during each project. These engineers thus constitute a virtual engineering community within the enterprise and beyond. The CoLinK system offers both document management and contact management.

- In "Conceptual Model of Target Activity as Tool for Developing Management and Support System for Dementia Care", Helena Lindgren presents a case study analysing the process of investigating suspected dementia in patient cases were analysed. The resulting model captures structures and required knowledge at different levels of care, while providing a perception of use context. The decision-support system DMSS (Dementia Management and Support System) is adapted to different use environments.
- In "On Problems, Requirements and Solution Approaches when Supporting Knowledge Intensive Processes in Industry", Christian Luetke Entrup and Thomas Barth aim at providing support of knowledge intensive processes by analysing similarities among product data, and by offering retrieval of the relevant knowledge-related documents in the context of a given process in the domain of automotive supplier industry.
- In "Third Generation Knowledge Management in Action: Relational Practices in Swiss Companies", Jens O. Meissner and Patricia Wolf show the relevance of third generation KM concepts to explain relational practices in contexts of face-to-face interaction and virtual communication. Scharmer's Concept of Self-transcending Knowledge and Snowden's Knowledge-Ecology-Approach 'Cynefin' enable to develop a third generation KM framework that highlights the critical role of relational practices for KM.
- In "Knowledge Management-in-action in EUD-oriented Software Enterprises", Bernhard Nett, Johanna Meurer and Gunnar Stevens use Business Ethnography methodology for analysing practices of small software enterprises and their potential to acquire, secure and use knowledge about end-users of their products, so as to enhance End-User Development.
- In "Business Finder – A Tool for Regional Networking among Organizations", Tim Reichling, Volker Wulf and Benjamin Moos present Business Finder, a tool for improving mutual awareness among small and medium enterprises (SME) in a regional network. The design of this tool is based on an empirical study into networking needs among SME in the IT domain. Relying on text matching algorithms and integrated into the usual document management, this tool allows creation and search of profiles of organisation competencies and activities, so as to identify potential partners.
- In "Knowledge Management Capability Framework", Birinder Sandhawalia and Darren Dalcher present a Knowledge Management Capability framework based upon an empirical case study on a software project organisation. They study the development of the organisation's KM initiative from its initial state, to an organisational state where the KM practices are institutionalised

and embedded within the daily activities and work methods of the organisation. KM capabilities tackled are KM infrastructure and KM processes. The proposed framework helps organisations to analyse potential imbalance between their KM initiative and their actual needs.

- In "DYONIPOS: Proactive Support of Knowledge Processes", Silke Weiß, Josef Makolm, and Doris Reisinger, present the research project DYONIPOS offering a context-sensitive and agile assistant based on semantic and knowledge discovery technologies, so as to support the knowledge workers with the currently needed knowledge automatically, in a non intrusive way.
- In "A Community of Knowledge Management Practitioners: Mirroring Power across Social Worlds", Hiroko Wilensky, Norman Su, David Redmiles and Gloria Mark distinguish two spaces: a community of KM practitioners and their respective work organisations. The authors notice that power relationships in work organisations are transferred into the community: they influence the community processes and enhance the knowledge sharing practices among the members. Strauss's social world perspective helps to understand how the actions and interactions outside of the community impact the community.

Acknowledgements

We thank very much the members of the program committee and the additional reviewers for their careful reviews of the papers, thus ensuring a high-quality conference. We are grateful to the members of the organisation committee, to IFIP and to WG12.6 for the conference organisation.

Mark Ackerman
Rose Dieng-Kuntz
Carla Simone
Volker Wulf

Invited Talk: Taking a Knowledge Perspective - The Future of Knowledge

Laurence Prusak

Executive Director, Institute for Knowledge Management, U.S.A., larry@laurenceprusak.com

Abstract: The loss of the monopoly of "useful" scientific and practical knowledge that has been held by the US, Western Europe and Japan since the mid-19Century is surely one of the defining events of our time. We are just beginning to see how the subsequent global dissemination of this sort of knowledge is affecting our economic and social institutions within the current phases of globalization.

Concurrently, and as both a cause and effect of this global dissemination, is the plummeting of information transaction costs. This is both a technical as well as an economic event-allowing codified information to spread round the globe at unforeseen speed. However the same forces have not caused the costs of knowledge to drop. Knowledge transaction costs have actually risen considerably, in all the developed economies. This in turn has focused attention on how much we pay for knowledge and how we better understand what we are paying for.

Many and varied experiments are also underway to allow organizations to better exploit and explore knowledge within their own boundaries and across the globe. Hard and soft technologies are being developed that take us far from the rigid, command and control hierarchies that evolved in the 19 century to work with traditional resources such as land, labor and financial capital. These new processes, roles and forms focus on how knowledge is to be developed, retained, and transferred.

Another new development are the ways we have of understanding knowledge itself. There has been much research into how human and social capital dynamics work to increase wealth and understanding based on knowlegde. Since it now thought that up to 60% of an organization's non-capital expenditures are on intangibles, and since knowledge is the predominant intangible, it isn't surprising that there is such strong interest.

There is also much work going on as to how to better understand the diverse forms of knowledge that we all use everyday, how can it be measured, and how can any entity "knows what it knows"?

Lastly there is a growing knowledge "democratization" movement in firms and in societies. This is strongly allied to the rapid growth of personal technologies and the erosion of traditional cognitive authority. However this movement is very

Please use the following format when citing this chapter:

Prusak, L., 2008, in IFIP International Federation for Information Processing, Volume 270; *Knowledge Management in Action*; Mark Ackerman, Rose Dieng-Kuntz, Carla Simone, Volker Wulf; (Boston: Springer), pp. 1–2.

much a double edged sword. In the age when "everyone knows everything" how will knowledge be evaluated for use, how will decisions be made and by whom, and on what basis will knowledge investments of all sorts be made?

Short biography: Larry Prusak is a researcher and consultant and was the founder and Executive Director of the Institute for Knowledge Management (IKM). He has had extensive experience, within the U.S. and internationally, in helping organizations work with their information and knowledge resources. He currently co-directs "Working Knowledge," a knowledge research program at Babson College, where he is a Distinguished Scholar in Residence. A noted authority in his field, Larry Prusak has lectured and been published widely. His most recent book publications include co-editing Knowledge Management and Organizational Learning (Oxford University Press, 2005), and co-authoring Storytelling in Organizations (Elsevier, 2004Larry Prusak has lectured at several important universities and schools, e.g., the Harvard Business School, M.I.T., New York University and the University of California Berkeley.

Core Knowledge Management in a Designer Community of the Automotive Field

Stefania Bandini[1], Sara Manzoni[1], and Fabio Sartori[2]

[1] CSAI, Viale Sarca 336, 20126 Milan (ITALY), {bandini, manzoni}@csai.disco.unimib.it
[2] DISCO, Viale Sarca 336, 20126 Milan (ITALY), sartori@disco.unimib.it

Abstract: The competencies in defining design strategies and the know-how necessary to manufacture innovative products are the effective knowledge capital for enterprises that operate in competitive sectors. Within this framework, the paper discusses a conceptual and computational approach to the design of a Core Knowledge Management system that supports people involved in the design and manufacturing of complex mechanical products. In particular we describe the design process and context in which the system is operating to acquire, represent, share and exploit expert designers' knowledge in Fontana Pietro SpA, an Italian enterprise leader in the development of dies for automotive industry.

1. Introduction

Knowledge Management Systems [13] provide methods, computational tools and technologies to acquire, represent and use heterogeneous data and knowledge, in order to tackle the challenge of supporting the complex and continuous evolution of organizations. Knowledge and competencies that concur to the maintenance of cohesion level of an organization to reach its objectives are several and heterogeneous. Among different kinds of knowledge necessary to allow the existence and growth of any organization involved in the design and manufacturing of innovative products, the Core Knowledge is the important one [9][6]. The context of Core Knowledge refers to the set of formal and experiential competencies that allow managing both routine working steps and new problem solving scenarios.

In this paper we illustrate a successful case study of Core Knowledge Management focused on supporting a community of experts involved in the design and manufacturing of complex mechanical products, namely dies for car body production that operates within Fontana Pietro S.p.A. (FP). Fontana Pietro S.p.A. is the Italian leader in engineering and manufacturing of dies for the deformation of sheet metal, in particular for the automotive sector. The enterprise is divided into Business Units: *FP Engineering*, *FP Die Manufacturing*, *FP Pressing*, and *FP Assembling*. FP Die Manufacturing, FP Pressing and FP

Please use the following format when citing this chapter:

Bandini, S., Manzoni, S. and Sartori, F., 2008, in IFIP International Federation for Information Processing, Volume 270; *Knowledge Management in Action*; Mark Ackerman, Rose Dieng-Kuntz, Carla Simone, Volker Wulf; (Boston: Springer), pp. 3–15.

Assembling are devoted to manufacturing and delivering of dies; FP Engineering aims at the design of the product, through the adoption of opportune technologies (e.g. CAD) and tools, in particular CATIA V5[1]. In particular, the Core Knowledge Management project presented in this paper aimed at supporting FP Engineering community in the management of its core competencies focusing on their design process and their jargon. *Intelligent Design System* (IDS) [4] is the name of the software system that has been developed to this aim.

The paper is organized as follows: In Section 2, after an overview of the different actors involved in the engineering of dies and their related interaction flow and the main steps of their decision making process, we focus on FP designers to describe their working environment and how they conceptualize the design activity. Section 3 describes knowledge engineering tools that have been adopted in the acquisition and representation of designers' knowledge. Then, a brief description of the system and its interactions with preexistent tools (i.e. CATIA) is provided in section 4; this section focuses also on results provided by the introduction of IDS in the design process, both from the organizational and computational point of views. Finally, some conclusions are briefly pointed out.

2. The Die for Car Bodies: A Complex Mechanical Product

A die is a very complex mechanical product composed of hundreds of parts with different functions that must be assembled into a unique and homogeneous steel fusion. A car body is the result of a multi–step process in which a thin sheet metal is passed through different kinds of presses (each one equipped with one of four main kinds of dies[2]). Each die is the result of a complex design and manufacturing process involving many professionals and it is basically made of pig iron melts on which other elements and holes can be added to fulfill specific die function (e.g. blades in Cutting dies).

In IDS project we have focused on the Forming Die but results can be easily extended to other die types. A Forming die is composed of a two main components (upper and lower shoe, respectively) that are fixed to and moved by the press in order to provide the desired final morphology to sheet metal. The main components responsible for the forming operation are the punch, the binder and the die seat, which are placed in the lower shoe (see left part of Figure 1[3]). *Punch* is the die component responsible for providing the sheet metal with the

---

[1]http://www-306.ibm.com/software/applications/plm/catiav5

[2]*Forming die* provides the sheet metal with the final morphology of the car body die (the presented project focused on this die type); *Cutting die* cuts away the unnecessary parts of the sheet metal; *Boring die* makes holes in the sheet metal, in order to make it lighter without side–effects on its performance; *Bending die* is responsible for the bending of some unnecessary parts that the Cutting die is not able to eliminate from the sheet metal.

[3] Picture published with the agreement of Fontana Pietro SpA.

required. Its geometry is designed according to the car body part (e.g. door, trunk, and so on) to be produced with it. The *binder* is the component of the die that allows the sheet metal to be perfectly in contact with the punch, by blocking the sheet against the upper shoe before the punch is pushed on it. Finally, the *die seat* contains both the punch and the binder and allows the die to be fixed to the press. The upper shoe of the die contains only a negative copy of the punch, usually called *matrix*.

The design of a die aims at obtaining a die that can actually give the sheet metal the desired final shape and it involves three main kinds of actors: the customer, (the automotive industry requiring the final die), the analysts and the designers. The right part of Figure 1 summarizes actors of professionals' community involved in a die design and the related interaction flow: Customer, Analysts and Designers. In particular, the *customer* provides a collection of norms and constraints that should be respected during the design of the die that summarize relevant information about presses and other machineries the die will be mounted on and some technical suggestions about specific design activities of die parts.

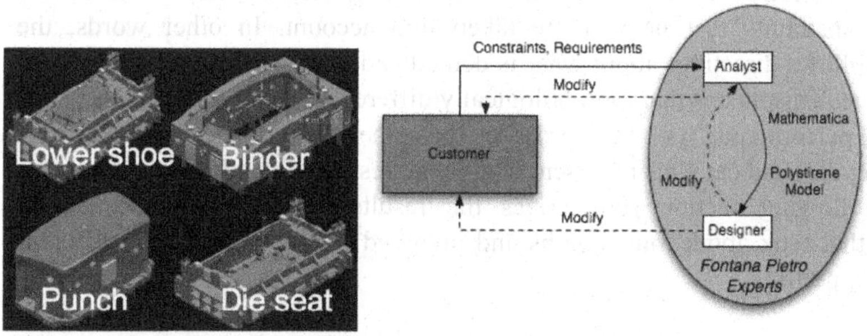

Figure 1. The components of a Forming die (on the left) and a schema of actors involved in the design process of a die and a simple interaction flow illustrating contracting activity occurring in this community of professionals (on the right).

Customer information is elaborated by a group of Analysts, which produce a mathematical description (model) of the geometrical properties of different parts of the die, named in the community jargon simply as die "mathematics". Analysts define the profile of the Forming Die and its skin, which is a 3D elaboration of the die profile, dimensions and shape of the sheet metal in input to the manufacturing process and the layout of the final car body part at the end of the production process. Moreover, the analysts produce the 1/1 scale final product in the form of polystyrene model of the die shape. Designers exploit all the available information (i.e., constraints of the costumer, mathematics, layout of the involved car body parts, and polystyrene model of the die) to obtain a die design that satisfies all customer requirements. In their decision making process, designers may be allowed violating some constraints and, thus, producing a final die shape that can be slightly differ from the polystyrene model produced by analysts. Of course, in constraints violation designers take into account and do not hinder die performance. This process is sometimes formalized and designers may ask analysts to modify the polystyrene model, or customer to relax some constraints.

In their decision-making process, every designer generates a conceptualization of the die as a collection of parts, each one delivering a specific functionality. The role of die parts and the meaning of design actions that can be accomplished on them are recognized quite instantaneously by die designers but often they result to be tacit and intrinsic in the design operations [10]. Moreover, it does not exist a unique way to intend the decision making process of die designers and the functional role [5] of a given component can change according to different functional contexts (e.g. a screw is used to fix a part to another one, but is it true that a screw is used to fix a part to another one in all the functional components of the die?). This conceptualization emerges from working experience of designers in the field as well as from their acquired competencies and studies (e.g. geometrical aspects of the die).

Therefore, die design is somehow a creative process and it does not exist a well-defined set of rules, a procedure, to be followed. Every designer follows guidelines reflecting his/her own style, evaluating step–by–step if there are possible constraints that have to be taken into account. In other words, the designer follows directives about what is denied and his/her creativity about what can be done. This means that morphologically different designs can have the same functional performance (i.e., they provides the same shape to sheet metal in case of Forming die) and can thus represent equivalent results of the design process.

The following section summarizes the results of knowledge acquisition activities that took about four months and involved five designers with different roles and expertise.

3. Representing Knowledge Involved in Die Design

As a result of the knowledge acquisition campaign to study the complex and heterogeneous nature of information and knowledge concerning the decision making process of a die designer, three different kinds of knowledge have been identified and have been categorized into: Functional knowledge [8], related to the representation of function performed by die parts (e.g. the screw allows to fix the die to the press); Procedural knowledge [16], related to the representation of constraints and order of design steps (e.g. the part B should be necessarily designed after the part A); Experiential knowledge, related to heuristics coming from the stratified knowledge of the company on the domain, and increased through the experience of the professionals (e.g. among fixing elements, screw is to be preferred, when part C has to be fixed). In the remaining of this section we describe in more details the computational approach that has been adopted for core knowledge representation and management in the design of IDS system about domain knowledge.

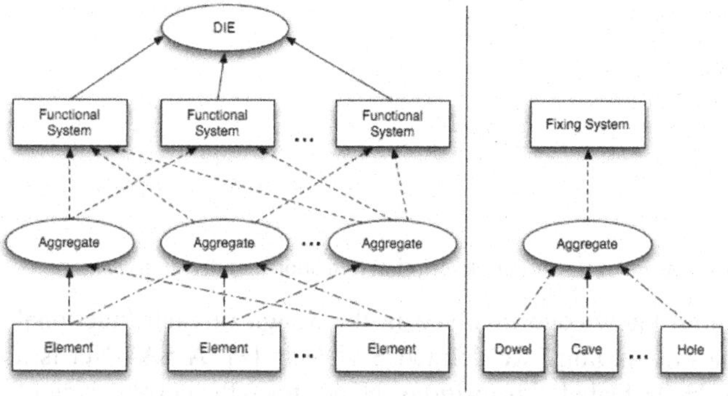

Figure 2. On the left, Relationships between components of a die and functional roles of object structure. Different levels of abstraction can be identified: functional systems, aggregates and atomic elements. On the right, examples of functional systems, aggregates and elements.

Functional knowledge has been represented according to an approach based on an ontological conceptualization of the domain [11]. The complex object to be designed is represented according to functions it will perform (similarly to the designer decision making process) rather than to its elementary parts (as in traditional CAD system like CATIA). Functional knowledge representation adopted in IDS (see Figure 2) consists of a hierarchical structural decomposition of the die, based on classificatory capabilities of the senior design professionals, but also on knowledge involving the functionalities of the involved mechanical parts (not captured by *is-a*, *part-of* relations) and functions that the die is requested to perform. A die is described as a collection of one or more *Functional Systems*, conceptual parts of the die that performs a function. For example, forming die must provide the sheet metal with a desired initial morphology and this function will be accomplished by a given group of die elements. But the forming die must also be moved from a press to another one, and other die parts accomplish *movement-ability function*. Each functional system can be fairly complex and usually designers conceive them as a composition of lower level *Aggregates of elements*. *Elements* are elementary parts (generally semi-manufactured, e.g. screws instance) whose role can be different according to the aggregate (and thus functional system) they belong to, while aggregates are groups of semi-manufactured components that can be grouped together to design a Functional System.

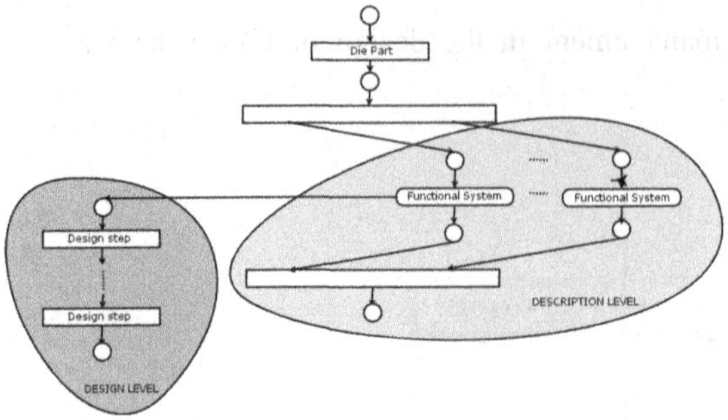

Figure 3. A SA*-Net has two classes of transition, description transition and design transition.

To represent procedural knowledge involved in the design of each functional system described in the die ontology we defined SA*-Nets [5]. A SA*-Net is a graph made of set of *nodes* and labeled *transitions*. Nodes trace the current state of the project, while transitions identify design steps. Two different classes of transitions have been considered in the design of SA*-Nets: *Descriptive* transitions that are labeled with the name of a functional system considered in the die ontology, link the description of a part to the related design process; *Design* transitions specify all the design steps necessary to complete the definition of the corresponding descriptive transition. Figure 3 shows a sample SA*-Net, where it is represented a sketch of a die part (i.e. die seat, punch, binder or matrix) as a set of descriptive transitions (boxes with round corners in the figure) where the naming of functional systems is defined by the die ontology. Each descriptive transition is linked to one or more design transitions (boxes in the figure) and defines how the functional system is configured in terms of aggregates and elementary parts of the die ontology.

SA*-Nets have been inspired by Superposed Automata Networks (SA-Nets) formalism (De Cindio et al., 1981), a sub-class of Petri Nets previously defined in the area of languages for the analysis and design of organizational systems and the study of non-sequential processes. Unlike traditional SA-Nets, SA*-Nets are characterized by a semantic completely defined by their transitions; in fact, while in the SA-Nets nodes act as *tokens*, with the consequence that a transition can be activated if and only if all its entering nodes are marked, in SA*-Net nodes allow tracing the design process and identifying, at each design step parts of the die to be designed next. Since design activities are composed of steps not necessarily sequentially ordered, SA*-Nets are provided with syntactic elements to manage sequential, concurrent and binding processes. A *sequential process* is a collection of design steps that must be necessarily accomplished according to a sequential order; a *concurrent process* is a collection of design steps that can be executed at the same time; a *binding process* is a collection of design steps belonging to *different* descriptive transitions where the execution of the transitions must preserve specific order constraints. While the first two compositions are the basic tools to build single part design processes, the latter allows the specification of relations among design processes of different parts.

While SA*-Net syntax inherits from SA-Nets syntactic elements to deal with sequential and concurrent processes, the management of binding processes has requested to represent and manage *constraints* between subnets. Constraints link design transitions of different descriptive transitions, and their representation and management strongly support designers in preventing potential negative side effects of wrong choices allowing them to freely define personal design path being notify about potential problems.

IDS provides specific functionalities to support in designing SA*-Net functional system by activating a set of rules for each design transitions to be accomplished (Figure 4) and warn the user about SA*-Nets relationships to prevent negative design side-effects. The specific design path within SA*-Net structure is the result of designer actions through the CAD system interface. Rule system execution evaluates functional system attributes and suggests parameters for the part coherently within the current design state.

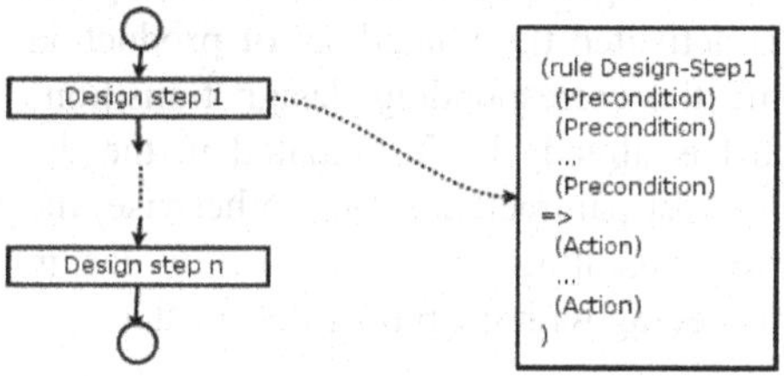

Figure 4. One or more rules are activated when a functional system is being designed

A rule is activated if all its preconditions (i.e. the left hand side) are verified. Rule precondition in IDS can be a test on a constraint or other information about the project: customer reference norms, the type and dimensions of customer presses (customer requirements introduced in Section 2, for example, a customer could require use of dowels instead of screws in the definition of Fixing System). In order to exemplify how rule preconditions can represent constraint specification we refer to the case depicted in Figure 5. Since the binder profile is adjacent to the punch one, the binder should be generally designed after the punch, as in Part A of the picture. However, a designer could decide to describe the binder first. In this case, possible side-effects like the one drawn in Part B of the picture could happen, where the punch dimensions exceed those of the binder. In this situation, when the user adds a binder to its design through his CAD interface, IDS notifies him about the fact that the punch design should have been executed before in order to generate useful information for the binder design (e.g. similarly this type of heuristics refer to holes and screws).

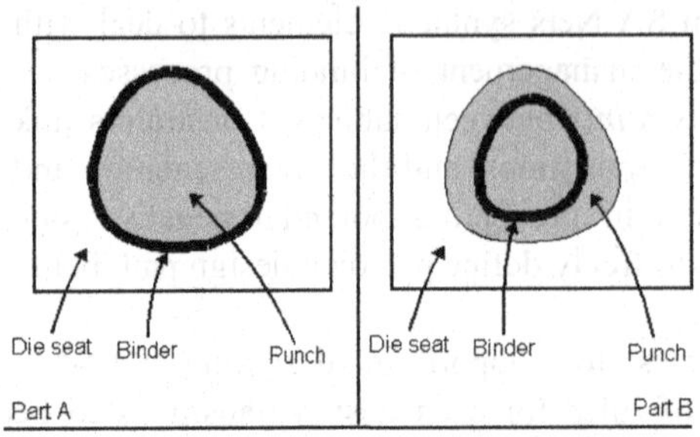

Figure 5. In Part A, the binder has been correctly designed after the punch, since the punch must slide inside it. In Part B, the binder has been defined before the punch, with a violation of geometrical constraints.

The binder is typically designed after the punch because its width and length are equal to the ones of the punch. Thus, there is a constraint between the punch and binder SA*-Nets such as the one shown in the right part of Figure 6. During the design of a binder width and length, it is activated the related set of production rules representing the constraint involving the corresponding design transitions and punch in the SA*-Net. If the punch has already be instantiated in the die ontology, its parameters can be used to suggest parameters set-up, otherwise, the user will be notified about the need for executing the *define width* design transition in the punch SA*-Net before proceeding with the binder design step.

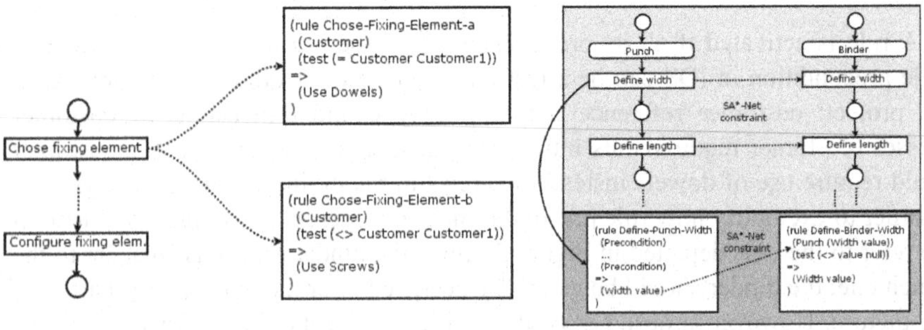

Figure 6. On the left, the same design step could be specified by different group of rules according to different preconditions. Here, the choice about the use of dowels or screws in building the Fixing System depends on the name of the customer. On the right, how to represent constraints between design transitions in the corresponding rules.

4. Implementation

Figure 7 shows a sketch of the architecture of the IDS system. It is a collection of knowledge–based and communication modules that interacts with CATIA V5, the CAD tool used by expert designers of Fontana–Pietro in their daily activities. The system has been implemented exploiting the client-server architecture, where CATIA acts as the client and IDS as the server. The system is made up of three logical components: the knowledge-based module, the CATIA-IDS connector and the knowledge repositories. There are three knowledge repositories, one for each type of knowledge identified: a collection of Java objects, a collection of XML files and a collection of production rules.

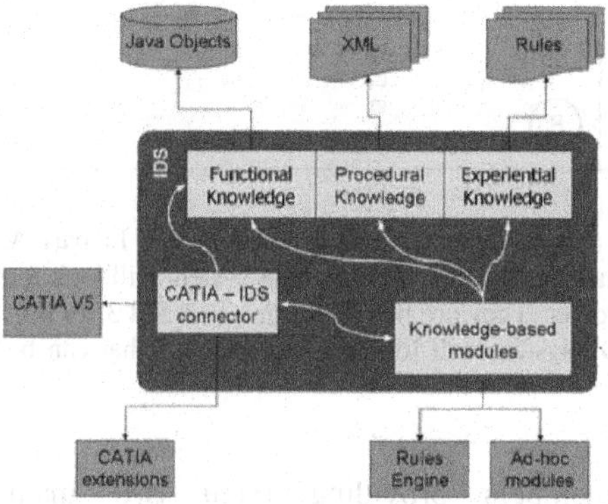

Figure 7. The IDS High Level Architecture.

Java objects implement the IDS ontology: every part of the die has been represented, starting from the functional systems up to elementary components. XML files have been adopted for the implementation of the SA-Net to describe procedural knowledge as well as the SA-Net Manager, a software module that allows browsing the SA-Net and managing it by adding new states, transitions, constraints and so on. Finally, a collection of files containing rules for implementing experiential knowledge is integrated into IDS knowledge base. Knowledge based modules communicate with CATIA (designers CAD tool in FP Engineering based on parametric hierarchical representation of complex objects) through the ad-hoc developed software module called *Catia-IDS connector*. Although CATIA promises an easy interconnection by standard mechanisms like CORBA, we have verified that it is not simple to use these functionalities, due to the difficulties in obtaining useful documentation. Thus, CATIA and IDS communicate through a TCP socket connection that is managed by CATIA. An communication syntax has been defined for message exchange between CATIA and IDS (a message contains at least the name of the required service, a list of parameters to be valued). To allow the communication between CATIA and IDS, an extension of CATIA has been made by *Fontana Pietro* R&D department, with the creation of a personalized GUI.

Today, IDS is in use by FP Engineering business unit and the upgrade of its functionalities is continue thanks to members of FP Research and Development Area.

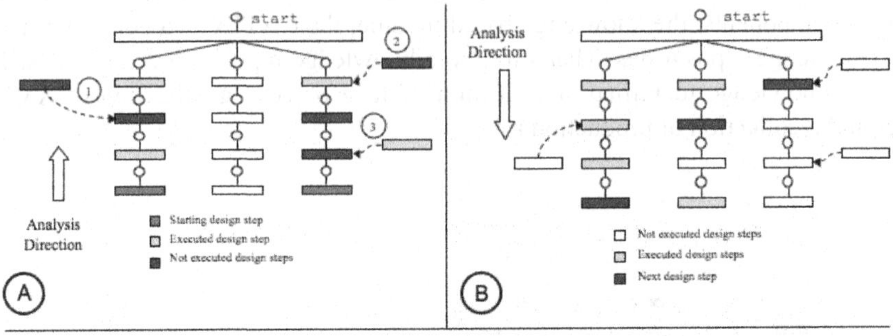

Figure 8. Functionalities of IDS (the dashed arrows represent binding processes): In part A starting from the two design steps labeled as "starting design steps", the IDS system will look for previous transitions that have not been executed yet. They are the transitions 1, 2 and 3. In part B, given the current stat of the project, the IDS system will look for design steps that can be executed, three in the figure.

IDS supports FP engineering members providing them two main functionalities: at each design step, without forcing the user in following a given design path, it suggests next design step to the user (i.e. *Next Step* functionality, part B of Figure 8); moreover, at each design step, IDS notifies the user about potential violations of procedural constraints (i.e. *Procedure Analysis* or *Project Procedure Analysis* functionalities, part A of Figure 8). When the Next Step functionality is called, the IDS system, starting from the *start* state, explores the SA*-Net looking for the first transition that have not been visited yet. When the Procedure analysis is invoked, the system, starting from the current design step, looks backward for possible transitions that have not been executed in the past, violating in this way precedence constraints. While Next Step is a *top-down* functionality (i.e. given an executed design step it defines the next one), the other two are bottom-up functionalities (i.e. given a design step, they identify all the design steps that have not been executed although they conceptually preceded it).

5. Conclusions

In this paper we have presented the IDS project, a knowledge based system to support designers of Fontana Pietro SpA in their decision making process about the design of dies for car body manufacturing.

The system is currently in use by FP Engineering: although no quantitative data about its evaluation are available at the moment, the implemented functionalities allowed expert designers to improve their day-by-day activities, through a significant decrease of design errors and the automatic management of some routine activities by the direct collaboration of IDS system with CATIA V5 (the CAD tool adopted by Fontana Pietro S.p.A.).

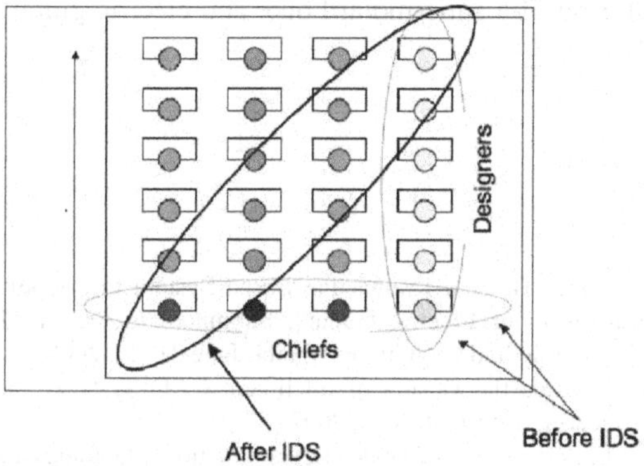

Figure 9. Organizational impact of IDS. Before the introduction of IDS, designers at FP Engineering were spatially organized into lines according to their role and the project they were involved in and this spatial organization reflected the structure of knowledge sharing within the organization. The introduction of a unified functional description of the object to be designed, strongly improved the access to information about design experiences of FP Engineering.

Qualitative evaluations can be done also from the organizational impact perspective. First, the introduction of IDS (see Figure 9), with its proposal of a unified and shared model of the die represented by functional ontology and procedural and experiential knowledge management tools, has fruitfully contributed to define a transversal way of designing different kinds of products. A major contribution to designers' collaboration is given by the possibility of designers to access to information about design choices made in every project by every member of FP Engineering. We can observe that the unified and shared conceptualization of the die promoted negotiation processes among designers similar to a community of practice [12]. Moreover, as a consequence of this work Fontana Pietro S.p.A. organized a new division that collects people from both FP Engineering and FP Research and Development business units. The major advantage of this organizational intervention is on designer performances that have strongly improved with a more direct collaboration with organizational roles devoted to the identification of innovation and customer needs and requirements. Finally, also newcomers in FP are strongly advantaged by the introduction of IDS, since also them can easily access to a shared conceptualization of the design tasks and be productive and autonomous with shorter training times.

From the Knowledge Management standpoint, the IDS project has allowed the definition of a computational methodology that can be easily reused in similar projects in the context of mechanical products design and manufacturing. Indeed, in every complex mechanical product can be identified functional and procedural aspects that can be captured by tools like Functional Ontologies and SA*–Nets. Two examples of the IDS model reusability can be found in [2] and [1], where functional ontologies have been adopted in the development of other KM systems to support the design and manufacturing of a supermotard bike and electric guitar, respectively.

References

1. Bandini, S., Bonomi, A., Sartori, F., Guitar Hero, a Knowledge Based System to Support Creativity in the Design and Manufacturing of Electric Guitars, Submitted to the Third International Conference on Design Computing and Cognition, Atlanta, June 21–25, 2008.
2. Colombo, G., A. Mosca, F. Sartori, Towards the Design of Intelligent CAD Systems: an Ontological Approach, Advanced Engineering Informatics 21, 2007.
3. Colombo, G., Mosca, A., Palmonari, M., Sartori, F., An Upper-Level Functional Ontology to Support Distributed Design, In Micucci, D., Sartori, F., Sicilia, M. A. (eds.), Proceedings of ONTOSE 07, 2nd International Workshop on Ontology, Epistemology and Conceptualization of Software and System Engineering, Milan, June 27–28, 2007.
4. Bandini, S., F. Sartori, Industrial mechanical design: The IDS case study, in: J. Gero (Ed.), Proceedings of Second International Conference on Design Computing and Cognition, Springer-Verlag, 2006.
5. Bandini, S., G. Colombo, F. Sartori, Towards the Integration of Ontologies and SA-Nets to Manage Design and Engineering Core Knowledge, Proceedings of the International Workshop on Ontology, Conceptualizations and Epistemology for Software and Systems Engineering, Alcalà (SP), 2005.
6. Bandini, S., S. Manzoni, Modeling Core Knowledge and Practices in a Computational Approach to Innovation Process, in Model Based Reasoning: Science, Technology, Values. Kluwer Academic/Plenum Publishers, 2002.
7. Gero, J., Computational Models of Creative Designing Based on Situated Cognition, Proceedings of the Fourth Conference on Creativity and Cognition, ACM Press, New York, NY, USA, 2002.
8. Scrivener, S.A.R., Tseng, W.S.-W, and Ball, L.J., The impact of functional knowledge on sketching. Chapter in Hewett T. and Kavanagh, T. (Eds.): Proceedings of the Fourth International Conference on Creativity and Cognition: CC 2002. New York: ACM Press, 2002
9. Prahalad, C. K., and Hamel, G., The Core Competence of the Corporation. In: Strategic Learning in Knowledge Economy: Individual, Collective and Organizational Learning Process, (R.L. Cross, S.B. Israelit eds.), Butterworth Heinemann, Boston, 2000.

10. Brown, D.C., Intelligent Computer-aided design, Encyclopedia of Computer Science and Technology, 1998.
11. Guarino, N., Some Ontological Principles for Designing upper level Lexical Resources, Proceedings of the First International Conference on Lexical Resources and Evaluation, Granada, Spain, 1998.
12. Wenger, E., Community of Practice: Learning, meaning and identity, Cambridge University Press, Cambridge, MA 1998.
13. Takeuchi I., Nonaka H., The Knowledge creating Company: How Japanese Companies Create the Dynamics of Innovation, Oxford University Press, 1995.
14. Chandrasekaran, B., A.K. Goel, Y. Iwasaki, Functional Representation as Design Rationale, IEEE Computer 26 (1), 1993.
15. De Cindio, F., De Michelis, G., Pomello, L. and Simone, C., Superposed Automata Nets. In Girault, C., Reisig, W., (eds.): Application and Theory of Petri Nets, Selected Papers from the First and the Second European Workshop on Application and Theory of Petri Nets, Strasbourg 23.-26. September 1980, Bad Honnef 28.-30. September 1981.
16. Friedland, P., Acquisition of Procedural Knowledge from Domain Experts. Proceedings of International Joint Conference on Artificial Intelligence (IJCAI), pp. 856-861, 1981

"KT" CarePacks - Collaboration Patterns for Knowledge Transfer: Learning from IS/IT-Outsourcing Case at a Swiss Financial Institution

Malgorzata Bugajska

Department of Informatics, University of Zurich, Switzerland, bugajska@gmail.com

Abstract: Organizations now more than ever focus on fostering team work in their daily activities to secure better results for their stakeholders. Team work and collaboration are especially important for inter-organizational outsourcing relationships where these qualities are crucial for the successful knowledge transfer conducted throughout all phases of outsourcing relationship. Knowledge workers involved in such complex, inter-organizational collaboration processes require support to secure structured and well managed collaboration. Consequently, there is a strong need of service receiver organizations to use sustainable approaches for the knowledge transfer to satisfy recurring transfer processes in forthcoming sourcing activities. Idea of "pattern" offers encapsulated approach for describing solutions for recurring problems and is already successfully used within the IT domain. In this paper we present the concept of patterns for the sustainable knowledge transfer for outsourcing relationships. We introduce CarePacks – reusable patterns for supporting act of the collaborative knowledge transfer and present lessons learned from introducing them at a Swiss financial institution while conducting six knowledge transfer pilots in three consecutive trials.

Keywords: Knowledge transfer, IS/IT outsourcing, Patterns

1. Introduction

Knowledge transfer is one of pthe critical factors that increases risk throughout all IS/IT sourcing relationship phases (Bloch, 2005; Carmel, 2005). It is therefore imperative to work towards achieving desired knowledge balance before deciding on a renewal, redefinition or termination of an outsourcing relationship and insource IS/IT services back home. To achieve the successful knowledge transfer between organization outsourcing IS/IT activities (the client) and the supplier of

---

Please use the following format when citing this chapter:

Bugajska, M., 2008, in IFIP International Federation for Information Processing, Volume 270; *Knowledge Management in Action*; Mark Ackerman, Rose Dieng-Kuntz, Carla Simone, Volker Wulf; (Boston: Springer), pp. 17–36.

IS/IT services, both parties need not only a measurable and result oriented transfer process, but also ability to support their transfer teams with tools (analog and electronic alike) and processes that help to achieve anticipated transfer results.

The knowledge transfer process within an organization has been researched extensively (Davenport, 2000; Davenport, 2005; English, 2006; Nonaka, 1995; Szulanski, 1999; Von Krogh, 1998). However, there still appears to be limited research on inter-organizational knowledge transfer, although researchers do point out that it is most likely a more difficult and complex task (Darr, 2000; Kim, 2000).

To understand the inter-organizational complexity of the knowledge transfer, it is important to analyze the factors influencing the transfer of knowledge. Based on researching approximately 100 pairs of client and service providers (consulting services), researchers (Ko, 2005) have modeled factors influencing the knowledge transfer between the clients and consultants. They list: communication (encoding and decoding content as well as source credibility), knowledge (absorptive capacity, shared understanding or arduous relationship) and motivational (intrinsic, extrinsic motivation) factors which influence the knowledge transfer. On a more general basis, researchers conclude that frequency and depth of person-to-person contact (Rulke, 2000), as well as congruency of organizational and individual goals (Jensen, 1976), play a role in defining quality of transfer within a company. Additionally, researchers describe the limitations in terms of transfer of expertise (expert to novice) which has been investigated at cognitive (availability bias, course of knowledge or "not invented here" syndrome) and motivational/intentional levels (reward systems, culture of trust) (Hinds, 2003). Consequently, understanding of organizational culture of the client and outsourcer is named as one of the most important factors of managing and deriving value from offshoring businesses (Carmel, 2005). Consequently, being aware of factors influencing the knowledge transfer it is important to use right transfer methods and tools for particular transfer situations (Davenport, 2000; Dixon, 2000). Appropriate transfer tools or instruments need to support the team of client and supplier in their transfer activities, since failing proves too expensive and risky for the client organization or significantly impedes attracting new clients in case of service providers (Carmel, 2005; Cohen, 2006).

This paper is organized as follows: in the next chapter we present the research question which we explored in the field project. Further, we describe the design methodology and data collection for our explorations. Consequently, we present the pattern approach for the knowledge transfer in the IS/IT outsourcing domain. From there we present an example of a CarePack followed by lessons learned acquired during our three implementation trials in the field (carried out by us at a Swiss financial institution, the "Institution"). We conclude by presenting practical implication for the use of pattern based CarePacks approach for the knowledge transfer.

2. Research question

Contract bound knowledge transfer in IS/IT outsourcing is executed jointly and collaboratively by two organizations during all outsourcing phases. Therefore, unsurprisingly there are enormous benefits (monetary, time based as well as organizational) to be gained from facilitating repeatable transfer approaches. Such approaches are already part of the value proposition of the IS/IT service provider champions (compare IBM or XANSA for Business Process Outsourcing). These organizations are committed to understanding the processes at client organizations as quickly and accurately as possible. The service provider teams are trained for achieving maximum progress in transferring knowledge (both explicit and implicit) from the client company to their own. Furthermore, well designed and sustainable knowledge transfer during the whole outsourcing cycle, as well as mutual systems for managing knowledge, contribute significantly to the quality of the relationship, increasing the likelihood of a prosperous relationship and consequently engaging new clients for the business (Gottschalk, 2007).

However, transferring knowledge proves difficult for majority of companies outsourcing their IS/IT activities (Carmel, 2005). Often an outsourcing service recipient lacks an appropriate set of instruments and methods to make the collaborative knowledge transfer sustainable. Furthermore, their skills for sharing knowledge between their own teams and teams of the service provider are often not mature enough. Consequently, the client as service recipient often follows set of unstructured activities, which are parts of processes designed by service providers. In many cases these are the only available transfer approaches at hand so the client will likely use them. Obviously, following parts of "foreign" processes which are not designed to secure strategic goals of the client does not necessarily contribute to the successful knowledge transfer for the client's organization. Therefore, redesigning or terminating the outsourcing relationship by the client is often described as difficult (and expensive) experience for the entire organization.

Sustainable knowledge transfer is a critical success factor for building competitive advantage for organizations wanting to profit from sourcing projects and not making it a costly mistake. Successful transfer needs to be based on the inter-organizational collaboration to meet the transfer goals agreed upon in the IT/IS outsourcing contract. Therefore, there is a need for well designed collaboration processes for knowledge workers involved in the transfer process. The value of collaboration for accomplishing organizational tasks is widely known and admitted (Briggs, 2003). In inter-organizational collaboration, the complexity is significant since the goals are to be accomplished by a team with whom the members most likely do not share the culture, communication and coordination processes. The importance of teams for accomplishing sourcing projects is confirmed by research (Carmel, 2005); therefore, any support given to the teams which could improve their performance is of value to organizations. The support for the collaborating team is often provided by collaboration facilitators. Although this is a very good solution, it is costly and does not guarantee sustainability of the solution if the facilitator is not available. As such the challenge for the organizations is to reduce the involvement of collaboration facilitators without endangering the drop in quality of the support for the teams and securing the sustainability of the collaboration support processes. The question thus arises how to design and implement the collaborative knowledge transfer to achieve a more sustainable approach within the inter-organizational set-up. Based on the methodology of work sciences, we designed our research as explained in the following chapter.

3. Research design and data collection

Together with the Institution, our research partner in Switzerland, which was in the process of remodeling relationships with their long term outsourcing partner, we designed the three year research project (with a total effort of about 10 person years) called Knowledge Transfer in Outsourcing Relationship. We used this relationship as a base example for researching the knowledge transfer in IS/IT outsourcing to design the sustainable knowledge transfer. During the outsourcing relationship, the Institution and its IS/IT service provider transferred the knowledge on a "need-based" basis. Whenever there was an operative need for the transfer, the transfer was performed. Since the Institution wanted to redefine its outsourcing relationship, it also started to rethink processes concerning the knowledge transfer. The Institution committed itself towards a more sustainable and measurable process for the knowledge transfer. Currently, its outsourcing partner develops and retains maintenance of a strategically important transaction processing software bundle. This software bundle is not only used by the Institution itself, but it is also used to provide a great number of services to other banks. Therefore, our objective in this project was to design a method to moderate the sustainable knowledge transfer process and to provide tools which can be reused for dealing with recurring problems in transferring knowledge between organizations. Results reported in this paper were achieved while focusing on in-sourcing the knowledge from the service provider back to the client in the last phases of their outsourcing relationship. The use of the method for earlier phases had already been tested with positive results.

Our research is design oriented (Heinzl, 2001; WKWI, 1994). Its objective is to develop solutions to generic types of problems on a medium level of abstraction, e.g. in the form of an architecture (in the tradition of computer science research), a reference model (Becker, 2004), or a methodology (Braun, 2004; Heym, 1993). Therefore, we use design methodology referred to as a "theory for design and action" (Gregor, 2006), which explains "how to do" something through defining principles of form and function and methods. Contribution of such design theory is seen as "utility to a community of users, novelty of artifact, and the persuasiveness of claims that is effective "(Gregor, 2006). In the context of our investigation:

1) we provide the users with the utility by supplying the practitioners with the artifacts - the CarePacks to provide or improve sustainability to the knowledge transfer processes; since a thorough literature review (Bugajska, 2006; Voigt, 2007) shows that no comparable methodology has yet been developed, particularly none that relies on replicable patterns for action);

2) Our approach is new, drawing creatively from interdisciplinary research (using available frameworks (e.g.(Hutzschenreuter, 2004; Thatchenkery, 2005), methodologies (Mulder, 2007) and techniques (e.g., after action reviews, 5-why etc. see (Dixon, 2000; English, 2006)) for KT and to draw conclusions for methodology development (see also (Bugajska, 2007); The literature review uncovered only methods either for the knowledge transfer (e.g. (Davenport, 2005; Dixon, 2000; English, 2006; Nonaka, 1995)), for managing IT/IS-Outsourcing relationships (most importantly: (Carmel, 2005; Cohen, 2006; Willcocks, 2006)) or for repeatable patterns of collaboration (Briggs, 2003; de Vreede, 2006), but none in the intersection of the three;

3) Through the multiple trials/pilots and cyclical usage of the CarePacs, we demonstrate the persuasiveness of our design. In such cyclical process the "knowledge is used to create works, and works are evaluated to build knowledge" (Owen, 1997).

3.1. Data collection

An important starting point was to understand the demand for the transfer to uncover which knowledge (packaged as "knowledge items") needed to be transferred, what were its distinctive characteristics and understand underlying causes for existing imbalance of knowledge. Additionally, to get more insight into cultural and communication approaches taken by different teams as well as to better understand the domains of the knowledge workers, we conducted job-shadowing and visited informal meetings of communities of practice. Furthermore, evaluation of the pilots contributed to the design of the next round of pilots. Altogether there were three rounds of trials and the fourth round is currently being prepared.

Ability to define and describe knowledge considered for the transfer and define the most successful way to implement it as well as secure its strategic fit requires full attention of the outsourcing client. Therefore, the important part of the knowledge transfer processes is to analyze the demand for the knowledge transfer in the first place.

The DEAN (The DEmand ANalysis for Knowledge Transfer) methodology allows for mapping the demand for the knowledge transfer in outsourcing relationships. We used this method to define which knowledge needs to be transferred from the outsourcer back to the client organization. The DEAN methodology (with its five phases) is described in detail in (Bugajska, 2006); it uses "knowledge item" as the smallest package of knowledge to be transferred between organizations. Since knowledge is by definition networked, there are no natural knowledge packages and therefore the packages need to be constructed with help of definitions describing organizational tasks. The suitable granularity is usually found in job family descriptions (e.g. job family - software architect) used within the organization.

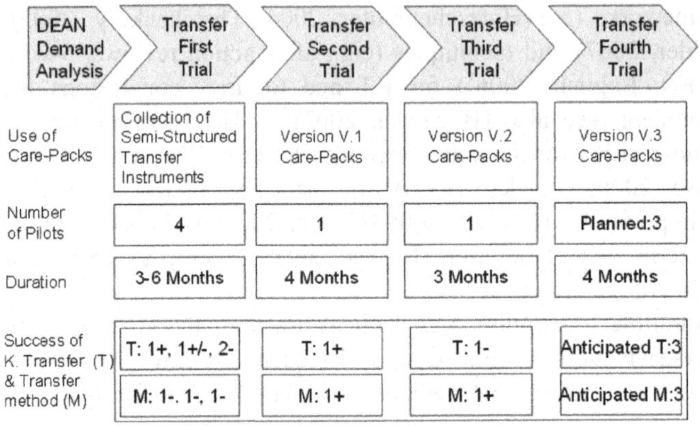
DEAN Demand Analysis
Transfer First Trial
Transfer Second Trial
Transfer Third Trial
Transfer Fourth Trial
Use of Care-Packs
Collection of Semi-Structured Transfer Instruments
Version V.1 Care-Packs
Version V.2 Care-Packs
Version V.3 Care-Packs
Number of Pilots
4
1
1
Planned:3
Duration
3-6 Months
4 Months
3 Months
4 Months
Success of K. Transfer (T) & Transfer method (M)
T: 1+, 1+/-, 2-
T: 1+
T: 1-
Anticipated T:3
M: 1-. 1-, 1-
M: 1+
M: 1+
Anticipated M:3

Figure 1: Summarizes the evolution of the method based approach, number of pilots, the duration of each trial as well as the success (marked with "+") of the knowledge transfer and/or the transfer method used. The reasons behind the success and failure of the approaches are described in text.

During these trials we observed how the transfer instruments, which later evolved into CarePacks, were improved and what was achieved in terms of transfer of knowledge within teams. During and after each trial we performed interviews and workshops with the main actors from both the management and user levels of the two organizations. During the 18 months of the project, the project members conducted a total of 38 (structured) interviews, 22 workshops (including 4 large group workshops using GroupSystems technology) and eight feedback sessions with 29 distinct actors including the CIO of the client and the CEO of the service provider organization. Notes were taken during all data gathering, but only some of the interviews were transcribed. In order to verify the data and to ensure objectivity to the largest extent possible, the author engaged in an additional round of six interviews immediately prior to the publication of this paper. Additionally, the author again reviewed documents form all meetings (pilot and expert meetings as well as project steering committee meetings) and corresponding meeting notes. Furthermore, the interviews conducted by a project member working on all trials have been supported with analysis of data available in (not restricted and project related) email communication streams exchanged with the Institution and its service provider.

4. "CarePacks" patterns for sustainable knowledge transfer

To explore our research question and to address the needs of our business research partners we turned towards the growing domain of collaboration engineering. Collaboration engineering researchers stress that there is a need to structure and manage collaboration processes to make the involved individuals focus more on achieving joint goals (de Vreede, 2005). This builds on the idea of pattern language (Alexander, 1977; Alexander, 1979) which was proposed to allow for anticipating predictability of particular architectural design activity by creating patterns incorporating a description of context, problems and solutions. Building on that pattern language created for the building environment, the software engineering patterns emerged (Gamma, 1995; Lukosch, 2006) offering reusable blocs for approaching recurring problems in software creation domains. Further, this methods and approaches are used for exploring collaboration processes which are recurring in nature and proposing approach for "packaging" the experience of collaboration facilitators ("ThinkLets - "reusable, predictable and transferable facilitation techniques" (de Vreede, 2006)). Commitment towards designing routine collaboration procedures significantly helps in securing achievement of the knowledge transfer goals set by the recipient of services. Important for introducing and supporting routine behavior in the organization are collaboration instruments which can be used by employees to conduct the transfer of knowledge with reduced presence of the facilitators.

Therefore, when the management of the Institution (which was in the process of in-sourcing the knowledge back to the organization) requested a more formalized approach for preparation and execution of the various pilots currently executed in the organization the opportunity for designing a more sustainable approach for this and future transfers emerged. Our answer was to design a set of CarePacks-based patterns for preparation as well as execution of the knowledge transfer initiatives within an outsourcing relationship. The facilitator and the team leaders involved in the transfer used CarePacks for preparation and execution of various transfer pilots. The knowledge keeper (an expert in the team of service provider) and knowledge receiver (the client's team member – a novice) followed the method as described in CarePacks to deploy the pilot and effectively conduct the transfer of knowledge without the support of external facilitator.

5. Structure of the CarePack

The knowledge transfer CarePack is a document which describes a method for transferring knowledge between individuals or groups within a specific transfer context (e.g. inter-organizational transfer) with particular transfer purpose or goal. The name "CarePack" was coined by the knowledge transfer project leader from the Institution and was quickly accepted by the organization and our research department. The CarePack is characterized through its structure including exemplary usage and description of resulting organizational context emerging after deployment of the CarePack. The CarePack reflects well the idea of engineered value of documented procedures created for sustainable care, maintenance and support for the organizational wide knowledge transfer initiatives. The CarePack is structured as follows:

Context and Name	Context of the CarePack usage - a description of Real-World Scenario (e.g. preparation for the transfer or transfer implementation).
	Goal of the CarePack (what will be achieved) and its addressees (who may use it)
Forces	What event triggered the usage of this CarePack? (e.g. change of service's supplier)
	What are the collaboration principles of the CarePack? (e.g. on-site but asynchron online meetings)
	How use of the CarePack supports confidence and trust in transfer team?
	What factors support collaboration processes in transfer teams?
	How is the collaborative goal achievement controlled?
	What is the contribution to the sustainability of knowledge transfer process?
Problem	Transfer problems and issues (e.g. transfer of knowledge from individual "memories" to the group "memory")
	Purpose and transfer goal of this CarePack
Solution	Core Idea:
	Factors dominating the use of CarePack
	Applicability – When to use this CarePack?
	Non-applicability of the CarePack .
	Procedural description of the CarePack (step-by-step)
	Link to templates and guidelines supporting the execution of this CarePack (and which has already been used within the organization)
	Involved actors: e.g.: knowledge keeper, knowledge receiver, transfer team leader.
	Use of artifacts/tools: e.g. Blog, Competency Development tools.
	Cooperation and Collaboration processes for transfer team members
	Tips: (Solution applied)
	Here the tips for introducing this CarePack within the organization are presented. E.g.: how to deal with possible lack of managerial engagement or what can be used to help coworkers to deal with uncertainness of discussing taboo issues.
E – tools	E-Tools supporting CarePack usage (e.g. Learning Diary-Blog, WIKIs, SharePoint space)

Example	Description of exemplar execution of this CarePack in the organization (step by step) Known applications of this CarePack within or outside the organization
Related Patterns	Related CarePacks – other CarePacks which can be considered for use CarePacks supporting the execution of this CarePack CarePacks to be used before using this CarePack (e.g. "Pilot Preparation" CarePack,) CarePacks to be used after using this CarePack (e.g. "Self Learning" CarePack)
Resulting Context	Foreseen changes in the organizational behavior after executing this CarePack Advantages and disadvantages of the CarePack usage.

Table 1. Structure of the CarePacks for the knowledge transfer process in outsourcing relationships.

As presented in Table 1, the CarePack structure carries the elements of the pattern already proposed by Alexander (Alexander, 1979) and used by Gamma (Gamma, 1995). A CarePack is identified by its name and contains a brief context of its usage, a description of the recurring problem that it can be applied to, a proposed solution and a resulting context. Additionally, we list the forces shaping the transfer situation for which we suggest to use a particular CarePack. A CarePack document also includes other elements which are the standard components of internal documents within many organizations, such as an explanation of used terms and abbreviations or other referred documents (e.g., links to organizational library of processes). It is important to mention that CarePacks always offer "Tips" (particularly important in the solution section) along the document which provide a practical link between an abstract content of the document and real-world situations of the outsourcing-based knowledge transfer. "Tips" are often derived from organizational "lessons learned" or "best practices" created or collected while using CarePacks.

The structure of the CarePack evolved during the trials performed at the Institution. We enhanced it significantly after the third trial adding: "Collaboration Principles of the CarePack", "Electronic Tools" and collection of known "Triggering events" for deploying the CarePack (forces of the CarePack). Collaboration Principles are introduced to support the collaborative character of the knowledge transfer. This should help not only to better understand the effect of collaborative work in achieving the transfer goals, but also determine how such collaboration can be better planned or deployed in the future.

The concept of "Resulting Context" which is often used in a pattern structure is an important element for understanding what can be anticipated after certain CarePacks are used for the transfer. Usage of certain CarePacks can lead to the improvement of specific skills in members of the team and thus impact the triggering of the organizational change process which needs to be addressed.

Further, we plan to enrich the CarePack documentation with links to other teams within the Institution which have already successfully used a CarePack or collected best practices of using particular CarePack for a particular knowledge transfer. This may improve the matching of the CarePack to a particular transfer situation and enrich the list of ill-suited usage of a particular pattern for the industry.

6. Example: "Project Reflection" CarePack

CarePacks are particularly effective for teams in outsourcing relationships since they offer a structured and detailed approach for the transfer team (or teams). yet they are still flexible enough to be re-modeled and improved to suit a particular context or situation. Consequently, as a consecutive user of a certain CarePack the transfer team profits from the information about the previous usage of the CarePack and its possible modifications. Here we explain how the use of CarePack is incorporated into the transfer process and further present the "Project Reflection" CarePack in more detail. This is one of twelve CarePacks we designed and used in the field (some of the others include Buddy Support, Self-Study, Tandem or Management Coaching CarePack).

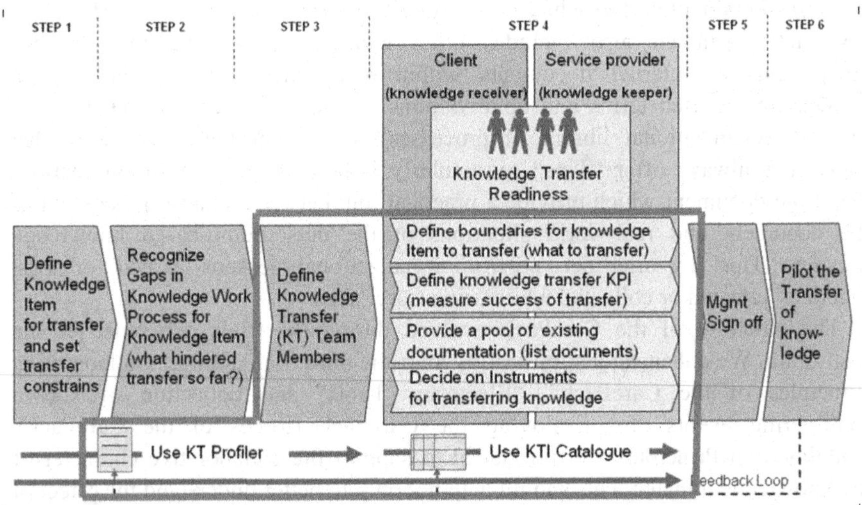

Figure 2: Process of designing pilots for the knowledge transfer in IS/IT outsourcing relationship as proposed by (Bugajska, 2007). The procedures of steps 3 and 4 as well as tools (KT Profiler and KT Instrument Catalogue) can be defined in form of a CarePack for reusable and therefore more sustainable knowledge transfer procedures within organization.

Consider following scenario: A LocalBank sets up an outsourcing project and invites a SoftwareHouse firm to support their own IT department to develop crucial software for bank operations. After some years of partnership a service provider has an immense knowledge about the design of this software. However, the bank IT team was never really involved in the design part of the software and their knowledge about the further development of this software does not allow them to continue this project without external support. Furthermore, the skills needed to perform more sophisticated software coding are not any more available in the bank team and have to be regained or bought. As the bank needs to regain the knowledge and starts to in-source back the knowledge from their service provider, the bank team – now in the role of "a novice" – needs to gather more expertise in activities so far performed by the service provider. Apart from documentation (its transfer or creation) – a transfer of tacit knowledge (experience) is essential. The service provider has been leading projects and took responsibility for the timely delivery of the service (e.g. software updates, design of new software modules) as well as appropriate distribution of tasks during the projects (including tasks for the bank team). Both teams need to participate in the knowledge transfer projects with well designed goals of completing a transfer (e.g. design of sub-module of software). The transfer process needs to be constantly present and should not be reinvented every time there is a need for transfer. It means that the group of professionals has to now incorporate another set of activities to their daily schedule of the software production - activities which from now on are part of the organizational routine for both organizations. The organization uses CarePacks to support their transfers and support the transfer routine.

Example: "Project Reflection" CarePack

Context and name: Project Reflection CarePack is to be used shortly after a jointly (client and service provider) executed project to reflect on the transfer of knowledge between client and service provider which has been performed in such a project. This pattern supports structured exchange of insights among members of the project. This CarePack is based on the transfer instrument called After Action Review which was developed by and for the US Army (Dixon, 2000) to help the individuals involved in a group activity to share knowledge among project members and contribute to the organizational memory of the project team after "the action" (often a military based field intervention) took place.

Forces: Use of this CarePack is triggered by the need of sharing views about the knowledge transfer in a project in the open forum consisting of all involved project members. The collaboration principles include: openness toward views of others, contribution towards a much richer "group view" and also understanding value of the team based improvement. Confidence and trust in the transfer team is strengthened through the project members' joint creation of the view on the project without imposing any hierarchical and organizational factors on the members expressing their point of view. Collaborative goal achievement is controlled through the level of active participation during Project Reflection meeting. This CarePack contributes to sustainability of the knowledge transfer through imposing a behavior of sharing during specially designed meeting where the meeting results are available immediately and the team (consisting of the client and service provider members) is actively involved in the process.

Problem: To understand if the knowledge transfer project (or project module) accomplished what was planned and if not, to understand what accounted for a change. This is a collectively built understanding where members of both the client and its service provider project members (two different organizations) need to contribute jointly.

Solution:

The knowledge transfer leader or a project leader prepares a collaborative meeting which leads towards building an understanding of transfer activity just performed. Such meeting takes place in a critical time/space of the collaborative work – which is right after completion of a particular jointly executed project. This is often a moment preceded by a considerable stress with great temptation for not to prolong the project through additional activities regardless of the achieved results. On the other hand, this is also a great moment for a group based reflection. The pursued project activities are still fresh and involved actors are still available for discussion and opinion. Therefore, the "Project Reflection" meeting is an essential part of wrapping up the knowledge transfer activities. It needs to be carefully prepared and communicated. Such meeting requires a presence of all the actors involved in this multi-organizational project. The procedural description of the CarePack describe step-by-step how such meeting need to be organized what artifacts are needed for the meeting, agenda, activities and the tips for the moderator. It is important to make sure that all the involved actors are invited (using communication guidelines of respective organizations), that they understand the goal of the meeting, are aware of the meeting agenda (3-Point agenda), understand and follow the rules of the meeting (explained below) , and can actively participate in the meeting. The goal of the meeting is to build a shared understanding about the project completed by a team consisting of a service provider and client organization. Therefore, it is crucial that all the members of the project can describe transfer activities (and issues) as they have experienced them without the need to consider company (or particular group's) politics, fear of losing a face in the company or losing a job. This kind of a meeting does not require "meeting minutes", however a personal note taking is allowed. Through sharing different views on particular issue or activity the whole group can better understand the complexity or origins of problems which can be avoided or redesigned in the future. Furthermore, particularly successful decisions can be validated and supplied as a guideline for further use in the organization(s). The project leader may point out a person which helps the meeting members to stick to the rules set up for this meeting.

This CarePack can not be used to collect information which is to be used against the subordinates as a proof of their wrong-doing or possible mistakes of a particular individual during the project.

E-tools: This CarePack procedures are to be used during face-to-face, synchronous discussions. However, if face-to-face meetings can not be conducted the transfer team may decide to use electronic communication tools. It is important to remember that use of electronic tools often allows for a very detailed way of tracing the comments to their authors and for this reason the comfort of open information sharing in this context needs to be provided.

Example and Related Patterns:

Example: The teams of both outsourcer and service provider are involved in a project which provides a company with a semi-annual update (release) of a crucial software (adding functionality and improving software performance). Part of this project is to transfer knowledge about the particular software module. After the new software release is implemented the team meets to discuss following aspects:

- what was planed to be transferred during this project (knowledge about the software module which allows the novice to create new libraries)
- what was actually achieved (new libraries are created but there is a loose of all old ones – a costly mistake). The team discusses what accounted for a change: expert believes the novice made a fatal mistake and was aware of the risk; the management of both teams think that there is a need for a better "safety net" for a novice working on a software module; the knowledge receiver is convinced that a novice took the risk but he was not aware of the consequences.

The team improves the transfer procedures and makes sure that both the novice and the expert are still able to perform joint activities.

Related CarePacks are listed; e.g. "Transfer Preparation" CarePack with information and procedures for successful start of the transfer pilot projects which, among others includes communication guidelines for organizations involved in outsourcing project. Use of "Transfer Preparation" CarePack results in the choice of appropriate group of knowledge keepers and receivers, identifies responsible management, identifies knowledge items for the transfer, defines time and methods for such transfer and provides a document which includes this information and is signed by the management of both organizations.

Resulting Context section lists advantages and disadvantages of this CarePack. A clear advantage of this CarePack is its structured approach used for enriching a group memory through group based reflection conducted after completing the project involving the knowledge transfer. A disadvantage for this CarePack is that if the project members are not able to follow rules of the meeting as described in the CarePack (e.g. forget about the organizational hierarchy while discussing the outcomes of the project) there is a possibility the team may face more challenges than before the meeting.

This CarePack facilitates the structured approach for: understanding what was the knowledge transfer supposed to achieve, assessing if it was achieved and identifying what accounted for a change during a jointly executed project. It supports the project leaders in designing a meeting with a "3- Points" meeting agenda and offering a set of rules for participants to support an open exchange of insights and views. Furthermore, the tips collected by previous "users" and added to the CarePack help to deal with e.g. particular "organizational culture" related issues experienced by the participants in previous meetings. Furthermore, it supports the enhancement of organizational memory of the teams helping them performing better in the future.

7. Introducing CarePacks at a Swiss financial institution

We had an opportunity to conduct three trials and we worked on improving the design methodology for the sustainable knowledge transfer at a Swiss financial institution. Here we report our observations and first lessons learned from designing and implementing CarePacks-patterns for the knowledge transfer in outsourcing relationships:

First trial:

Introduced artifacts to support the transfer: In our first trial we used "Knowledge transfer instrument catalogue". Based on the extensive literature research we created a catalogue of "methods" explaining how the knowledge (tacit, implicit or explicit) can be transferred between groups or individuals and also what qualities of involved individuals are needed for successful transfer (Bugajska, 2007). Transfer instruments can be accessed at: www.swissprimary.ch. Furthermore, we offered first electronic support for the transfer teams e.g.: "Online learning diary" (in form of a Blog) to describe the transfer process. Additionally, "wiki" space for the transfer team was created to foster sharing of information about knowledge items which are to be transferred together with contacts and repository for transfer related e-documents.

What we have learned: Catalogue of methods for the knowledge transfer is a great tool for team leaders to help propose appropriate instrument to their transfer teams. However, a relatively short description of the instrument did not suffice to convince or engage the team to implement it for their field activities. It offered too much "open space" without precise directions. Furthermore, while working on several pilots simultaneously, we (the transfer facilitators) realized that there is a strong need to define routine approaches for the same activities (e.g. transfer preparations, procedures for choosing a transfer method, complementing with communication processes of both organizations). Consequently, proposed e-tools were not used effectively. One e-tool called "Online learning diary" (offered as an online Blog) was not used willingly due to the lack of openness of one's activity toward the group. Furthermore, "wiki pages" introduced as a collaboration platform to describe knowledge items for transfer (to be used by both organizations) were still not user friendly enough. Overall, the introduced activities were perceived as considerably slowing down operational activities. Additionally, interview conducted with one knowledge receiver revealed the existence of transfer instruments created by the knowledge receiver himself which (unfortunately) ended up hidden from the rest of the team (and not shared). This clearly shows that the transfer between organizations needs to be connected to the internal knowledge management processes and needs to inform internal management of the improvements realized as part of the process.

What we addressed: We proposed to introduce a more formalized approach for the knowledge transfer. We proposed a contract like agreement which included transfer goals, results and measurements (KPIs) for each knowledge transfer item and the involved transfer team. Furthermore, we offered an approach for internal knowledge build-up as an alternative for transferring the knowledge (e.g. internal trainings or "buying" the knowledge keeper). Moreover, we concentrated on designing a more sustainable approach for conducting the knowledge transfer without the constant presence of a transfer facilitator during the transfer meetings. Additionally, we built an organizational support for the idea of a more collaborative (client and service provider) knowledge transfer. This includes offering more visibility for the transfer team through the appropriate design of the transfer pilot. The transfer team needs to be recognized as a contributor to the overall group of the whole software development unit and, as such, receive adequate support for contributing to the group innovation and improvement of group performance.

Second Trial:

Introduced artifacts to support the transfer: We used set of CarePacks for preparation and execution of the knowledge transfer. We created more user friendly "wiki" pages and included an example for future users. We introduced a process for automatic upload of a "Learning Diary" which the user completes on his computer and share with group when he finishes it.

What we have learned: The collaboration requires a structured approach to support the transfer involving people representing different organizations and also find ways to support the client organization in distributing the knowledge across the team members. Moreover, successful transfer of knowledge requires collaboration between the knowledge keeper and knowledge receiver and it is important they take active part in designing the transfer. For example, one of the knowledge keepers reported that our self study template needed to be remodeled. He proposed his own template (for learning the software) which soon was accepted by the knowledge receiver. Such "filled" template is now used as a software-developer handbook by the team. From the perspective of use of patterns, we saw it as an interesting approach for using the pattern as a creative re-design and re-definition of routine processes to address the needs of the organization.

We also learned that the roles of motivator and transfer sponsor taken by the team leader were essential for the success of the knowledge transfer initiatives. Important element of the transfer was the choice of the CarePack to support the transfer team according to the personal characteristics of the knowledge keeper and receiver. Furthermore, linking the knowledge transfer initiatives to internal knowledge management processes requires that middle management understands well their challenges in the process of transferring knowledge within organization ("Middle-up-Down Mgmt Style", (Nonaka, 1995))

What we addressed: We offered design approach for improving the transfer processes by introducing the CarePacks patterns of which structure accepts and invites their re-design. For the CarePacks, we decided to introduce a grid of clearly defined milestones allowing the team leader to check if the knowledge receiver is still on track. Often, if the transfer is successfully accomplished, the knowledge receiver (novice) becomes an expert of some sort. Therefore, it is important to reflect that in the talent development process within the organization. Furthermore, successful transfer reflects the ability of the receiver to absorb the knowledge under given circumstances.

Third Trial

Within this trial we introduced "train the trainer" initiatives for the Knowledge Transfer Coach as well as Coaching for middle-managers to act on their "Middle-up-Down Mgmt Style" for more successful knowledge transfers.

What we have learned:

Only some portion of the process becomes "the regular and predictable behavioral patterns [...] that are coping with a world of complexity and continuous change" (Pavitt, 2002). Therefore, the role of KT Method Coach is to recognize them and to deal with the rest of the situations which shape the uniqueness of every knowledge transfer individually (which can lead to re-design of the CarePack).

It is important to note that the design of CarePacks needs to reflect the duality of routines and the unique approach by securing a balance between covering every possibility, issue and situation in a collaborative transfer of knowledge and formulating transfer routines for successful inter-organizational transfer. Additionally, the knowledge transfer profits from a better incorporation of transfer results into the periodic organizational performance reviews.

What we addressed:

We offered a creation of "How-to-Design a CarePack" to help the Coach in new designs. Furthermore, we improved the presentation of the patterns. As a communication instrument, a coherent and short presentation of a CarePack additionally stresses the value of such pattern as a portable accommodation instrument for new design paradigms discovered by collaborating teams. Especially for the collaboration within the outsourcing relationship set-ups, an ability to find a common ground for collaborating team members by proposing a one or maximum two page document, instead of a sixty page book, would be of a great value for all involved.

We also believe that the organization needs to address a structured approach to the competency mapping and competency development of the employees. This could enhance the role of the CarePacks in supporting the development of the employee; on the other hand, the competency map could be used for choosing appropriate CarePack for skills of particular knowledge receivers and identify candidates with the ability to disseminate the knowledge across the organization.

8. Conclusion and practical implications

Initial efforts to support the knowledge transfer in our field project strove to determine the specific demand of the involved organizations and to design a set of routine processes for the knowledge transfer activities on the level of the knowledge transfer episode. The efforts focused on collecting proven designs for transferring knowledge such as "after action reviews" (Dixon, 2000), "peer assist" (Collison, 2004) etc. These proven designs were incorporated in the initial CarePacks. The collection of the CarePacks proved to be useful, but of course on their own they are not sufficient to fully implement the knowledge transfer. In contrast to workshops and meetings (i.e., the traditional application areas of collaboration engineering (de Vreede, 2005)), the organizational "surroundings" frequently interfered with the collaborative processes in the form of interruptions, change in priorities, lack of guidance, de-motivated employees, hidden agendas and other obstacles. In traditional workshops and meetings, moderators have the possibility to control the meeting process, motivate and focus the participants and keep interruptions away from them. Yet it is not feasible to have a moderator present each time the knowledge transfer activities were to take place. The knowledge transfer is by nature far too much embedded in work activities and having a moderator there is too expensive and sometimes may prove counter productive. Thus the task of the moderator had to be taken over by the organizational surrounding and the participants. Collaboration engineering had to design a network of actors to fulfill this task and to enable them to do the work.

Care-Packs are addressing the need for sustainable, routine-based repeatable collaboration instruments which can support the knowledge transfer during IT outsourcing relationships between organizations. Furthermore, Care-Packs are designed not only to empower teams involved in the knowledge transfer process without showing disrespect for the complexity of the transfer, but also to support individuals sharing their knowledge about the tasks, needed skills, information and know-how between the two organizations.

Based on the experience that we have gathered throughout the knowledge transfer project between the Swiss financial institution and their IT service provider, we offer important practical implications for conducting and managing transfer of knowledge during the IT outsourcing projects. Judging by the current developments in sourcing initiatives led by biggest banks (e.g., sourcing initiatives of UBS Bank) and insourcing tendencies seen in North America (Fowler, 2006), we believe that preparing organizations to successfully conduct transfer of knowledge can only gain importance in the future. We believe that there is a strong need for developing and deploying CarePacks - like instruments for the knowledge transfer in IT outsourcing - since they not only offer sustainable processes for handling the transfer, but also because the knowledge transfer routines allow the employees to develop skills important for knowledge sharing and further shape the culture of the organization. CarePacks follow the structure of patterns and can profit from qualities associated with them. Another important quality of the CarePacks is that the usage of patterns fosters development of new and better (for both the transferring and receiving teams) methods of the knowledge transfer in an outsourcing relationship. Finally,, such patterns provide a platform for community-based altering or creating new patterns which are of great value for communities of sourcing organizations to work on. Such platforms, in turn, enable exchange of the knowledge transfer patterns to help service receivers in balancing the knowledge with service providers during the course of IT outsourcing relationships.

If designed and implemented properly, Care-Packs could be put into practice by numerous companies as well non-profit organizations struggling to manage one of the most significant long-term risks inherent in each outsourcing relationship: erosion of knowledge and skills. It oftentimes proves to be very costly in cases where an organization needs to redefine or terminate an existing outsourcing relationship due to changes in the chosen strategy or external ramifications.

Acknowledgements: We would like to thank the project sponsor Gerhard Schwabe for valuable ideas and comments and support during the project and project member Mr. Ben Voigt for data collection and analysis, sharing his insights on the knowledge transfer process as well as providing feedback to this paper.

We thank the reviewers of this paper for their insights and feedback contributing to making this work a better tool for transferring our insights.

References

Alexander, C. (1979) *The Timeless Way of Building,* Oxford University Press, New York.

Alexander, C., Ishikawa, S., Silverstein, M., Jacobson, M., Fiksdahl-King, I., Angel, S., (1977) *A Pattern Language: Towns, Buildings, Construction,* Oxford University Press, New York.

Becker, J., Delfmann, P., (Ed.) (2004) *Referenzmodellierung - Grundlagen, Techniken und domänenbezogene Anwendung,* Springer.

Bloch, M., Jans, Ch., (2005) *Reducing risk in offshoring projects,* The McKinsey Quarterly, No.3

Braun, C., Hafner, M., Wortmann, F., (2004) *Methodenkonstruktion als wissenschaftlicher Erkenntnisansatz,* University of St. Gallen, St. Gallen.

Briggs, R. O., Vreede G.J., De, Nunamaker J.F, Jr., (2003) *Collaboration Engineering With ThinkLets To Pursue Sustained Success With Group Support Systems,* Journal of Management Information Systems, 19 (4), pp.

Bugajska, M. (2007) *Piloting Knowledge Transfer in IT/IS Outsourcing Relationship. Towards Sustainable Knowledge Transfer Process. Learnings From Swiss Financial Institution.,* ACIS, Keystone.

Bugajska, M., Schwabe, G., Voigt, B., (2006) *DEAN: Demand Analysis Method for Knowledge Transfer in IT Outsourcing Relationships*, Proceedings of Third International Conference on Knowledge Management, London.

Carmel, E., Tija, P., (2005) *Offshoring Information Technology,* Cambridge University Press, Cambridge.

Cohen, L., Young, A., (Gartner, Inc.) (2006) *Multisourcing. Moving Beyond Outsourcing to Achieve Growth and Agility,* Harvard Business School Press, Boston, Massachusetts.

Collison, C., Parcell, G. (2004) *Learning to Fly: Practical Lessons from one of the World's Leading Knowledge Companies,* Capstone, Oxford.

Darr, E. D., Kurtzberg, T. R., (2000) *An investigation of partner similarity dimensions on knowledge transfer,* Organizational Behavior and Human Decision Processes, 82 (1), pp. 28-44.

Davenport, T., H., (2005) *Thinking for a Living. How to Get Better Performance and Results from Knowledge Workers,* Harvard Business School Press, Boston, Massachusetts.

Davenport, T., Prusak, L., (2000) *Working Knowledge. How Organizations Manage what they know,* Harvard Business School Press, Boston, Massachusetts.

de Vreede, G.-J., Briggs, R.O. (2005) *Collaboration Engineering: Designing Repeatable Processes for High-Value Collaborative Tasks*, HICSS, International Conference on System Sciences, Vol. 03, Hawaii.

de Vreede, G.-J., Kolfschoten, G.L.,Briggs, R.O. (2006) *ThinkLets: a collaboration engineering pattern language,* International Journal of Computer Applications in Technology, 25 (2/3), pp. 140-154.

Dixon, N. (2000) *Common Knowledge. How Companies Thrive by Sharing what They Know.,* Harvard Business School Press, Boston, Massachusetts.

English, W., Baker, W., H., Jr. (2006) *Winning the Knowledge Transfer Race,* McGraw-Hill, New York.

Fowler, B. (2006) *Is Insourcing the New Outsourcing?* CIO.

Gamma, E., Helm, R., Johnson, R., Vlissides, J., (1995) *Design Patterns, Elements of Reusable Object-Oriented Software,* Addison-Wesley.

Gottschalk, P. (2007) *Knowledge Management Systems: Value Shop Creation,* IGI Publishing.

Gregor, S. (2006) *The Nature of Theory in Information Systems,* MIS Quarterly, 30 (3), pp. 611-656.

Heinzl, A. K., W.; Hack, J., (2001) *Erkenntnisziele der Wirtschaftsinformatik in den nächsten drei und zehn Jahren,* Wirtschaftsinformatik, 43 (3), pp. S. 223-233.

Heym, M. (1993) *Methoden-Engineering: Spezifikation und Integration von Entwicklungsmethoden fuer Informationssysteme,* Rosch-Buch, Hallstadt.

Hinds, P., Pfeffer, J., (2003) *Why Organizations Don't "Know What They Know": Cognitive and Motivational Factors Affecting the Transfer of Expertise.,* In Sharing Expertise. Beyond Knowledge Management(Ed, Ackerman, M., S., Pipek, V., Wulf, V.) MIT Press, Boston.

Hutzschenreuter, T. (2004) *Evaluator for knowledge transfer*, Otto Beisheim Graduate School of Management.

Jensen, M. M., W., (1976) *Theory of the firm: Managerial behavior, agency costs and ownership structure,* Journal of Financial Economics, (3), pp. 305-360.

Kim, L., Nelson, R.R., (2000) *Technology, Learning and Innovation: Experiences of Newly Industrializing Economies.,* Cambridge University Press, Cambridge, UK.

Ko, D., Kirsch, L., J., King, W.,R. (2005) *Antecedents of Knowledge Transfer from Consultants to Clients in Enterprise System Implementations,* MIS Quarterly, 29 (1), pp. 59-85.

Lukosch, S., Schümmer, T. (2006) *Groupware development support with technology patterns,* International Journal of Human-Computer Studies, 64 (7), pp. 599-610.

Mulder, U., Whiteley, A., (2007) *Emerging and capturing tacit knowledge: a methodology for a bounded environment,* Journal of Knowledge Management, 11 (1), pp. 68 - 83.

Nonaka, I., Takeuchi, H., (1995) *The Knowledge-Creating Company. How Companies Create the Dynamics of Innovation,* Oxford University Press, New York, Oxford.

Owen, C. (1997) *Design Research: Building the Knowledge Base,* Journal of the Japanese Society for the Science of Design, 5 (2), pp. 36-45.

Pavitt, K. (2002) *Innovating routines in the business firm: what corporate tasks should they be accomplishing?* Industrial and Corporate Changes, 11 117-123.

Rulke, D. L., Zaheer, S, Anderson, M., (2000) *Sources of managers' knowledge of organizational capabilities,* Organizational Behavior and Human Decision Processes, 82 (1), pp. 134-149.

Szulanski, G. (1999) *The process of knowledge transfer: A diachronic analysis of stickiness,* Organizational Behavior and Human Decision Processes, 82 (1), pp. 9-27.

Thatchenkery, T. (2005) *Appreciative Sharing of Knowledge: Leveraging Knowledge Management for Strategic Change,* Taos Institute Publications, Chagrin Falls, Ohio.

Von Krogh, G., (1998) *Der Wissenstransfer in Unternehmen: Phasen des Wissenstransfers und wichtige Einflussfaktoren,* Die Unternehmung, 52 (5), pp. 235-253.

Voigt, B., Novak, J., Schwabe, G., (2007) *How to manage knowledge transfer in IT outsourcing relationships - towards a reference model,* AMCIS, Keystone, Colorado.

Willcocks, L., P., Lacity, M., C., (2006) *Managing knowledge in outsourcing: Cases in financial services.,* In Global Sourcing of Businesses and IT Services(Ed, Willcocks, L., P., Hindle, J., Feeny, D.,Lacity, M., C.) Palgrave Macmillan, New York.

WKWI (1994) *Profile of Information Systems Research,* Wirtschaftsinformatik, 36 (1), pp. S. 80-81.

Knowledge Artifacts as Bridges between Theory and Practice: The Clinical Pathway Case

Federico Cabitza[1], **Carla Simone**[1], **and Marcello Sarini**[2]

[1] Dipartimento di Informatica, Sistemistica e Comunicazione. Università degli Studi di Milano-Bicocca, Italy, {cabitza, simone}@disco.unimib.it
[2] Dipartimento di Psicologia. Università degli Studi di Milano-Bicocca, Italy, sarini@disco.unimib.it

Abstract: This paper discusses how Clinical Pathways (CPs) are defined, used and maintained in two hospital settings. A literature review and observational study are combined to illustrate the composite nature of CPs and the different roles they play in different phases of their life-cycle, with respect to the theme of bridging medical knowledge with the related practices by which physicians deal with a specific care problem. We take the case of the CP as a paradigmatic case to stress the urgent need for an integrated approach with the computer-based support of information and knowledge management in rapidly evolving cooperative work settings.

Keywords: Knowledge artifact, Clinical pathway, Electronic patient record, Medical knowledge, Hospital work

1. Artifacts that put knowledge in practice

In the last few years the concept of *Knowledge Artifact* (KA) has been introduced in relation to a whole series of studies on how to *support* knowledge, as well as its creation, sharing and management. In fact, knowledge is often operationally defined in terms of a meaningful collection of rules, principles, criteria and informative notions that enable people to interpret a given situation, make decisions, solve problems, communicate and cooperate. Rather than focusing on knowledge itself (whatever it is), this notion leads to focusing on *what is used* when people have to deal with knowledge, i.e. on the physical *artifacts* that are created to somehow *embed and reify* the knowledge that is externalized for a particular purpose. Often, the concept of KA is used intuitively as a mere juxtaposition of the concepts of knowledge and artifact.

Please use the following format when citing this chapter:

Cabitza, F., Simone, C. and Sarini, M., 2008, in IFIP International Federation for Information Processing, Volume 270; *Knowledge Management in Action*; Mark Ackerman, Rose Dieng-Kuntz, Carla Simone, Volker Wulf; (Boston: Springer), pp. 37–50.

This is often done without giving KA a precise connotation with the risk of loosing the understanding of its role in managing knowledge "in action". This is probably due to the fact that in the literature there are several definitions of KA that mainly differ in respect to how the represented knowledge characterizes a specific community of practitioners. Limiting ourselves to the organizational domain, the definition of KA given by Holsapple and Joshi within their Organizational Knowledge Resources Framework [1] emphasizes its generality and ability to be further specialized. In fact, a knowledge artifact is any object that conveys or holds *usable* representations of knowledge. As any object, KAs can be transferred, shared, and preserved. Moreover, *usability* of a KA is interpreted as its ability to be put into action by a human actor in an organizational context: however, there is no explanation about how a KA can make this happen. Accordingly, Seiner keeps the characteristic of *representability* and *usability* that are intrinsic in the previous definition, but goes one step further. He also stresses the aspect of *shareability* by defining a KA as any "defined piece of recorded knowledge that exists in a format that can be retrieved to be used by others" [2]. By using the term "recorded" the latter definition hints both to an act of encoding, and also to an accumulation that the knowledge artifact must somehow permit, in order to grow *within* the community of its users and *together with* their competencies, experiences and knowledge. The fundamental role of the memory characterizes the acceptation of KA proposed in [3], where the authors focus on how such artifacts support the process of *knowledge creation* [4] and management due to the fact that they are *collectively defined* as the result of a progressive stratification of experiences, local practices of use and lessons learned to solve a problem. Then, KAs support practitioners only for their capability of being usable, i.e., to actually be artifacts open to human interpretation and capable of evolving in virtue of the constant negotiation of intended goals, involved incentives and responsibilities within the community.

In light of the last definition, we denote artifacts as *knowledge artifacts* whenever they are *primarily* used to *objectify* how people within an organization and community organize their "memories" and the involved "knowledge" and how people are able to put it into use to make proper and timely decisions. As reported in [3], this can also happen in the presence of underspecified knowledge: in fact, the common ground of the community provides the key to the right interpretation in the given context. This makes underspecification an economical way of maintaining usable knowledge within the community.

Organizational settings, and more generally cooperative settings, provide a wealth of significant examples of the *social* and *participatory* nature of the core knowledge involved, as well as of the *dynamic* and *cumulative* nature of the knowledge artifacts reifying it: almost any knowledge representation that has been collaboratively edited and that can be updated and annotated as necessary by its "consumers" can be considered a knowledge artifact, as long as it "incorporates" core competencies and "best practice" in which members of a community *recognize themselves* successfully solving problems and adding value to their activities.

In this paper, we focus on *Clinical Pathways* (CPs) and interpret their role in the hospital setting in terms of KA: in Section 2, we provide a general definition of CPs and briefly discuss their relationship with clinical guidelines. Section 3 discusses the composite nature of CPs and outlines their general structure and the types of knowledge they encompass in terms of different and complementary artifacts. In Section 4, we illustrate the main findings of our observational study with regards to the different ways CPs are used during their life-cycle. Lastly, Section 5 discusses these findings in the light of the advocated integration between CPs and clinical records and, more generally, between knowledge management technologies and actual work practice.

2. Clinical pathways for the clinical practice

For its apparent variability, interpretability and context-dependability, medical knowledge is something that cannot be simply learned from university textbooks and by putting practice aside. To this aim, clinicians have always relied on a number of different representations specifically conceived to provide quick and concise access to the relevant procedural knowledge, i.e., knowledge on *how* to apply notions of human anatomy, physiology and pathology to the pragmatic management of single and peculiar clinical cases. These representations have been called algorithms, protocols, procedures, plans and other similar terms: these terms are endowed with semantic nuances that usually depend on the extent to which clinical context is reported and in what detail, although the related concepts often end up simply overlapping. All of these representations share the idea that an *ideal way* to cope with a specific health problem exists, whereas *ideality* relates to the presupposed ability to minimize risks and to optimize chances of full recovery. The medical community achieves and improves on these effective ways of coping with sick patients as part of its daily work. Doctors report on this in specialist publications and literature contributions that are periodically digested and summarized in what they call *guidelines*, i.e., “a collection of systematically developed *statements* to assist practitioners [. . .] for specific circumstances” [5] to cope with their indeterminacy and unpredictability. These statements are expressed in terms of discursive and punctual recommendations towards “best practice” where all non-essential elements from the original context have been expunged to reach the necessary generality.

Clinical Pathways (CPs) have been proposed as a way of *combining* all the recommendations pertaining to a typical course of illness and of *articulating* them along the temporal and organizational dimension, i.e., in terms of who does what or when. Notwithstanding the apparent plainness of their function, a recent survey on PubMed literature identified more than 70 slightly different definitions of the term "clinical pathway" in more than 500 papers [6]. Most of these definitions define a pathway as an artifact which provides easy and convenient access to the whole body of useful notions that regard a specific treatment plan. The treatment plans are usually agreed upon by a group of clinicians to establish a reference in the management of a particular disease, and hence of any patient who could suffer from this disease, in order to reduce the odds of inappropriate interventions. This ambitious goal is not always reached: actually, what is more often obtained is a reduction of unnecessary variability of treatment that enables a more reliable and precise benchmarking among healthcare facilities. It also fosters the discovery and adoption of clinical evidence due to the better comparability and reproducibility of outcomes.

The reason why a medical staff decides to consolidate "best" or "usual" practices in specific CPs out of their usual interventions generally involves considerations based on either volume, cost, or risk of treatment [7] but also personal interests and academic drives . Usually establishing a CP in a clinical arrangement requires a team of healthcare providers to meet to combine the practitioners' multidisciplinary personal knowledge, usual practices and preferences with the existing medical literature and guidelines. They do that in order to establish what they consider the best treatment for a medical problem in their own settings. In this combination and adaptation to local needs, practitioners tend to consider any aspect that characterizes their own situations, e.g., organizational and resource-related constraints that would make the "ideal theory" of guidelines unfeasible.

3. Debundling clinical pathways

In order to have a clear picture of the interrelated aspects that characterize a CP, we undertook an observational study of how clinical pathways are designed, used and maintained in two Neonatal Intensive Care Units (NICU) of two important hospitals in Northern Italy, respectively the 'Alessandro Manzoni Hospital' in Lecco and the 'Giovanni Fornaroli Hospital' in Magenta (in the following denoted as NICULe and NICUMa, respectively).

We decided to focus on two NICU settings for a number of reasons. Neonatology is still a young discipline devoted to life-saving care of ill and premature newborn infants. Like in other intensive care disciplines, the practitioners involved in neonatology are faced with challenging standards with respect to efficiency, timeliness and effectiveness of intervention. Even more than in other similar disciplines, the increasing effectiveness of neonatal interventions relies on constant and continuous innovation, in regards to both technological equipment (e.g., mechanical ventilation), drug treatment (e.g., pulmonary surfactant replacement) and process improvement. This orientation towards continuous improvement and modernization has dramatically improved the survival rates of extremely premature infants and decreased the rates of disabling complications. For our studies, we undertook ethnomethodological observations in a number of hospital settings, including geriatrics, cardiology, orthopedics and internal medicine departments. Yet, neonatologists were the practitioners who showed the most enthusiasm towards computer-based support for their work and who were willing to consider their own practice from an objective point of view. We decided to focus on their work setting and practices, since we observed how neonatologists were deeply and sincerely committed to taking full advantage of the use of clinical pathways as a concrete and time-saving artifact that could actually improve their practice.

Indeed, both in the NICULe and NICUMa we saw that CPs were a significant case of *composite knowledge artifact*. In fact, the CPs we studied contained a wealth of documents, sheets, sections, maps, diagrams and forms [8, 9]. These heterogeneous artifacts differ for a number of reasons: e.g., because they bear different amounts of description and specification or they have been conceived for different purposes by practitioners with different competencies. They have been put together in order to provide practitioners with all the necessary notions and tools to make the "care plan" clear, to recognize its applicability to a specific clinical case and to help them in keeping the care trajectory "on track" with respect to that plan. Usually a CP is a collection of pre-existing documents of this kind that are put together to support a process of care "as a whole" by providing convenient access to a heterogeneous palette of indications related to the procedural, organizational, and medical knowledge that is available in a specific hospital setting, aimed at directly supporting different phases and episodes within the intended path. A significant example of these enclosures are the nomograms: graphical tools that support the predictive ability of practitioners which are intended to reify a sort of statistic knowledge about odd ratios and diagnostic / prognostic probability of test outcomes. Besides the nomograms, a CP can also encompass templates and structured forms: they provide an obvious support for compilation and data collection, but they also reify the knowledge indicating the minimum set of data to consider in order to undertake an intervention that is compliant to the law and local norms. Likewise, numerical scales and threshold-based criteria reported in the CP can be seen as cognitive aids conveying knowledge about the optimal heuristics to make clinical decisions that reduce the risk of adverse events. Classification schema and taxonomies succinctly reported at the end of a CP are intended to provide practitioners with indications regarding what conceptual categories must be considered in the interpretation of relevant clinical phenomena. To this same aim, even simple check-lists can be seen as tools conveying knowledge about what steps are to perform and what facts to consider in what loose order as a general and not prescriptive rule. Since activities and supportive tools are chosen according to the latest and most reliable guidelines, CPs are also endowed with references or short excerpts of those single recommendations from the guidelines that are applicable in each step of the pathway. Most of the time, recommendations are reported along with the strength of the related clinical evidence and degree of reliability.

Besides these knowledge-oriented components, CPs also encompass sheets which are purposely conceived to help practitioners to either monitor the performance of the care process with respect to specific output indicators extrapolated from the guidelines, or to keep track of the occurrence of variances during the progress of the illness of the patient with respect to the intended plan. Despite other names used in the literature, we refer to these artifacts as either *monitoring forms* and *variance records*, respectively. Variance records are those specific artifacts where clinicians are supposed to report "all the unexpected events which occur during patient care events which are different from those predicted in the pathway" [10]. Monitoring forms are artifacts by which clinicians can collect data needed to monitor the output of the most critical activities that are associated to performance indicators (e.g., number of times the patient has received a specific treatment in the last 48 hours with respect to the standard indicated by the guidelines). Both variance reporting and data monitoring are activities intended to facilitate the aggregation of data from multiple applications of the same pathway and enable its post-hoc analysis. This latter activity allows for the progressive tuning of the CP with respect to either the latest clinical evidences or the local best practices as we will see in more detail in the next section.

4. Clinical pathways in action

Once the composite structure and intended goals of a CP were identified, the next step of the study was to understand the actual role of CPs within medical practice in the two hospital wards we studied. The interviews, observations and their analysis highlighted four different phases where CPs play a different role: creation, use, evaluation, and update.

4.1. CP creation

The physicians and nurses interviewed at the NICUMa told us that the decision to embark the process of definition and adoption of a new CP is usually driven by two alternative criteria: *frequency* of cases and *seriousness* of illness. For example, gastroenteritis was chosen since it is a frequent disease in newborns and infants, although the problems that it causes are not severe. However, the high number of cases requires some shared and agreed criteria that can be expressed within a CP in order to admit patients only when they really require hospitalization. On the other hand, the criterion of seriousness was, e.g., applied when there was an unexpected outburst of meningitis cases at the hospital. In such a critical situation, decisions must be made quickly, often in an emergency context: therefore, the clinicians decided to make a trustworthy reference available to all staff involved and hence put it into a corresponding CP for meningitis.

The definition of a CP can be framed into the more general issue of resistance to changes. The problem of resistance to changes in healthcare settings is well acknowledged in literature (e.g., [11]). To deal with this issue, some strategies are recommended: in particular i) to not involve all practitioners in innovation, but only the so called "early adopters", i.e. only practitioners who have a positive attitude towards it; ii) to make early adopters' activity visible so that more prudent practitioners can also realize the effects of innovation. This last point is relevant in order to reduce the resistance to change of the more skeptical adopters. We observed similar strategies also in the hospitals under study. Our observations confirmed that the definition of a CP is a social process involving some representatives of the practitioners working in a specific hospital unit where the need for a CP is perceived. Then CPs are tested by these representatives and successively explained to the rest of the staff. During the definition process, the possibly discordant local practices that clinicians rely on when dealing with a well defined problem are discussed and confronted in the light of the current scientific evidences regarding the particular pathology. This process is not free of problems even if it is carried out by practitioners who have worked together for a long period. We observed three paradigmatic possible outcomes: i) practitioners reach an agreement about a local practice, which possibly conforms to the theory expressed by the guidelines; ii) an agreement cannot be easily reached: in this case, the indications given by the related theory are considered as a sign of a controversial point to be further discussed; iii) the compromise was the outcome of an asymmetric relationship that gave more influence to one of the discussants involved. In the following, we outline three vignettes illustrating the above listed different levels of agreement. The first two cases are about the CP designed for the treatment of neonatal infections due to the beta hemolytic streptococcus group B (GBS), which is often associated in severe gastroenteritis; the last case involves the definition of a CP to manage cardiac decompensation.

The first vignette illustrates how the theory (guidelines) was "arranged" by clinicians on the basis of a set of locally agreed best practices that are usually deployed to deal with the GBS problem. The head physician of the NICULe told us that the definition of the CP required the identification of what tests should be prescribed in order to formulate a sound diagnosis of the GBS infection. While the related international guidelines suggest the prescription of a wide battery of tests, physicians agreed on the usual practice to prescribe the complete battery of tests only for non-routinary cases, when further investigation is needed. In fact, since some of the recommended tests are too invasive for the infants, physicians preferred to save them from pain and possible complications unless strictly necessary. The structure of the CP reflected this choice: the first activity prescribes the first subset of tests, then a medical assessment has to be performed;

if a clear diagnosis can not be formulated, another activity recommends the other (more invasive) tests. The choice to prescribe the complete battery of tests only for non-routinary cases also satisfied the requirement of cost reduction advocated by the hospital administration, since the most invasive tests are often also the most expensive ones. Notwithstanding, this criterion was not considered to be the leading one, but simply a positive addendum.

The second vignette illustrates a case in which participants were not able to reach an agreement. The NICULe head physician described the case in which the physicians involved had discording opinions (even if with slight differences) about which was the best time interval to keep the newborn under observation in order to understand whether the signs of GBS infection had manifested or not. This time is crucial in order to avoid unnecessary treatments that can negatively impact the infants' health. Since after a lengthy discussion an agreement was not reached, the 48-hour time span proposed by the guidelines with strong evidence helped them to overcome this deadlock and deliver the CP that was to be timely issued. Physicians decided to conventionally use that time span as a purely hypothetical value indicating a still open issue to be further investigated. This conventional use has been possible because it was fully under the control of a coherent community, whose members work at arms-length, and continuously confront the practices used to deal with the different clinical situations. In any case, the selected value also protected the patients from too severe drawbacks, should the CP be used by occasional practitioners or novices, and it also protected clinicians from legal liabilities.

The last vignette illustrates a case where the CP was defined but turned to be practically unusable. The case regards the definition of a CP to manage cardiac decompensation, a condition that necessarily involves different wards and specialties. In this specific case, clinicians belonging to two groups (cardiologists and internists) conducted the negotiation in a way that raised an irreconcilable conflict: on the one hand, the cardiologists wanted to consider the ECG as a routinary exam to formulate a diagnosis for cardiac decompensation and wanted to build the CP accordingly. On the other hand, internists did not deem this exam as necessary, both for clinical motivations (i.e., other simpler, almost equivalent, diagnostic exams are available) and for organizational reasons: in their ward the ECG machine is not available, and hence performing this exam would require time-consuming and expensive interactions with external facilities. This conflicting situation led to discussions that frustrated the physicians of the internal medicine ward: they quit their active participation in the definition of the CP, whose final version was written taking into account only the cardiologists' point of view but basically never came into practice. This case shows how crucial and fragile the identification of who has to be involved in the definition (and subsequent use) of a CP is. The presence of a common ground is a fundamental precondition that cannot be surrogated by the simple fact that a group of people is dealing with the same disease on the same group of patients. One could object that this happened only because the CP concerned an inter-ward process. This is not completely true: the practitioners interviewed reported similar failures that also happened when a single ward was involved, typically when the head physician did not pay enough attention and effort to establish the right preconditions for the CP definition, or when a CP defined for a ward was transported as is into an apparently similar one. Therefore, when looking at a CP as a knowledge artifact, locality either in terms of background and elaboration, plays an unavoidable role.

4.2. CP in use

When observing and interviewing practitioners about CPs put in action, the basic question is: do CPs outlive their definition or do they disappear as soon as they have played the role of supportive artifact of the externalization of tacit knowledge? And, in the positive case, are they used only by newcomers or also by the people who built them? In our investigations we had a clear indication that CPs are not "dead letter". In fact, the physicians interviewed reported to us that they take CPs into constant consideration during their work: CPs are usually printed and kept by physicians as separate and unofficial artifacts that complement those pertaining to the clinical record. This habit shows a continuous need of practitioners to be supported in bridging the gap between theory and practice, to have a memory ready-at-hand of how to perform usual or critical practices when for any practical reason the content of this memory is difficult to be aptly retrieved and timely applied to the current case.

CPs do not play a role only for the individual decision-maker. Our observations highlighted how the participatory way in which CPs are defined (when successful), as well as their pervasive presence in the ward, facilitates the creation of a more collaborative relationship between doctors and nurses. From this point of view, CPs can be seen as boundary objects between these two complementary roles [12]. From doctors to nurses, they convey medical knowledge that helps the latter ones to better understand and contextualize doctors' decisions and their follow-up in the activities that nurses perform. The other way round CPs support the transfer of information pertaining to the decision of a doctor to the colleagues who will assess the same patient later. In this specific case, CPs define a clinical context to which this information can be related and become more reliable from the doctor's point of view. As the head-nurse of the NICULe told us: "by means of CPs, nurses are empowered to act as active and prompt reminders about activities due while surveying cases during the ward round and they become more confident in their ability to assist doctors on specific activities".

CPs are not used only as a part of and in combination with the whole clinical record: at the NICULe, a small number of main reference CPs are also printed and pinned on the walls of the small kitchen that physicians use for their informal meals and meetings. Sometimes discussions spring up in front of the CP diagram during coffee breaks, especially in regards to the most interesting cases which occurred a few hours earlier [13]. The presence of CPs hung on the walls of the dinette seem to facilitate storytelling and the exchange of experiences, as well as foster the exchange of opinion among peers who have dealt with similar cases: to this aim, CPs constitute a map where critical decisions are located and their consequences are analyzed in a discursive and visual manner.

The usefulness of CPs to deal with concrete problems (either routine or not) is acknowledged by most of the practitioners: notwithstanding, the head physician of NICULe clearly stated to us that CPs are still used as an "external" reference and hence their inclusion in the current practices is not facilitated at present: this is still perceived as an open issue even for those CPs that are actively used. The most advocated solution is to make CPs an official artifact that is fully and seamlessly integrated within the clinical record so that it is possible to more easily draw correlations between the entries of the clinical record and the activities referred to by the CP, and viceversa. This recurrent requirement opens up new possibilities to conceive feasible ways to introduce a computer-based technology supporting the full usage of clinical records: we will come back to this point in the concluding section.

4.3. CP evaluation and update

The deeply contextualized nature of CPs makes them a live artifact that evolves together with its context. This evolution can be defined in terms of both *evaluation* and *update*: these two phases are strongly correlated since the evaluation gives indications for the changes characterizing the latter and the updating phase justifies the additional effort involved in the former for the sake of continuous quality improvement. In this twofold phase, CPs play two complementary roles with respect to their capability of bridging theory and practice. On the one hand, CPs allow new medical knowledge to come into practice. In fact, once the CP has been consolidated, its updating is triggered by the appearance of new scientific evidence in the specialist literature for the pathology at hand. In this case, the responsible for the CP, a role that is usually defined among the physicians who are expert in that pathology, has to update the CP and notify the updates to the other colleagues accordingly. This usually happens as soon as new evidence become available which contrast or only complement the indications reported in the current CP. Even when new evidence is not available, a revision on average every two years is a common practice in the settings we have studied. On the other hand, CPs facilitate the monitoring of how current behaviors within the ward comply with the intended local best practices embedded in the CPs; CPs also permit the post-hoc evaluation of the performance of the overall caring process that they describe. These two kinds of information should be collected in specialized components of the CP: the variance records and the monitoring forms we mentioned in Section 3. While the first role traces back to the themes concerning the CP definition, the second role raises more serious problems when CPs are put into action. In fact, the filling in of the two above mentioned components is a typical case of effort that in theory is well understood and accepted by all of the involved practitioners, but which in practice is difficult to perform because of the chronic lack of resources shown by the medical settings in Italy. To this regard, the head physicians see the introduction of technological solutions for the management of care information as a way of facilitating physicians in compiling the necessary forms at the place and time of the execution of the activities. This returns to the point that CPs and clinical records need to be more integrated.

At NICUMa, the problem to have information about monitoring behaviors and evaluating performances collected on different specialized components of CPs led to an original solution. Variance records and monitoring forms have been unified into a single form in order to concentrate the compilation effort and to keep some of the context of the inscriptions. The driving goal was to monitor the performance of the process in terms of outputs and of their compliance with the standard indications contained in the CPs. For this some performance indicators have been identified within the organizational unit where CPs are used and inserted in the monitoring form: those indicators refer either to clinical aspects of the care, e.g. whether an antibiotic has been administered in the presence of bacteria for meningitis within the first hour since admission; or to more organizational aspects: e.g., whether a patient has been observed for a few hours after having slight dehydration in gastroenteritis cases; or to more patient specific topics: e.g., whether relatives received clear recommendations about the proper dietetic regimen to follow after their child has been discharged from the hospital. Each indicator has associated a reference value as specified by the local interpretation of the standard values posed by the theory (i.e., the guidelines). The same form contains sections where the free-text description and justification of the deviation from those values have to be inserted. This local solution has several advantages. First, the indicators point to specific activities or their pre/postconditions that are deemed as particularly critical in the process map contained in the related form of the composite CP: this information supplements the process description since it gives a measure of criticality of the activities it contains [9], although the correlation is only implicit. In fact, the two kinds of information are contained in different forms and the connection is dynamically reconstructed only in their practical use. Second, practitioners are better supported in the documentation of the variances. In fact, the presence of all the information on the same sheet lets the above criticality indicate which variances are really relevant to be traced and makes the documentation of the possible variances contextual to the activities and indicators to which they refer to, besides the obvious advantage of avoiding unproductive repetition of the same information on two sheets [14]. When the indicators show that current practice for a particular disease is not performing as well as indicated in the related standard and that the variances occurred exceed a physiological amount (due also to the initial tuning of a new CP), the responsible of the CP goes through the justifications reported therein and decides whether measures have to be taken to improve compliance with the practices indicated in the CP, or the latter one has to be modified according to the new current behaviors. The head physician of the NICUMa, who is responsible for the CPs, told us that the strategy is to gather all practitioners together once a month and to call a meeting where practitioners are informed about the indicators whose values do not reach the standard values. These meetings are also intended to facilitate the promotion of knowledge internalization and externalization; in fact, disseminating knowledge about those indicators that fall short of the standard is a way to promote self reflection (internalization) and to raise discussions among the practitioners involved (externalization) in order to find an agreed way to improve team performance with respect to the problematic activities. In all of the considered settings, evaluation and tuning is perceived as a collaborative process that is worth taking up part of a clinician's scarce time for the positive impact on the cohesion of the clinical community and for the improvement of the caring process with respect to patients and their families.

5. Implications on technologies

The paper outlined the main findings of a study concerning the definition, usage, evaluation and updating of CPs in two hospital wards. The study showed that this kind of composite knowledge artifact is a carrier of that procedural knowledge that combines the indications of an ideal behavior, as defined by guidelines derived from clinical research, with the constraints imposed by the current setting adopting the CP. Moreover, our study outlined some positive and problematic issues that arise when these knowledge artifacts are put into action. These positive and negative aspects concern the more general issue of how to reconcile the ways practitioners manage data in their daily work with the ways practitioners manage the knowledge they need in order to make sense of the data. This relationship is often problematic, especially since it is generally neglected in the design and development of computer-based information systems (ISs) and knowledge management systems (KMSs). In almost all the application domains, work is based on a set of core pieces of knowledge and on data that are used and produced in virtue of (and according to) that knowledge. Yet, knowledge and data are seldom considered tightly bound together as they are in practice, either by the management of an organization or by the designers of the organization's information system. Within the same organization, the technological solutions dealing with both aspects, ISs and KMSs respectively, are usually under the responsibility of different departments, or, in any case, within different programmes of work automation. This usually results in interoperable components which are logically disjointed. Our point is that if ISs and KMSs look at data and knowledge from irreconcilable perspectives, they end up by forcing behaviors that are hardly mutually supportive of cooperative and knowledge work.

We are well aware that it is dangerous to propose generalized approaches intended to fit every context, especially when knowledge management is involved. Notwithstanding, the healthcare domain is a paradigmatic case where the production of data and the access to the related knowledge are naturally combined in everyday practice. In fact, data and knowledge are managed by the same community of heterogeneous practitioners who closely interact with each other around the same set of patients and the same set of caring problems. The point we make here is that the development of both ISs and KMs has to take into account this obvious, but usually neglected, fact: actors perceive and need these systems to be integrated as two sides of the same coin. They are not that integrated, especially in all those cases in which data disappear quite quickly after their production either in the rows of a database or in the verbose pages of an almost unusable documentation. They are also not integrated in any other case where the constant and progressive stratification of experiences, solutions and best practices is not fostered or, worse yet, is practically hampered. In these cases, designing towards a strongly interconnected system is almost impossible and the use of loosely-coupled and partial solutions seems unavoidable, at least at the initial stage of introduction of KMSs. In other cases, the integration between data and knowledge occurs already in the everyday field of work, where practitioners are also supposed to use consolidated information management technologies that have a strong cultural and pragmatic impact on how they have their work done: here, the integration of knowledge management functionalities could be proposed on top of these existing systems and more importantly, could evolve jointly with them. This is an opportunity we detected for the healthcare domain [15], where Electronic Patient Records (EPRs) were introduced years ago and are being increasingly used in the hospital domain. Since the introduction of a new EPR in a hospital setting is still problematic [16], and since the relevance of CPs as a means to improve the quality of care is constantly increasing among the practitioners of that domain, this is a unique occasion to face the two sides of the same coin within a unified project. In such a project, the interaction functionalities that are typical of both ISs and KMSs could be jointly designed. In this light, EPR would stop looking as a set of templates reflecting the tables of the underlying database and it would become a more flexible, context-aware, and user-centered support that would also encompass knowledge-oriented tools as CPs are. These, in turn, would become closely integrated with clinical data, easy to be updated and tuned, and endowed with a dynamic interface integrated with the EPR that could support timely decision making, and make quality assessment and monitoring a reasonable effort. The above considerations have inspired both our methodological [17] and design-oriented [15] researches so far towards the fulfillment of the urgent requirement of integration which we collected from our participatory and observational studies in the last three years in the hospital domain.

Acknowledgements: The work presented in this paper has been partially supported by the Italian fund F.A.R. 2007. The authors would like to thank the management and personnel of the Neonatal Intensive Care Units of the Alessandro Manzoni hospital of Lecco and of the Giovanni Fornaroli hospital of Magenta for their kind collaboration.

References

1. C.W. Holsapple, K.D. Joshi, Organizational knowledge resources, Decis. Support Syst. 31(1), 39 (2001)
2. R. Seiner, Metadata as a knowledge management enabler, TDAN.com & KIK Consulting Services The Data Administration Newsletter. 15 (2001)
3. S. Bandini, E. Colombo, G. Colombo, F. Sartori, C. Simone, The role of knowledge artifacts in innovation management: the case of a chemical compound designer, Communities and technologies, pp. 327–345 (2003)
4. I. Nonaka, H. Takeuchi, The Knowledge Creating Company. Oxford University Press, Oxford, UK (1995)
5. M. Field, K. Lohr (eds.), Guidelines for Clinical Practice: from development to use. Institute of Medicine, National Academy Press,Washington, DC (1992)
6. D. Bleser, Depreitere, D. Waele, Vanhaecht, Vlayen, Sermeus, Defining pathways, Journal Of Nursing Management 14, 553 (2006)
7. T. May, Clinical pathways: Cure guide or cost-cutter?, Business First of Columbus (1997)
8. F. Cabitza, M. Sarini, On the pathway towards ict-support for a better and sustainable healthcare, In ECEH07 Proceedings of the second European Conference on eHealth, Lecture Notes in Informatics -GI-Edition, vol. P. Gesellschaft fur Informatik, pp. 89–100 (2007)
9. F. Cabitza, M. Sarini, C. Simone, Providing awareness through situated process maps: the hospital care case, In GROUP'07: Proceedings of the 2007 International ACM SIGGROUP Conference on Supporting Group Work, ACM Press, pp. 41–50 (2007)
10. J. Cheah, Clinical pathways – an evaluation of its impact on the quality of care in acute care general hospital in Singapore, Singapore Medical Journal 41, 335 (2000)
11. D.M. Berwick, Disseminating innovations in health care, JAMA 289(15) (2003)
12. S.L. Star, G. Bowker, Sorting Things Out: Classification and its Consequences (MIT Press (1999)
13. D.G. Bobrow, J. Whalen, Community knowledge sharing in practice: the Eureka story, Reflections, the Journal of the Society for Organizational Learning 4(2), 47 (2002)
14. F.. Cabitza, M. Sarini, C. Simone, M. Telaro, "When once is not enough": The role of redundancy in a hospital ward setting, In GROUP'05: Proceedings of the International Conference, ACM Press, pp. 158–167 (2005)
15. F. Cabitza, C. Simone, "... and do it the usual way": fostering awareness of work conventions in document-mediated collaboration, In ECSCW'07: Proceedings of the Tenth European Conference on Computer Supported Cooperative Work (ECSCW), pp. 119–138 (2007)
16. M. Berg, Health Information Management, Routledge (2003)
17. F. Cabitza, C. Simone, A language for executable specification of coordinative functionalities for electronic document systems, In CHItaly'07, Proceedings of the Fifth Symposium on Human-Computer Interaction (2007)

Managing Knowledge in Urban Planning: Can Memory Support Systems Help?

Adele Celino, Grazia Concilio, and Anna De Liddo

Dipartimento di Architettura e Urbanistica Politecnico di Bari, Italy, [a.celino, g.concilio, a.deliddo]@poliba.it

Abstract: When dealing with environmental plans, participation is considered crucial but hard work still has to be done in order to make participatory knowledge really operative. Tools and approaches to knowledge management are required that make participatory knowledge, which is produced, shared, and used along the planning action, available to the action itself. Starting from an experience of participatory planning in the context of Torre Guaceto natural Park, authors first reflect on the possible meaning of knowledge management in the planning process; secondly authors envisage the relevance of memory support systems in such processes as means to capture the argumentation chains which, explaining the action, are produced along the action and supporting it. Finally the paper presents the first results of a research project aiming at developing a memory support system dedicated to the Torre Guaceto Park Agency.

Keywords: Participatory knowledge management, Memory support, Argumentation, Long-term plans

1. Introduction

Participatory planning processes ask for and handle with knowledge collaboratively generated and validated. This knowledge is multiple (it comes from different peoples, sources and uses), plural (it is expression of different people needs and try to accomplish different tasks) and evolving (it changes in terms of time, space, social context settings and interpretations).

When dealing with environmental plans, participation is considered crucial but hard work still has to be done in order to make participatory knowledge really operative. More then in other domains, the need to keep trace of the assumptions, values, experiences, conversations, and decisions as they evolve along time is mainly oriented to enable reflection for the action-oriented plans development. Tools and approaches to knowledge management are required that make

Please use the following format when citing this chapter:

Celino, A., Concilio, G. and Liddo, A.D., 2008, in IFIP International Federation for Information Processing, Volume 270; *Knowledge Management in Action*; Mark Ackerman, Rose Dieng-Kuntz, Carla Simone, Volker Wulf; (Boston: Springer), pp. 51–65.

participatory knowledge, which is produced, shared, and used along the planning action, available to the action itself.

The paper argues the need to combine the concept of knowledge management with the concept of organizational memory in order to represent, take trace, and give reason to this knowledge process.

The paper starts from an experience of participatory planning in the context of Torre Guaceto natural Park, and represents it as just one of many planning stories where the ability to monitor and manage knowledge in participatory planning action is crucial for the effectiveness of the action itself. Following the reflections stimulated by that story, the authors first reflect on the possible meaning of knowledge management in the planning process, secondly envisage the relevance of memory support systems in such processes as means to capture the argumentation chains which, explaining the action, are produced along the action and supporting it. The perspective of "memory support systems" is discussed as an opportunity to orient knowledge management to action in participatory planning processes.

Finally the paper presents the first results of a research project aiming at developing a memory support system dedicated to the Torre Guaceto Park Agency.

2. The story: Planning the Torre Guaceto wetland

This case considers the activities carried out by the Park Agency of the Torre Guaceto wetland and the results obtained in its planning activity (Celino and Concilio, 2006a). Our analysis mainly focussed on the agency ability to reinterpret its planning tasks out of institutional protocols and to develop with the local community a communication framework, rather different from what it usually is in Italy. Since the very beginning of its activity the Park Agency approached participation practices conceiving participation not as a pre-structured planning protocol or simply one of the several activities of the planning process. Participants could not be captured into the planning process and simply managed as additional cognitive inputs. Two main conditions affected and still affect the interaction between the Park Agency and the local community.

1. The most recurring task for the Park Agency of Torre Guaceto is mainly oriented to plan and regulate in the area both agricultural uses and practices which are directly and heavily affecting the economic revenue of agricultural activities; discussions on the necessary modification of the agricultural practices could not avoid conflicts thus making interaction deeply lacking in communication and/or mutual learning and understanding.
2. A large number of land owners characterizes the area each representing a potential participant to be involved in the planning process. They are not

only strong individual actors, due to their deep interest in the productivity of their activities; they also represent, all together, a rooted community whose communication dynamics gives shape to a complex and compact network. This network is difficult to be entered and cannot be summarised by one or two of its representatives.

The Park Agency developed the ability to act within the community as a part of it. It initially shaped its communication skills coherently with the communication mechanisms of the community network and subsequently, together with it, started to evolve. Coherently with the dynamics just described, a planning path out of codified protocols of the Park Agency can be outlined when looking at the Torre Guaceto activities.

The story we want to tell refers to the decision making process related to a specific portion of the Land Use Norms (part of the Reserve Spatial Management Plan): prescriptions for biological olive tree cultivation and olive oil production (Norms for Olive Oil Production, NOOP).

Constraints imposed onto land use practices usually activate strong reactions of individuals affected by the constraints. Also in Torre Guacteo deep aversion to the first version of that NOOP was given by the local agricultural community. Subsequently, new different versions of the NOOP, always less restrictive, have been proposed for the park area but no agreement with the agricultural community has been reached and norm, as means for innovating agricultural practices, has been temporarily abandoned.

A second version of the NOOP has been developed to restart the discussion among the Park Agency and the Torre Guaceto Agricultural Community each supported by their own consultants. In this second participatory phase the Park Agency tried to involve in the process all the cognitive actors recognized and accepted by the agricultural community thus shaping a new participatory environment characterized by knowledge flows, cognitions and actors different form those involved in the previous phase. Still, and similarly to the previous phase, collective discussions were organized, in the form of forum, in order to give rise to collaborative interactions. Also this second version of the norms has been deeply opposed since, may be, it was not considered by the agricultural community a product of its own reflection and decision.

Starting from an analysis of the agricultural community needs and requirements and using funds of an INTERREG project for supporting innovative agricultural practices in wetlands, a new communication protocol, out of the formal/institutional participation protocols for norms and plan adoption, has been activated. The new communication protocol involved the agricultural community in developing and testing a new practice for olive oil production: the agricultural community become the privileged actor of an experimental agricultural practice mainly due to its experience and practice.

A fourth version of the NOOP is currently being developed in form of Regulation of the Producers Association of Biological Olive Oil in Torre Guaceto and it is more restrictive than the first version of the NOOP elaborated by the park agency.

This story shows some elements which we consider crucial referring to the issue of making participatory knowledge operational for the decision.

Both the Agency and the Agricultural Community have shown cognitive openness: their availability to be involved in regional, national or international projects gave them the economical opportunities to start experimentation to find out protocols for innovative agricultural practices. This initial openness is now transformed: neither the Park Agency nor the agricultural community present solutions to each other. They are always looking for new practices making their productions no more impacting the wetland and no solutions is considered as such unless it is the result of a collaborative cognitive effort: knowledge is managed not to defend predetermined solutions bur rather to collaboratively create new ones.

The Park Agency continuously reframes its tasks within the area and has identified a new role for itself in park management. Within the general goal of guaranteeing the re-naturalization of the wetland and the sustainability of the surrounding areas, the Park Agency became a "process interpreter": its effort is no longer oriented to attract cognitive resources into a predetermined planning process, it rather observes the community mechanisms from its inside (it is now a component of that community, it behaves and is considered as in charge of some of the strategic community activities) and, contemporarily, from outside (it keeps its institutional managerial and monitoring tasks) and is able to continuously reshape the planning process, i.e. the action. In this way planning action is no longer the result of a pre-designed protocol, it is an emerging process which can be described by the interpretation of the continuous acting and deciding of the community and the Park Agency as a whole.

New agricultural practices have been tested and implemented looking for products which traditionally grown in that area although with a lower productivity. They are not completely new practices: they are the result of a creative search combining the re-use of traditional cultivar with modern agricultural techniques and transformation processes. Looking for possible solutions becomes a creative process based on cognitive collaboration. The enlarged community (Park Agency included) behaves like a pulsating entity: while searching solutions, it incorporates new components or, depending on the problem at hand, becomes part of other communities then returning to its previous condition although not unchanged. The modification required for an effective search did not only added new and operative knowledge, it rather represents a mode developed by the community to develop and manage knowledge throughout their participatory planning action: the planning action shapes itself around knowledge and its dynamics.

3. Managing knowledge in participatory planning environments

The story of Torre Guaceto represents just one of many planning stories where the ability to monitor and manage knowledge in participatory planning action is crucial for the effectiveness of the action itself.

Although participation is considered fundamental in environmental planning activities (Tress and Tress, 2003; Kangas and Store, 2003; Mostert, 2003; Pellizoni, 2003), stories like this one highlight the crucial role of cognitions being produced, shared and used throughout such processes. The construction of environmental plans cannot be considered a mere addition, analysis and assessment of information and data: the construction of environmental plans is more and more intended as a social activity producing highly cognitive visions able to guide collective action and make it converge.

When building plans within participative processes, new methodologies and approaches for knowledge management are required since predictive knowledge needs either direct approaches to knowledge communication and exchange (vis-à-vis meeting, web-based discussions) or relational approaches for social and institutional arenas management (communication, cooperation network management, public relations) (Jasper et al., 2004).

In the last years, a great effort has been carried out on the characterization of knowledge produced, shared and made operatively available during participative processes for plans development (consider for example the great discussion on lay and local knowledge); it is a distributed knowledge, scarcely structured, non-formalized and/or hard to formalize, organized and transferable in very different and particular forms (stories, traditions, practices, life styles, …) difficult to acquire and, most relevant, difficult to manage within traditional knowledge management approaches.

Jasper, Banthien and Mayers-Ries (2004) introduced the concept of Participatory Knowledge Management (PKM) that is a knowledge management able to consider "soft facts of knowledge such as structural or cultural behaviour patterns, perception frames, values and opinions, implicit, practical and local knowledge" (Jasper et al., 2004: 69).

The problem of participatory knowledge management shows its peculiarity in both the specificity of involved cognitions and the modalities through which that knowledge is explicated, generated, and archived; it is a knowledge which:

- is multi- o trans-disciplinary,
- is highly flexible and reflexive,
- is produced in a variety of sites (formal or informal) and/or in virtual/ephemeral networks,
- needs new modes for quality control (attention has been recently paid to the knowledge assessment issue; EEA, 2001; Risbey et al., 2005).

Such knowledge is generated in action (Hage et al., 2006), and partially revealed and/or explicated only in action. Therefore action becomes the space in which modes for participatory knowledge management have to be defined and implemented. Obviously it is not possible to determine a priori such modes but it is possible to consider some very general rules, taking into account the peculiarity of participatory knowledge together with its strong relation to action.

This close relationship between knowledge management and action becomes crucial in participative processes for environmental planning: in such processes it is necessary to consider knowledge management as an activity able to give structure to action.

4. Memory support systems: What perspectives

As above remarked, the construction of environmental plans must be intended as a social activity in which evolving plans are (judged) able to guide the participatory action and make it converge. In such cases, the knowledge (often tacit) coming from participative processes could be considered as a value and utility only when it is able to stimulate collective, practical and more or less shared reflections (Celino and Concilio, 2006b).

The access to the knowledge developed by the decision making process during the process itself is particularly relevant for the plan development process since it strengths the support for reflection, enables re-experience considered fundamental mechanism for learning, (Celino and Concilio, 2006b) and widens the opportunities for decision making.

A plan developed in a participatory environment should focus not only on the substantive character of medium/long term visions but also, and especially, on the decisional system explaining those visions. Such a plan needs to evolve together with its decisional system and, consequently, to incorporate the continuous modifications that collective reflections produce on existing prospects, interpretations of the involved actors, and preliminary remarks explaining the decisions (Celino and Concilio, 2006b).

The need to explore the concept of organizational memory in participatory planning experiences starts from the stance to consider information and knowledge (used and produced in these processes) not as passive records to be stored in a repository but as dynamic contents living and changing along the time and coherently with the organization evolutions. It is important not only capturing and storing the history of the decision making process but also making it accessible for further and continuous interpretation and exploration along the process itself and by all the members of the organization, i.e. the stakeholders involved in building and using that memory day by day. As Fischer pointed out "organizational memory must be: i. extended and updated as it is used to support work practices, ii. continually reorganized to integrate new information and new concerns, and iii. serve work by making stored information relevant to the new task at hand " (Fischer, 2001:353).

In environmental planning, capturing the Decision Rationale (DR) underlying the process itself and making it available to participants (Karacapilidis and Papadias, 2001; Santos et al., 1997; Alvarado et al., 2005) could be considered functional to the need to mediate between the short-term organizational memory and the long-term organizational memory.

Long-term organizational memory refers to those structures and contents of organizational memory being stable like values, principles, cognitions shared throughout the planning organization; short-term organizational memory represents essentially working memory (Miyake and Shah, 1999; Baddeley, 1986); deeply related to a specific decision making process it is an evolving entity supplying contents and knowledge to long-term memory throughout the DR considered as an intermediate memory and a stepping stone towards long-term organizational memory.

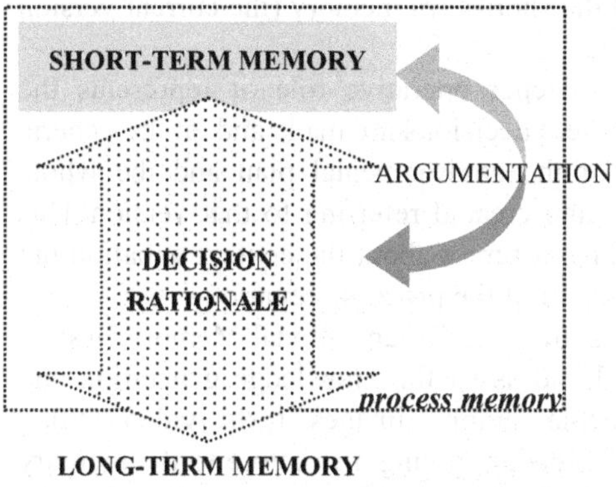

Figure 1: The mediation role of Decision Rationale

Argumentation becomes crucial. It has a double role both in: i. making DR explicit, and ii. explaining the modifications of the short-term memory (or working memory) along (Shum, 1991; 1996) such modification process as a sequence of cognitive transactions (Wegner, 1995; Zeleny, 1989; Brauner and Becker, 2006) from one version of plan to the subsequent.

Our interest is not only in knowledge in itself but also in the underlying context of knowledge and in the process that created that context of knowledge at the time it is created (Miyake and Shah, 1999). Information systems, supporting such processes, need to be developed having a content repository and a context repository, both structured and organized in a process memory. In these systems argumentation would represent not only a relevant component of the DR (Tweed, 1998; Celino and Concilio, 2006b) but also the power engine of the plan evolution. Therefore, the process memory, referring to the tracing of the DR, has to include both the knowledge evolution and also the argumentative base explaining such evolution.

In order to consider the temporal dimension of both the plan generation process and the plan itself, ICT systems should support the dynamic representation of the memory of the organization involved; indeed, such representation of the memory has to be considered a tool to "store" and exchange knowledge but also a mean:

i. to make explicit (and then visible to the users and system manager) the cognitive conditions and the argumentations generating the transactions from one version of the plan to the subsequent and
ii. to explore the operability of the current plan.

Starting from the model briefly described above, we are exploring the opportunity to represent dynamically the process memory within ICT environments by enabling the development of what we defined *process-scenario* that is a scenario which evolves together with its related decision making contexts and with the action itself (Celino and Concilio, 2006b). In a sense, the *process-scenario* includes the process-memory (the "Design Rationale as the reasons behind spatial planning decisions) and the short-term memory (the current version of the plan).

The *short-term memory* has got a deeper operative role: it represents the support of the operative environment where decisions are made and, at the generic time t, contains the current version of the environmental plan and the whole cognitive content developed, acquired and created referring to that version This last would promote shared understanding at time t about the context situation but does not have long-term value; it is just part of the process-scenario.

Coherently with the considerations above, the Organizational Memory System we are developing allows: i. to record and assist the knowledge generation and management (expressed in several media: graphs, images, texts, video, audio, etc.), ii. to keep trace of the history of decision, giving a structure to the memory of the complex "ephemeral" organization (Lanzara, 1983) emerging all around the participatory planning process, iii. to extract from history specific or new contents which are, or become during the process, "the focus of discussions and actions"; finally, iv. to trace the contents evolution and modifications along the process.

The Organizational Memory System allows users to create new knowledge rather than restricting them to the consumption of existing knowledge. Following the philosophy of meta-design (Fischer, et al., 2004), the system aims to support a reflective community in a collaborative design process; in such a way, the system is an open system that users can modify and evolve (Celino and Concilio, 2005).

5. The architecture of the memory support system for Torre Guaceto

In the following paragraph we present an experiment we are carrying out in Torre Guaceto in order to support a new starting project aiming at producing tomatoes in a biological perspective. This new project aims at implementing a memory support system assisting the community while developing new cultivation strategies and practices and is supposed to involve mainly the same community of the Torre Guaceto story told above. The system aims at tracking the memory of the decision making process thus making the knowledge produced along the action available for the action itself. That group of cultivators, collaborating with the Park Agency, is now interested in expanding its activities and possibly widening the community; all this with the help and supervision of the Park Agency to which it now recognizes a coordination role.

Starting from the lesson learnt from the NOOP Torre Guaceto story and described in paragraph 2, we designed a system prototype that can support the Agency in:

a. describing and monitoring the planning process and its main decisional steps;
b. capturing actions and decisions of the community and the park agency as a whole;
c. showing the knowledge network dynamics;
d. structuring and representing meetings contents and results;
e. detecting the features of the emerging community.

In other words the system would help the Agency to monitor the process and then to build new knowledge to put into the action of the on-going work.

The Park Agency acting as *participatory process tracer* can develop and improve its ability to manage knowledge within action. Process tracing is here considered the activity of tracing the development of a plan, i.e. to build the process memory related to the plan development.

The question to unfold is: is a memory system the right tool to orient knowledge management to action?

We start from the base assumption that any kind of reasoning and reflection about both process and knowledge needs to consider several aspects of knowledge itself, which are highly context dependent (Ackermann, 1982). When this process is collaborative and knowledge intensive, like participatory planning processes are, the context is rapidly changing and deep reflections are needed in order: 1. to distinguish in the process between changing and resistant features, and 2. to interpret and make sense of what is happening. Observation, reflection and action often rely on personal participants' skills, in particular to their ability or practice to carry out effective actions in rapidly changing contexts. We argue that ICT tools devoted to memory tracing can offer a valuable support to combine eventual community skills with more systematic benefits coming from more structured process of memory exploration.

Memory building activities can bridge knowledge to action in three ways at least:

1) putting knowledge in multiple-contexts,
2) showing the effects of past actions in similar or different contexts,
3) understanding the reasons for that context to be.

By performing these activities the Memory Support System would enable:

a. better-informed actions, based on multiple-context explorations and cross-temporal comparisons with other cases (other knowledge applied to the same action, or other actions derived from the same knowledge);
b. higher transparency and understanding of the scopes behind actions (exploring reasons behind decisions helps in understanding where the process is going and why, so that we can monitor and eventually change, on going, the process direction; this helps to better orient actions toward the goals of the actions themselves).

We designed a memory system focusing on the points 1 and 3 stated before: we tried to represent knowledge in multiple contexts and to trace the decisions rationale, that is to say explaining reasons behind decisions and actions.

The system is being developed in the Compendium (Bachler et al., 2003) environment. Compendium is a hypermedia and sense-making tool used as a Knowledge Management Tool to store, structure and represent dialogical contents. The dialogical contents are extracted from argumentative dialogues performed along the participatory planning activities. Members of the community discuss problems, negotiate resources and select alternatives in order to reach collaborative decisions and actions. This dialogical process is often unstructured but it is stored referring to the key descriptors of the process (actors, time, problem environment, relations to other discussions, …) thus reducing the effect of interpretation and structuring effort needed to convert real discussions in what we define argumentative-discussions (Hitchcock, 2002). Argumentation needs to be recognized within contents but contents are pre-structured and can easily support the re-tracking of argumentation chains. Contents of dialogues are extracted from meeting recordings and/or from meeting notes obtained with dialogue mapping techniques (Conklin et al., 2001).

In order to reduce the influence of subjective interpretation, contents are stored according to key descriptors of process which are organized coherently with five dimensions of participatory planning processes: conceptual, social, spatial, temporal and causal. A Soft System Methodology has been used to test the use of the hypermedia environment as knowledge management tool to represent and manage deliberation in participatory planning processes. As a first step we defined a conceptual model of knowledge object taxonomy. We recognized and defined the aspects (memory objects) of memory that need or use to be recollected during a Participatory Planning Process. Memory object types are: knowledge claims, decisions, information, process details, social details, geographical details etc. Based on this analysis we defined the memory object taxonomy to tag the knowledge objects during the knowledge tracking. This taxonomy has been used as data collection framework to annotate and classify knowledge objects and then represent them in the hypermedia database. In the knowledge taxonomy five dimensions have been recognized as constitutive for participatory planning processes.

Actors: Being this process participatory a first constitutive dimension has been considered the social one: who are the actors and what they say?

Time: Furthermore, because dealing with a process of deliberation and design, the time dimension has been considered key to contextualize contents to actions: when in the process something has been said?

Space: Moreover the spatial dimension is considered constitutive because managing spatial planning activities: often the statements need to be referred to geographical areas or to spatial objects mainly because they refer to spatial issues.

Concepts: The conceptual dimension is considered constitutive of to represent dialogues and deliberation: in which dialogical and argumentative content a statement has been raised? In which context of dicussion?

Rationale: Finally what we defined "causal" dimension refers to causal chains of arguments. This is considered a key dimension because it motivates decisions then offering a representation of the design rationale.

The five dimensional knowledge object taxonomy have been tested in this pilot project to represent the contents of the Torre Guaceto project. Results of the application and evaluation of the memory system will follow in order to confirm or revise the knowledge taxonomy as in a soft system methodology approach.

In the following picture we show one view of the system enabling the access to memory from one of these dimensions (the conceptual one), in particular the figure 2 shows an image of argumentative dialogue extracted from one of the community meeting.

The dialogues are structured with an Issue-Based Information System (IBIS). IBIS is an argumentation model distinguishing between issues, positions on these issues, and arguments pro and con these positions (Kunz and Rittel, 1970). The IBIS argumentative model is used to represent contents of the meetings and then additional contents is performed to show and explore the contents through the five dimensions one by one. Following the argumentative chain it is possible to observe roles, trust relationships and decisional steps. The system allows monitoring the meetings and memorizing the contents.

Another view is the social one; it mainly consists of a list of participants attending the meetings; starting from the icon of each participant it is possible to explore general information, institutional roles in the project, his/her own network of relationships, list of the actor's statements and indexes to the video replay of the meeting (in case the meeting was extracted from a video).

The final result is a multiple-knowledge repository, organized in content and context sub-repositories, in which every actor's statement can be explored according with its temporal, conceptual, spatial, social and causal-argumentative context. These multiple "views" on knowledge offer :i. a knowledge-base for further analysis and evaluation ii. a detailed and multiple contextualization of information and knowledge produced during the process and iii. the tracing of the decision rationale in form of argumentative chains explaining decisions.

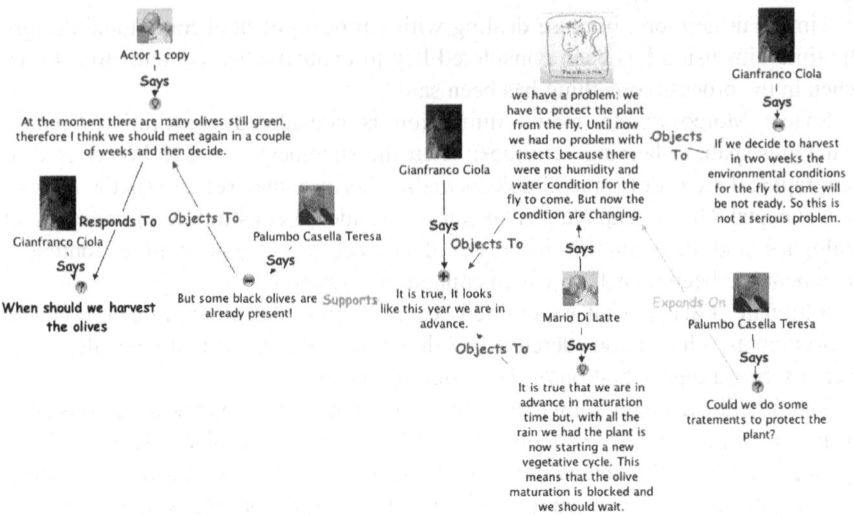

Figure 2. The conceptual view showing argumentative-discussions.

6. Conclusions

The paper explored the concept of organizational memory in participatory planning considering information and knowledge, used and produced in participatory processes, not as passive records but as dynamic contents living and changing along the time.

Since the ability to monitor and manage knowledge in participatory planning action is crucial for the effectiveness of the action itself, the paper proposes memory support systems as opportunities to orient knowledge management to action. In such systems the focus on the argumentation content is combined with the necessity to merge argumentation and environmental planning issues in a sort of memory, the *process-memory*, which is considered relevant for two main reasons: i. it supports effectively the environmental planning decision making process and; ii. it represents a sort of cognitive guide to orient action coherently with the indication contained in the environmental plan.

The memory system prototype we are developing for Torre Guaceto Park Agency stresses the tracing of the decision rationale; large effort still needs to be devoted to make this tracing more effective, less energy and time consuming and then consequently to produce contents which are available during the planning action so that these can be used from the community in order to support the action itself. The system is being developed to support the entire planning process by providing an integrated collaborative environment as structured space for participatory decision making. In such a collaborative environment knowledge is activated as a resource by the users who form relationships, act together, share and reflect collectively on their knowledge and beliefs.

At the moment using the system requires technical skills; both knowledge classification skills and technological training with the Knowledge Management tool are needed. Future research efforts will be devoted to complete the implementation of the memory system by improving functions oriented to the structuring and re-using the knowledge contents.

The reflections and the approach proposed in this paper derive from experiences and observations carried out in the environmental planning domain. It refers to plans development activities and, in particular, focuses on potentials of knowledge management in supporting the creation, management and use of evolving organizational memory in collaborative decision support systems. Our approach to KM focuses on a perspective in which workers as stakeholders create new knowledge as they carry out their work practices. Our goal is to enable innovative practices at a social level by supporting collaboration and communication. We see knowledge as an intrinsic aspect of collaborative practices production, in which stakeholders are integrating the knowledge they collaboratively construct into the (re)production of solutions and the practices themselves.

Generalizing, our reflections and approach could keep their validity in those domains where: i. decision making is characterized by collaboration and knowledge intensive interaction among stakeholder and ii. strategic planning activities are carried out in a futures visioning approach; ii. the dynamics of organizational memory is relevant for knowledge management and decision support.

Acknowledgements: The present contribution presents some results of a Research Work currently carried on in the Dipartimento di Architettura e Urbanistica of the Politecnico di Bari and funded by the Puglia Regional Administration: PE077 PARCHIAPERTI (POR 2000-2006).

References

Ackermann, R.. : Context Dependent Knowledge. Philosophy and Phenomenological Research, 42(3):425–433 (1982).

Alvarado, M. , Banares-Alcantara, R., and Trujillo, A.: Improving the Organizational Memory by recording decision making, rationale and team configuration. Journal of Petroleum Science and Engineering, 47:71-88 (2005).

Bachler, M., Buckingham Shum S., De Roure, D., Michaelides D., and Page, K.: Ontological mediation of meeting structure: Argumentation, annotation, and navigation. In: 1st International Workshop on Hypermedia and the Semantic Web. Nottingham, UK, 30th August (2003).

Baddeley, AD.: Working Memory, Oxford Univ. Press, Oxford (1986).

Brauner, E., Becker, A.: Beyond Knowledge Sharing: The Management of Transactive Knowledge Systems, Knowledge and Process Management, 13(1):62-71 (2006).

Celino, A., Concilio, G.: Supporting collaborative learning in environmental scenario building through an argumentative system. Knowledge Management Research & Practice, 4:240-249 (2006b).

Celino, A., Concilio, G.: E-Governance or environmental planning: perspectives of open content systems. In Dan Remenyi (ed.), Proceedings of the International Conference on e-government, Academic Conferences Limited Reading, UK, pp. 89-99. (ISBN 1-905305-11-7) (2005).

Celino, A., Concilio, G.: Managing open contents for collaborative deliberation in environmental planning. In F. Malpica, A. Oropeza, J. Carrasquero, & P. Howell, eds., *Proceedings PISTA 2006. The 4th International Conference on Politics and Information Systems: Technologies and Applications,* International Institute of Informatics and Systemics, pp.155-160 2006a.

Conklin, J., Selvin, A., Shum Buckingham, S., Sierhuis, M.: Facilitated hypertext for collective sensemaking: 15 years on from gibis. In: HYPERTEXT '01 Proceedings of the twelfth ACM conference on Hypertext and Hypermedia:123–124, New York, NY (2001).

EEA: Participatory integrated assessment methods: An assessment of their usefulness to the European Environmental Agency. Technical Report n.64. http://reports.eea.europa.eu/Technical_report_no_64/en/Technical_Report_64 (2001).

Fischer, G., Arias, E., Eden, H., Gorman, A., and Scharff, E.: Transcending the Individual Human Mind - Creating Shared Understanding through Collaborative Design. In J. Carroll (ed.) "Human Computer Interaction in the New Millennium", Addison-Wesley, pp. 347-372 (2001).

Fischer, G., Giaccardi, E., Ye, Y., Sutcliffe, A.G., and Mehandjiev, N.: Meta–design: A manifesto for end–user development, Communications of the ACM, volume 47, number 9, pp. 33–37 (2004).

Hage, M, Leroy, P, Willems, E.: Participatory Approaches in Governance and in Knowledge Production: What Makes the Difference? Working paper series 2006/3, Research Group Governance and Places, University of Nijmegen. http://www.ru.nl/contents/pages/141634/gapwp06-03.pdf. (2006).

Hitchcock, D.: The Practice of Argumentative Discussion. Argumentation, 16(3): 287-298 (2002).

Jaspers, M., Banthien, H., Mayer-Ries, J.: New forms of knowledge management in participatory foresight: The case of "Futur". Eu-us seminar: New technology foresight, forecasting & assessment methods (Seville, May) (2004).

Kangas, J., Store, R.: Internet and teledemocracy in participatory planning of natural resources management. Landscape and Urban Planning, 62:89-101 (2003).

Karacapilidis, N., Papadias, D.: Computer supported argumentation and collaborative decision making: the HERMES system. Information Systems, 26:259-277 (2001).

Kunz, W., Rittel, HWJ.: Issues as elements of information systems. Technical Report WP-131, University of California, Berkeley (1970).

Lanzara, GF.: Ephemeral organizations in extreme environments: Emergence, strategy, extinction. Journal of Management Studies, 20(1):71–95 (1983).

Miyake, A., Shah, P.: Models of working memory: Mechanisms of active maintenance and executive control. Cambridge University Press, New York (1999).

Mostert, E.: The Challenge for Public Participation. Water Policy, 5:179-197 (2003).

Pellizoni, L.: Uncertainty and Participatory Democracy. Environmental Values, 12:195-224 (2003).

Risbey, J., Sluijs, J., Kloprogge, P., Ravetz, J., Funtowicz, S., Corral Quintana, S. Application of a checklist for quality assistance in environmental modelling to an energy model. Environmental Modeling & Assessment, 10(1):63-79 (2005).

Santos, AC., Galina, SVR., Alves, AC. , Fagundes, LG.: Adapting a Decision Making Synchronous/Asynchronous Environment to a Distributed Hypermedia Concurrent

Engineering System. In: 30th Hawaii International Conference on System Sciences, 6 to 10 January, Maui - New York. IEEE, 1: 686-694 (1997).

Shum, S.: Cognitive Dimensions of Design Rationale. In: Diaper D, Hammond NV (eds) People and Computers VI: Proceedings of HCI'91. Cambridge University Press, Cambridge, 331-344 (1991).

Shum, S.: Analyzing the Usability of a Design Rationale Notation. In: Moran TP, Carroll JM (eds) Design Rationale: Concepts, Techniques, and Use. Lawrence Erlbaum Associates, Hillsdale, 185-215 (1996).

Tress, B., Tress, G.: Scenario visualisation for participatory landscape planning - a study from Denmark. Landscape and Urban Planning, 64:161-178 (2003).

Tweed, C.: Supporting Argumentation Practices in Urban Planning and Design. Comput., Environ. and Urban Systems, 22(4):351-363 (1998).

Wegner, DM.: A computer network model of human transactive memory. Social Cognition, 13:319-339 (1995).

Zeleny, M.: Cognitive equilibrium: a new paradigm of decision making?. Human Syst. Manage., 8: 185-188 (1989).

Building a Framework for Actions and Roles in Organizational Knowledge Transfer

Alexander Hoffmann

Johann Wolfgang Goethe-University, Frankfurt a.M., Germany, alexhfm@wiwi.uni-frankfurt.de

Abstract: In order to analyze and improve knowledge management (KM) initiatives, organizations must be enabled to systematically look into the processes of organizational knowledge transfer. They need to know what roles are involved in these processes and what actions are performed. We propose that only if the building blocks of organizational knowledge transfer are known, reasonable in-detail analyses of KM initiatives can be conducted. In this paper we present a framework that structures roles and actions relevant in organizational knowledge transfer scenarios and that is useful for identifying and classifying factors which leverage or prevent knowledge transfer. The identification of roles and actions is inevitable since they build the core structure of knowledge transfer in an organization and therefore represent appropriate starting points for analyses. Without a proper framework that shows these starting points it might be difficult to set up a thought-out research that grasps the characteristics of organizational knowledge transfer. Furthermore, by contrasting IT supported knowledge transfer with non-electronic knowledge transfer our framework helps in answering the question how KM systems can support knowledge transfer.

Keywords: Knowledge management, Knowledge transfer, Knowledge management systems

1. Introduction

Knowledge management (KM) is seen as one of the most important tasks of organizations (von Krogh, 1998). But KM projects and knowledge management systems (KMS) often do not fulfill the needs of organizations. For example, a survey about management tool usage in international firms in 2001 showed that amongst all 25 considered management tools, KMS are at rank 19 in terms of usage frequency (Rigby, 2001). Concerning customer satisfaction, KMS have been evaluated with 3.22 on a scale from 1 (not satisfied) to 5 (very satisfied). That corresponds to rank 25 of all 25 considered types of management tools. Similarly, a Fraunhofer study from 2004 arrives at the conclusion that a general

Please use the following format when citing this chapter:

Hoffmann, A., 2008, in IFIP International Federation for Information Processing, Volume 270; *Knowledge Management in Action*; Mark Ackerman, Rose Dieng-Kuntz, Carla Simone, Volker Wulf; (Boston: Springer), pp. 67–79.

dissatisfaction concerning KM exists: more than 75% of organizations from Germany, Austria, and Switzerland participating in the study were not comfortable with the current handling of knowledge, although KM projects had already been started (Decker et al., 2005).

In order to find out what leverages and prevents organizational KM, organizations need to have a tool that helps to set up a structured analysis, and researchers need a framework to find starting points for research. Both must be enabled to systematically look into the processes of organizational knowledge transfer, that is, they need to know what roles are involved in these processes and what actions are performed. Only if the building blocks of organizational knowledge transfer are known, efficient in-detail analyses of KM initiatives can be conducted. If KM in organizations includes information technology (IT) support, a comparison between knowledge transfer supported by KMS and non-electronic knowledge transfer is necessary in order to find out how IT can contribute to these processes. But a systematic comparison can only be conducted, if researchers and managers know what roles and actions in knowledge transfer are affected by IT support.

In this paper we present a framework that structures roles and actions relevant in organizational knowledge transfer scenarios and that can be used to identify the characteristics of knowledge transfer in concrete KM settings, enabling the organization to take specific actions to improve perceived problems. We see knowledge of roles and actions as inevitable for a reasonable analysis of KM projects, since they build the core structure of knowledge transfer in an organization and therefore represent appropriate starting points for research. Without a proper framework that shows these starting points it might be difficult to set up a thought-out measurement that grasps the characteristics of organizational knowledge transfer.

This paper does not describe how an actual analysis of problems or a research study concerning organizational KM should be conducted, but it provides a structuring and description of organizational knowledge transfer that might be useful for researchers and managers who plan to conduct analyses and research in a structured and efficient way. Our framework helps people to find out where to start looking for reasons of observed problems, but not how to actually conduct the research.

2. Related work

We define *knowledge* as mental concepts that represent the nature of perceived objects and relationships between these objects. The basis of these mental concepts is, on the one hand, the result of cognitive processing that is triggered by the inflow of new stimuli (Alavi & Leidner, 2001). On the other hand, concepts can be created or modified by applying common rules of conclusion to get insights based on these stimuli (Wittmann, 1979).

Following this view, knowledge has two fundamental attributes: first, since mental concepts belong to one person only, knowledge is always personal (Blair, 2002). It is bound to a person and is not an object that is concrete and easy to share, because it originates and is applied in the minds of people (Davenport & Prusak, 1998). According to (Miller, 2002) „knowledge is, after all, what we know. And what we know cannot be commodified." Second, knowledge is not bound to the use of language, so that non-linguistic knowledge can exist (Bloch, 1991). This view is supported by the often cited statement that "we can know more than we can tell" (Polanyi, 1983).

Polanyi's statement leads to the distinction of explicit and tacit knowledge: *explicit knowledge* can be expressed in words, drawings, equations, numbers, etc. and is therefore communicable to other persons (McBriar et al., 2003; Nonaka, 1994). To avoid confusion, we stress that explicit knowledge is different from articulated knowledge, since the former exists in people's minds and the latter is perceivable representations of knowledge. In contrast to explicit knowledge, a person is not aware of his or her *tacit knowledge*. Due to a lack of awareness, articulation of tacit knowledge is only partly possible, and according to some researchers actually fully impossible (Collins, 1974; Herbig & Büssing, 2003).

Knowledge transfer can be seen as the transfer of mental concepts from one person to another embedded in an act of communication (Garavelli et al., 2002; Ko et al., 2005). For knowledge to be transferred to other persons, the knowledge carrier has to represent its mental concepts in a way that they are perceivable for other persons. We call the process of making knowledge "visible" to the outside world, so that it can be perceived by others, *knowledge articulation*. Since knowledge is what people have in their minds and data is external perceivable structures, knowledge transfer is not identical to data transfer. Or, as (Garavelli et al., 2002) put it: "Even when knowledge can be materialized in an object [...], the transfer of that object does not necessarily fulfill the knowledge transfer process." That is because data has to be interpreted by people. Data is inherently meaningless, „it simply exists [...] – all waiting to be interpreted, all waiting to have meaning attached – by people." (Miller, 2002). But one can never be sure that two persons associate the same representation with the same object.

If we use the term knowledge without further explanation, we always mean explicit knowledge that can be articulated and therefore be transferred between persons, after it was actually articulated. If we talk about knowledge transfer in the narrower sense, we refer to articulation of knowledge into any form of representations, transferring the representations and interpreting them in order to create new knowledge. We use the term knowledge transfer in a broader sense referring to knowledge transfer in the narrower sense including the processes of identifying, contacting and brokering knowledge sources, as well as the processes of storage and retrieval of knowledge.

In the literature several frameworks can be found that structure the domain of knowledge management from different points of views. We analyzed some of these frameworks with regard to their appropriateness for helping the researcher to identify characteristics of organizational knowledge transfer. Additionally, we evaluated if and how these frameworks place KMS in the domain of KM.

(Ahmed et al., 1999) propose a holistic model of KM which captures key elements and dimensions of KM and helps in screening and evaluating KM projects. It supports monitoring and tracking of KM initiatives, which is important for leveraging positive effects from managing knowledge. Since the model gives a very general view on KM projects as a whole and includes extra-organizational elements like customers and suppliers, its usefulness might be restricted for the analysis of organizational knowledge transfer in particular. It does not cover actions and roles related to knowledge transfer in detail, making it more difficult for managers and researchers to identify what leverages and prevents knowledge transfer processes. However, the framework does consider the role of technology in KM and gives starting points for analyzing how IT can effect and improve KM.

A more detailed model concerning the characteristics of organizational KM is proposed by (Shin, 2004). The author combines resource based perspective, transaction costs perspective and agency perspective in a holistic framework that helps organizations to identify positive and negative effects on KM and KMS. While this model covers lots of factors influencing KM, it does not examine all relevant roles and actions in organizational knowledge transfer. Its focus is still too wide, so that it might not be appropriate as a basis for identifying and analyzing the building blocks of organizational knowledge transfer.

A model of different types of knowledge creation, knowledge transformation, and knowledge transfer that is widespread in KM literature is the so called SECI model (Nonaka, 1994). It is based on the assumption that new knowledge emerges from transfer and transformation of explicit and tacit knowledge in all possible combinations between two persons: from tacit to explicit, from explicit to explicit, from explicit to tacit, and from tacit to tacit knowledge. But within the model, the definition of explicit knowledge is not precise, since it remains unclear if the author sees explicit knowledge as articulated knowledge that is independent of an individual, or as knowledge that could be articulated but still resides in a person's mind. Tacit knowledge is merely defined as knowledge that is "hard to formalize and communicate". Although the model describes some building blocks of organizational knowledge transfer, its imprecise definitions of different types of knowledge make it difficult for researchers and practitioners to implement the framework in empirical settings. Additionally, the model does not explicitly consider the role of IT in creating, transforming and transferring knowledge.

Since we did not find frameworks that adequately represent both the characteristics of knowledge transfer in organizations and the role of IT in knowledge transfer, we propose a new framework that structures and represents knowledge transfer situations.

3. Roles and actions in knowledge transfer

In order to efficiently analyze organizational knowledge transfer and to find out how KMS can support knowledge transfer, we will identify roles that participants of knowledge transfer processes might adopt and actions they might perform. Additionally, in order to give starting points for in-detail analyses we will describe some factors that leverage and prevent these actions. As a result, we present a framework of organizational knowledge transfer that combines the roles and actions in a graphical representation. The framework is an artifact in the context of design science according to the conceptual framework proposed by (Hevner et al., 2004). Its design is based on everyday observations and concepts that can be found in the KM literature and the integration of these ideas into a coherent framework.

3.1. Roles in organizational knowledge transfer

The most obvious roles in a knowledge transfer process are *knowledge carrier* and *knowledge requestor*. The first role is adopted by persons that need knowledge about specific topics and the second role is adopted by persons that have knowledge about specific topics. Within an organization, people perform different tasks and are specialized in certain domains, so that each person holds different knowledge. Therefore, knowledge gaps between persons exist, which lead to the existence of knowledge carriers and knowledge requestors. Considering a specific topic X, knowledge carrier and knowledge requestor are different persons. That is, one person has knowledge about X, another person requires knowledge about X. Concerning different topics it is possible for a single person to be both a knowledge carrier for a specific topic X and a knowledge requestor for another topic Y. (Husted & Michailova, 2002) use the terms knowledge transmitters and knowledge receivers to refer to persons who have knowledge and to those who need knowledge. (Davenport & Prusak, 1998), who compare the processes of knowledge exchange with mechanisms known from markets for more tangible goods, introduce the terms knowledge seller and knowledge buyer, which we see as equivalent to knowledge carrier and knowledge requestor.

In order to preserve knowledge and make it accessible independently of a knowledge carrier, it must be articulated and stored in physical objects, which we call *knowledge repositories*. An IT system that can store and display articulated knowledge adopts the role of an electronic knowledge repository. These systems usually have mechanisms for acquisition, control, and publication of knowledge (Kankanhalli et al., 2005). Examples of electronic knowledge repositories are conventional document management systems (DMS), content management systems (CMS), or Wikis, storing and indexing electronic documents. If articulated knowledge is stored in non-electronic physical objects, we call these objects manual knowledge repositories, e.g. books or printed documents in files. Both knowledge carriers and knowledge repositories are knowledge sources and could be considered equal concerning the role they adopt in organizational knowledge transfer. But, as we argue in the following section, actions involved with knowledge repositories are different from those involved with knowledge carriers, so that knowledge repositories are adopting an individual role.

Knowledge carriers, knowledge requestors, and knowledge repositories can be connected via knowledge brokers, which are persons or IT systems that bring together "those who need knowledge and those who have it" (Davenport & Prusak, 1998; Hellström et al., 2001). A person or an IT system acting as a knowledge broker does not have the knowledge that a knowledge requestor is asking for, but knows where to find that knowledge, i.e. the person or IT system has structural knowledge.

Similar to knowledge repositories, we differentiate between electronic and non-electronic knowledge brokers respectively: a person adopting the role of a non-electronic knowledge broker is, for example, a librarian, who works in the corporate library and knows where to find knowledge about a specific topic. Of course, everyone else who has structural knowledge about a topic of interest can act as a knowledge broker. Another example of a non-electronic knowledge broker is a card-index system that is used for finding archived files. An IT system storing information about where to find required knowledge serves as an electronic knowledge broker. Examples of electronic knowledge brokers are search engines that identify virtual locations of electronic documents, and electronic library catalogues allowing its users to find books about specific topics and indicating their physical locations within a library.

An IT system can combine both the roles of an electronic knowledge broker and electronic knowledge repository if it stores both articulated knowledge and structural knowledge. The same is true for non-electronic objects storing both articulated knowledge and structural knowledge. For example, a DMS that stores articulated knowledge in a database and therefore acts as an electronic knowledge repository, always comes with a search engine, allowing its users to find the virtual locations of required documents. It therefore combines both the role of an electronic knowledge repository and an electronic knowledge broker.

Concerning individuals, the very same person can adopt all of the aforementioned human roles, i.e. knowledge requestor, knowledge carrier and knowledge broker. Depending on topic and context, a person might act as a knowledge requestor concerning a topic X, as a knowledge carrier concerning a topic Y, and as a knowledge broker concerning a topic Z. From an omniscient point of view, the described roles can easily be assigned to a person or an object. But from an individual's point of view, it might not be obvious what roles another person can adopt. Therefore, the identification of roles that a contacted person can adopt might be connected with additional costs.

The interaction between the described roles can be supported by *communication technology*, e.g. e-mail, telephone, and Instant Messaging. These systems help people and machines to make their communication more efficient by reducing communication time, effort and costs. Since these systems neither store articulated knowledge nor structural knowledge, they are not any type of KMS, but support actions relevant in knowledge transfer processes.

3.2. Actions in organizational knowledge transfer

Having identified different roles that persons or objects can adopt in knowledge transfer processes, we will now describe actions that relate to these roles. In the text, each action is labeled with a number, which corresponds to a number in figure 1 in section 3.3. Additionally, we will give a short overview of factors that influence these actions in a positive and negative way. However, the list of factors is by no means complete, but provides a starting point for further research.

Probably the most common action in knowledge transfer scenarios is a knowledge request: a person needs knowledge about a specific topic and asks another person or an IT system about it (1). Knowledge requests can be sent from knowledge requestors to persons that are assumed to be knowledge carriers or knowledge brokers, to electronic knowledge brokers, and to electronic and non-electronic knowledge repositories.

As described in the previous section, in case of a personal knowledge request a knowledge requestor might not know for sure if a contacted person is a knowledge carrier, knowledge broker, or unknowing concerning the requested topic. That is, a knowledge requestor may spend time and effort trying to find out what role an asked person can adopt and trying to contact other persons if the previously asked persons could not help (Gray, 2000). Therefore, if knowledge requests in an organization are analyzed, one has to consider time and effort a knowledge requestor has to accept in order to find a person that can be of any help.

In order to estimate efforts of personal knowledge requests, further aspects have to be considered. For example, psychological barriers can exist that bar a knowledge requestor from asking another person for advice. The knowledge requestor might be afraid to steal someone's time or he or she might feel uncomfortable to reveal knowledge gaps. Furthermore, a knowledge requestor might hesitate asking a person because he or she is afraid that the knowledge carrier or knowledge broker expects favors in return for sharing his or her knowledge. Further aspects are related to the knowledge carrier: If a knowledge carrier is not perceived as reliable, trustworthy, or knowledgeable, initiating knowledge transfer will be more difficult as if there is evidence that the source is reputable (Szulanski, 2000). According to (Husted & Michailova, 2002), a main reason for knowledge-rejecting behavior is the "Not-Invented-Here" syndrome: knowledge requestors might generally doubt the validity and reliability of other persons' knowledge and therefore develop preferences for generating own ideas and knowledge. These psychological barriers might impede organizational knowledge transfer, even if a proper knowledge transfer infrastructure is available.

Knowledge requests to IT systems are different from those to humans insofar as knowledge requestors have to formulate their requests in a way that they are understandable for the systems. Since IT systems do not understand human language to such extend that the knowledge requestor can formulate a colloquial knowledge request, he or she must accept certain effort to formulate the request in a form that IT systems can understand.

According to section 2, *knowledge transfer* (2) in the narrower sense includes three processes: articulating knowledge into any forms of representations or data respectively (2a), transferring data (2b), and interpreting them (2c) in order to create new knowledge. If only one or two of these three processes are executed, we do not speak of knowledge transfer, but of knowledge articulation, data transfer, and data interpretation instead. Since efficient data transfer is beyond the scope of this paper, we focus on articulation of knowledge and interpretation of data in the following paragraphs.

Articulation of knowledge depends on several criteria regarding the assumed receivers and other environmental conditions. If knowledge can be articulated at all, depends on the type of knowledge. As described in section 2, we only consider explicit knowledge that still resides in a knowledge carrier's mind and can be articulated in principle.

If and how this knowledge is turned in articulated form depends on the knowledge carrier's capability of expression and encoding competence (Ko et al., 2005). Considering the time and effort that a knowledge carrier must spend for articulation, he or she might experience a lack of motivation, since the time necessary to articulate knowledge might be spent more profitable and more productive and can therefore be considered as opportunity costs (Kankanhalli et al., 2005). Another factor considering motivation is the fear of losing power and individual competitive advantages: if a knowledge carrier makes his or her knowledge publicly available, the person gets exchangeable concerning this particular knowledge (Gray, 2001; Husted & Michailova, 2002; Stenmark, 2001).

Representations usable for knowledge articulation are restricted by the availability and type of communication channels that transfer the representations. For example, if articulated knowledge is transferred by e-mail or Instant Messaging, only textual representations of knowledge can be used. If knowledge is stored in a knowledge repository, articulation is restricted by the representations the repository can deal with.

If articulated knowledge is comprehensible for other persons, depends on the knowledge carrier's and receiver's interpretations of the representations. Since persons all over the world speak different languages, whereas language not only refers to natural languages like English, German or Spanish, but also technical languages like "mechanical engineer" or "field sales" (Davenport & Prusak, 1998), they have different representations for articulating their knowledge and different ways of interpreting these representations. Similarly, (Ko et al., 2005) identified common understanding based on shared values, norms, philosophy, and prior work to have a positive impact on the success of knowledge transfer. According to (Husted & Michailova, 2002), the fear of being misunderstood even prevents some knowledge carriers to share their knowledge.

In this context, it is relevant for the articulation process if the receiver is known and if he or she is assumed to have the same understanding of knowledge representations. If knowledge is articulated for storage in a knowledge repository, the future knowledge requestors might not be known, so that the representations of knowledge have to be unambiguous in order to avoid misunderstandings.

An electronic or non-electronic knowledge broker facilitates "contacts between knowledge need and such expertise" (Hellström et al., 2001), that is, the broker communicates structural knowledge. We call the process of transmitting structural knowledge *knowledge brokering* (3). Structural knowledge can point to knowledge carriers, knowledge repositories, or other knowledge brokers. In the last case, structural knowledge does not directly point to a knowledge source, but to another knowledge broker that might lead to the required knowledge.

Structural knowledge is transferred from knowledge brokers to knowledge requestors. This action can be conducted by both electronic and non-electronic knowledge brokers. Consider, for example, a situation where an employee asks the corporate librarian about where to find information about a specific topic. The librarian, adopting the role of a knowledge broker, conducts knowledge brokering by telling the knowledge requestor the name of a book containing the required knowledge.

Persons or machines that have been contacted as knowledge brokers can also forward a knowledge request to other knowledge brokers if they do not have the necessary structural knowledge to conduct knowledge brokering. They might even directly ask a knowledge carrier about the topic of interest or consult a knowledge repository. In these cases the acting person or IT system does not adopt the role of a knowledge broker any more, but that of a further knowledge requestor. After receiving the required knowledge, this requestor can either forward the received knowledge to the original knowledge requestor, adopting the role of a knowledge carrier, or conduct knowledge brokering by passing on contact information about the identified knowledge sources to the original knowledge requestor, facilitating direct contact between knowledge requestor and knowledge carrier.

For a knowledge broker to be successful, the available structural knowledge must be updated and extended frequently. Knowledge brokers known for little or expired structural knowledge will obviously only rarely be contacted by knowledge requestors. Therefore, knowledge brokers conduct *management of structural knowledge* in order to be up-to-date (4). Correspondingly, (Hellström et al., 2001) see the key tasks of knowledge brokers in identifying several knowledgeable persons and their respective competence areas, and in listing these persons.

For example, the well-known electronic knowledge broker "Google" frequently scans new web sites and re-visits already indexed web sites in order to extend and update its structural knowledge. Of course, knowledge brokers can interact with knowledge carriers as well. Considering persons adopting the role of a knowledge broker, (Davenport & Prusak, 1998) describe some of the intra-organizational knowledge brokers as knowledge entrepreneurs, who "intentionally set out to become experts on who has knowledge and how to exploit it." They invest time in moving around the organization, talking to people, listening, and establishing knowledge needs and corresponding expertise (Hellström et al., 2001).

A knowledge carrier may not have to wait for knowledge brokers to find him or her: the knowledge carrier can contribute actively to the actuality and scale of a knowledge broker by publishing his or her area of expertise and registering his or her contact details. For example, some social networking web sites allow organizations to register their contact details, line of business, and/or core competences for free. Having collected enough contacts, the web site can act as an electronic knowledge broker, so that knowledge requestors can use the site to find organizations that may have the required knowledge. Here, the knowledge carriers (the organizations) independently advertise their knowledge by contributing data to the electronic knowledge broker. We call the process of actively contributing structural knowledge to knowledge brokers *knowledge advertising* (5).

3.3. Framework for organizational knowledge transfer

In the previous sections we described four roles that persons or objects can adopt in knowledge transfer processes. In addition, we identified actions that can be conducted by the described roles. Figure 1 illustrates the relations between the described roles and actions in organizational knowledge transfer. The framework also shows the role of communication technology in knowledge transfer processes and delimits KMS from communication technology.

Since the mentioned roles and actions can be affected by external influences like incentive systems or the organizational knowledge sharing culture (Husted & Michailova, 2002), the framework additionally shows the environment of knowledge transfer processes.

Besides showing the building blocks of knowledge transfer, the framework provides a distinct terminology for the domain of KM, which is helpful for clearly addressing certain aspects in the domain.

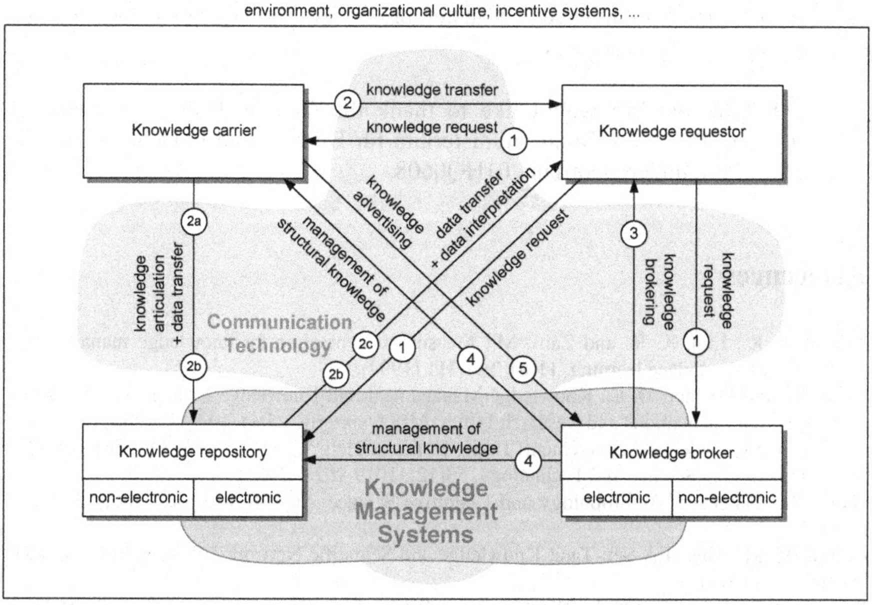

Figure 1: Framework for organizational knowledge transfer.

4. Conclusion and outlook

Our framework shows roles and actions relevant in knowledge transfer situations. Based on these roles and actions, in-detail analyses concerning knowledge transfer can be conducted. For example, an organization could check if each of the described roles and actions exist within the organization and what costs, barriers, and benefits are involved with each of the described roles and actions, allowing more specific and goal-oriented improvements in organizational knowledge transfer. Furthermore, our framework clearly shows what roles can be adopted by IT systems and what actions can be influenced by IT, allowing structured analyses of knowledge transfer with and without IT support.

We see our framework as a single iteration in the search for an effective solution to the problem of understanding and analyzing knowledge transfer in organizations and enhance the impact of KM activities. Since we only considered a subset of relevant factors from the environment, the framework may be satisfactory for some situations, but not useful enough for more complex settings. Therefore, this paper is only one contribution to the process of designing a framework that can adequately map the relevant elements of organizational knowledge transfer.

Further research projects will have to show that the framework is useful for analyzing concrete knowledge transfer situations, for identifying factors that leverage and prevent knowledge transfer processes, and for analyzing how IT systems impact these processes.

Acknowledgments: We would like to thank the German Federal Ministry of Education and Research (Bundesministerium für Bildung und Forschung), which funded this work under record no. 01HQ0608.

References

Ahmed, P. K., Lim, K. K. and Zairi, M.: Measurement practice for knowledge management. Journal of Workplace learning, 11(8), 304-311 (1999).

Alavi, M. and Leidner, D. E.: Knowledge Management and Knowledge Management Systems: Conceptual Foundations and Research Issues. MIS Quarterly, 25(1), 107-136 (2001).

Blair, D. C.: Knowledge Management: Hype, Hope, or Help? Journal of the American Society for Information Science and Technology, 53(12), 1019-1028 (2002).

Bloch, M.: Language, Anthropology and Cognitive Science. Man, New Series, 26(2), 183-198 (1991).

Collins, H. M.: The TEA Set: Tacit Knowledge and Scientific Networks. Science Studies, 4(2), 165-185 (1974).

Davenport, T. H. and Prusak, L.: Working Knowledge - How Organizations Manage What They Know. Boston, Massachusetts (1998).

Decker, B., Finke, I., John, M., Joisten, M., Schnalzer, K., Voigt, S., Wesoly, M. and Will, M.: Wissen und Information 2005. Fraunhofer IRB Verlag, Stuttgart (2005).

Garavelli, A. C., Gorgoglione, M. and Scozzi, B.: Managing knowledge transfer by knowledge technologies. Technovation, 22, 269-279 (2002).

Gray, P. H.: The effects of knowledge management systems on emergent teams: towards a research model. Journal of Strategic Information Systems, 9, 175-191 (2000).

Gray, P. H.: The impact of knowledge repositories on power control in the workplace. Information, Technology & People, 14(4), 368-384 (2001).

Hellström, T., Malmquist, U. and Mikaelsson, J.: Decentralizing knowledge - Managing knowledge work in a software engineering firm. Journal of High Technology Management Research, 12, 25-38 (2001).

Herbig, B. and Büssing, A.: Comparison of the role of explicit and implicit knowledge in working. Psychology Science, 45(3), 165-188 (2003).

Hevner, A. R., March, S. T. and Park, J.: Design Science in Information Systems Research. MIS Quarterly, 28(1), 75-105 (2004).

Husted, K. and Michailova, S.: Diagnosing and Fighting Knowledge-Sharing Hostility. Organizational Dynamics, 31(1), 60-73 (2002).

Kankanhalli, A., Tan, B. C. Y. and Wei, K.-K.: Contributing Knowledge to Electronic Knowledge Repositories: An Empirical Investigation. MIS Quarterly, 29(1), 113-143 (2005).

Ko, D.-G., Kirsch, L. J. and King, W. R.: Antecedents of Knowledge Transfer from Consultants to Clients in Enterprise System Implementations. MIS Quarterly, 29(1), 59-85 (2005).

Mcbriar, I., Smith, C., Bain, G., Unsworth, P., Magraw, S. and Gordon, J. L.: Risk, gap and strength: key concepts in knowledge management. Knowledge-Based Systems, 16, 29-36 (2003).

Miller, F. J.: I=0 (Information has no intrinsic meaning). Information Research, 8(1), (2002).

Nonaka, I.: A Dynamic Theory of Organizational Knowledge Creation. Organization Science, 5(1), 14-37 (1994).

Polanyi, M.: The tacit dimension. Doubleday & Company, Gloucester, Massachusetts (1983).

Rigby, D.: Management Tools and Techniques: A Survey. California Management Review, 43(2), 139-160 (2001).

Shin, M.: A framework for evaluating economics of knowledge management systems. Information & Management, 42, 179-196 (2004).

Stenmark, D.: Leveraging Tacit Organizational Knowledge. Journal of Management Information Systems, 17(3), 9-24 (2001).

Szulanski, G.: The Process of Knowledge Transfer: A Diachronic Analysis of Stickiness. Organizational Behavior and Human Decision Processes, 82(1), 9-27 (2000).

Von Krogh, G.: Care in Knowledge Creation. California Management Review, 40(3), 133-153 (1998).

Wittmann, W.: Wissen in der Produktion. In Handwörterbuch der Produktionswirtschaft. (Kern, W., Ed), pp 2261-2272, Stuttgart (1979).

CoLinK: Cooperative Knowledge Management for Engineering Teams

Michael Klingemann[1] **and Jürgen Friedrich**[2]

[1] University of Bremen, Center for Computing Technologies, Germany, klingemann@tzi.de
[2] University of Bremen, Center for Computing Technologies, Germany, friedrich@tzi.de

Abstract: Due to today's increasingly complex processes in planning and design, knowledge management (KM) is becoming a crucial factor of success in the engineering sector. In a participatory design project we created a prototype for a process oriented KM system (CoLinK), which allows engineers to jointly model projects with generic process descriptions, creating a virtual engineering community within the enterprise and beyond. During every project these process descriptions will be augmented with knowledge annotations. The CoLinK system includes a document as well as contact management module and lets users semantically link the corresponding information in the process context. With any finished project engineers can utilize the acquired knowledge to cooperatively improve the quality of the generic process descriptions.

Keywords: Knowledge management, Engineering, Cooperative work, CoLinK

1. Introduction

Knowledge Management (KM) in the engineering sector is becoming increasingly important and challenging. Due to global markets, companies have to face international competition and can, therefore, no longer focus on just national business. Dealing with international clients increases the required amount of knowledge (e. g. country specific requirements and regulations) and at the same time decreases the local availability of key players due to business travelling, which demands for a system that is accessible from anywhere via Internet connection. On the other hand, sharing knowledge not only improves the quality of engineering products but also enhances the quality of work of the engineers.

Our system analysis, which has been conducted in several iterations within four engineering companies, has shown that intensive knowledge exchange takes place

---

Please use the following format when citing this chapter:

Klingemann, M. and Friedrich, J., 2008, in IFIP International Federation for Information Processing, Volume 270; *Knowledge Management in Action*; Mark Ackerman, Rose Dieng-Kuntz, Carla Simone, Volker Wulf; (Boston: Springer), pp. 81–95.

within the cooperative solving of complex processes (e. g. discussing required changes to drawings). The key for successful knowledge management is seen by the participating companies in the ability to reuse existing project schemes for future engineering projects.

Based on the findings in our analysis we propose that knowledge acquisition in the engineering sector has to take place during the process execution. Knowledge exchange has to be facilitated by encouraging discussion about encountered obstructions and possible solutions. Storing this information in form of annotations in combination with links to related documents and contacts constitutes valuable process knowledge that can aid future projects. According to these assumptions we have created a system named CoLinK (Cooperative Linking of Knowledge), a knowledge management system for cooperative engineering teams.

2. Knowledge management in engineering – a deficit analysis

2.1. Methods: Analysis and inclusion

The subject of our analysis – knowledge transfer in engineering teams – requires a thoroughly chosen set of research methods: Engineering teams are complex social organizations. They have to cooperate in differentiated, dynamic, and vaguely determined work environments. The need for cooperation is twofold: First of all, the engineering projects are subdivided into processes which often are being performed by different engineers and which, therefore, need a high degree of horizontal cooperation. Secondly, they have to cooperate to organize the knowledge exchange between experienced and less experienced (younger) engineers. Each engineering project is different from the other. This is especially true in international engineering projects where legal frameworks, physical conditions, working attitudes etc. vary in a broad range. Also the team members themselves show a substantial degree of variation with respect to their level of qualification, professional specialization, work experience etc. Analysis and design of work organization and IT infrastructures in such an engineering environment require a set of concerted methods beyond traditional standardized tools like multiple-choice questionnaires.

The overall approach we followed was taken from the *Participatory Design* paradigm which is quite popular in computer science [1, 2, 3]: The IT development process, from analysis and design to implementation and testing, is no longer understood as a single sequence of steps following each other ("waterfall model") but as a repeatedly traversed cycle of development steps whereat each cycle results in a more elaborated prototype of the system ("evolutionary model"). Participatory design is especially useful in an area where engineering, planning or consulting tasks have to be performed [4].

To comply with the complex requirements of analyzing engineering work we have to deal with the problem "that users often are not sufficiently able to reflect their work situation and to express it appropriately in interviews. Users often do not have an adequate conceptual understanding of their role and behaviour in a work flow; many of their working methods are internalised and cognitively automated. Explaining those methods is difficult or even impossible for them." [2] This is what Polanyi described by the term 'tacit knowledge' [5] and what others call "tacit *knowing*" to indicate genuine dependency of this kind of knowledge on the human being. We tried to overcome this lack of explicitness by performing *intensive in-depth talks* with the engineering personnel – using a semi-structured guideline – as well as observing their task performance and communication behaviour at the workplace. Talks were performed with engineers, project managers, market researchers, external users, and the management. Conversations took up to four hours depending on the subject discussed. Topics of interest were:

- the organizational structure of the enterprise,
- the communication structure
- basic operational knowledge entities: projects, processes, tasks, documents (contracts, drawings), annotations, contacts (employees, supplier, experts) etc.
- kinds of knowledge, processes with special knowledge needs
- the formal and informal information flow
- knowledge exchange between local team members as well as with remotely operating members
- weaknesses in knowledge generation and distribution, and
- the IT infrastructure in use.

The analysis has been done in four different engineering companies, all of them SME with about 10 to 50 employees. The companies' profiles are as follows:

- **Company A** is planning huge chemical and pharmaceutical facilities as well as steelworks in several countries worldwide. The company runs branches in industrialized as well as developing countries and has to manage knowledge flows between engineers of hundreds of construction firms and suppliers.
- **Company B** is not only planning complex electrical and electronic installations and process controls for food industry, environmental technology and materials handling, but is also active in producing, assembling and maintaining control facilities for these businesses.
- **Company C** is a construction firm which mainly focuses on mechanical engineering as well as ship building industries (from passenger liners and cargo ships to container and navy vessels). Engineers in the large CAD departments provide the drawings which create the knowledge links to their customers.
- **Company D** is an engineering company specialized in the field of steel construction for electro-hydraulic engineering. Roll-on-roll-off ramps, quay facilities, bridge and sluice hydraulics as well as associated services characterize this company.

The companies have been chosen to cover a broad range of engineering tasks which enables us to compare knowledge demands in different engineering areas and maybe get some general findings which can be used for tailoring the organizational and technical support structure for engineering knowledge work.

Participatory design in the development phase meant that we discussed each prototype with the engineering staff and implemented their proposals in a feedback loop. To facilitate prototyping we used rapid development tools allowing us to produce "throw-away prototypes" which could be used by the engineers hands-on without complete functionality. Meanwhile the system is transferred to an evolutionary prototype which is already in use in the participating companies. Next step will be to evaluate the CoLinK prototype in real project environments of the partner companies. We are just starting to develop appropriate evaluation methods [6, 7].

2.2. System analysis: Empirical findings

The following paragraphs describe the aspects discovered during the system analysis that had major influence on the design of the CoLinK system.

Methodological competence of engineers
In the engineering sector the execution of processes requires methodological competence which is important for quality assurance as even small mistakes during the process can be critical. This makes it particularly hard for young engineers who are not used to the details of the company's methods.

To target this problem one of our partner companies attempted to build up a "knowledge library" on the central file server where employees could store process relevant documents, e. g. process descriptions, guidelines, etc. Since the complex processes require mainly implicit knowledge, they did not succeed in exploring and storing that knowledge.

While these problems can be generally approached with document management software, we discovered further aspects that require an approach that goes beyond document management. Within the interviews (with the management) it showed that while the general processes itself are similar in many projects, they have their particularities depending e. g. on the type of facility or the country where it is constructed. Accordingly, to make use of any stored information not only a project reference is required (e. g. meta-data) but also information about the project itself to identify similar projects and make use of information that is connected to it.

Further more, the need to link contact information to processes, e. g. to identify experts, was discovered, which was so far done in a separate database with only rudimentary functionality and no link to either projects or processes.

Project traceability

The traceability of projects is seen as an important factor by the participating companies and employees. Next to project oriented storage of emails on an exchange server, they attempted to log file transfers between different parties by putting copies of up/downloaded files into corresponding inbound/outbound folders on their file server. Having traceability for data exchange and correspondence partly in place, our partners lack support for tracing especially knowledge relevant project information. Even though they realized the importance of preserving knowledge creation and exchange within the processes they could not find a way to successfully implement it.

Distributed knowledge management

Due to business engagement in emerging markets e. g. in Asia and Eastern Europe staff members need to travel and are not always locally available. However, local presence is currently a key element for successfully conducting the engineering projects. To handle distribution, so far only VPN connection for remote file access and VoIP software is being used, however, this enables distributed knowledge exchange only to a certain extent. During the system analysis the high demand for distributed knowledge management became obvious. Since our partners are planning to extend the distributed work by installing subsidiaries in other countries to have a closer contact to their customers, support for distributed knowledge management becomes a central aspect for the CoLinK system.

Information technology infrastructure

The system analysis revealed a general lack of IT infrastructure in the participating medium sized companies, e. g. a document management system as a foundation for knowledge management was not used by any of our partners. Also existing standard components for shared email and calendar functionality and a central file server were not used to their full potential. While this situation caused the engineers to report many "standard problems" during our interviews, which complicated a clear focus on knowledge management issues in the beginning, it also enabled certain beneficial aspects:

- The importance of including information management techniques as a foundation for successful knowledge management was pointed out.
- Missing use of document management systems gave us clear evidence that including a DMS into the CoLinK system was a must.

The question arises how to bridge the gap between traditional information processing and future knowledge management by the use of adaptive ICT.

3. State of the art

3.1. Knowledge management and cooperation

In the context of CoLinK we have to consider two dimensions of knowledge and knowledge management: a) Knowledge as an individual property of humans vs. a collective resource of organisations. b) Knowledge management as a technology to extract knowledge from humans vs. a cooperative approach to organise knowledge within institutions.

Knowledge as an individual property – a research subject of cognitive psychology – deals with topics like the organisation of the brain, different kinds of knowledge representations, properties of short and long term memory, problem solving etc. The second interpretation of knowledge extends the view from the individual to the organisation: How is knowledge created, stored and exchanged in organisations? The concepts of "learning organisations" and "organisational memory" are widely accepted as models for explaining creation, acquisition, integration, distribution and use of knowledge in organisational contexts [8, 9, 10]. Knowledge as a social category describes the background of the CoLinK cooperation model.

Reviewing knowledge management literature, on the one hand KM is seen as a technology to extract, organize and save human knowledge – mainly by means of artificial intelligence – in computer systems (data mining). The goal is to systematically retrieve this knowledge by standardized methods from the centralized knowledge repository and to apply it to a given problem. On the other hand KM is described as a socio-technical system which comprises the knowledge worker, the working environment, the social activity of knowledge exchange, the individual or collaborative problem solving process as well as the information technology to support these processes. In this understanding KM is not a technology to extract knowledge from humans but to multiply knowledge by sharing it between humans (see also [11]). This second approach which provides the basis of our project strongly relies on a number of assumptions which have to be considered when implementing the CoLinK system. To mention only some:

- Knowledge always depends on the organisational *context* of its generation and use.
- Knowledge is *subjective* in a way that it depends on its creator or bearer. Dreyfus and Dreyfus [12] defined five stages of expertise from beginner to expert each of which can be described by special characteristics of the respective level of knowledge.
- Knowledge often has a *tacit dimension* (see above). Knowledge workers have difficulties in explicitly communicating this kind of knowledge to co-workers.
- Knowledge is *distributed* among team members. This raises the question of the relation between centralized and decentralized knowledge.

Providing support for coping with these problems is the challenge the CoLinK system has to face.

3.2. Knowledge management in engineering

Engineering constitutes the early stage of manufacturing, i. e. planning, conceptioning, requirements specification, construction, detailing of plans etc. It is a service provided as a crucial precondition to enable physical production. Therefore, knowledge management in engineering may be the key to a successful production management [13].

The reasons for developing KM strategies in industry and especially in engineering are: a) to preserve given and generate new knowledge within the company and b) to capture knowledge from outside the company and thereby strengthen the innovative power of the enterprise. Several instruments can be used to reach this goal: Exploring innovative knowledge sources, e. g. by cooperating with science and technology institutes. Not less important: using everyday liaisons with external partners like customers, subcontractors or consulting experts. The necessity of using these external knowledge sources often is underestimated especially by small and medium enterprises. Edler [14] proved this assumption in his case study about knowledge management strategies in German industry. The important role of knowledge intensive business services for the promotion of city regions as analyzed by Simmie and Strambach [15] underline these findings as well. The question is how to support this crucial success factor by an appropriate *contact management component* in the CoLinK system as well as a method to deal with *distributed knowledge* in internal and in externally related "communities of practice" [16].

3.3. ICT support for knowledge management in engineering

Considering the broad functionality of KM systems there are no common overall software systems targeting existing heterogeneous approaches. Because knowledge gathering, consolidating and exchange build up the centre of knowledge management, *CSCW* and *groupware systems* are most often mentioned with first priority. More than 20 years of research in this field [17, 18] shows a great potential for applying theories and practices of CSCW in the fields of engineering and design. There are several interesting approaches for applying groupware to engineering tasks, showing advantages and problems. Pipek and Wulf [19] tried to install the Answer Garden approach – originally designed by Mark Ackerman and Thomas Malone [20] – in the environment of maintenance engineering in a steel mill. Results showed that division of labour, competition between engineers, and rivalry between organisational units often obstruct effective cooperation within the Answer Garden framework which hardly can be addressed by groupware technology. Perry [21] applies CSCW and groupware to design activities in construction engineering. As a result of two case studies (design work in civil engineering, consulting engineers in building design) he stresses the fact that CSCW systems in engineering often consider organisations as stable units neglecting social dynamics and organisational change. In our approach we try to cope with this problem by providing a high degree of flexibility and perspectivity as properties of CoLinK.

Secondly, *document management systems* are a strong basis to build upon: Documents in most cases can be seen as "information", e. g. a drawing of a pump in mechanical engineering normally does not contain knowledge about the context of use (e. g. climate) or about dismantling for repair. Therefore, the semantics of document management systems has to be enriched by the pragmatics of use. One possibility to reach this higher level of semiotics is to add meta-data to the basic information.

Thirdly, in contrast to information, knowledge in most cases is connected to processes. Therefore, in enterprise environments *project management systems* serve the dynamic side of knowledge management.

The number of software houses providing components for knowledge management is huge. They often present an impressive range of features from a content library, a workbench, different discussion boards up to a task manager which allows project managers to assign tasks to team members and to keep a log of current status of each task. Most of the systems aim at big companies; the requirements of small and medium enterprises are often not in the focus of these systems: not appropriate, too big, too difficult to use, too expensive. The CoLinK system tries to meet the requirements of these smaller firms and to integrate necessary functions to an easy to use configurable, scalable and affordable KM system.

4. CoLinK system experience

4.1. General approach

The conducted interviews and observations revealed that it would not be helpful to concentrate on single aspects like document, project or contact management. Certainly, within each segment an improvement could be reached by extending the existing solutions, however, the highest potential for improved information and knowledge exchange was seen in the linking of these aspects within the project context.

Thereby, it was understood as a critical success factor that the system does not aim at replacing existing technologies but to seamlessly integrate into the companies' infrastructure. For the contact management a bidirectional synchronization tool has been developed that let the partner companies continue to use their existing tools for contact management (e. g. Microsoft Outlook and proprietary databases). Since all partners are running common file servers in their networks with a consistent folder structure for their projects a document management system (Alfresco) was chosen that provides a standard network share to access the repository.

Therefore, no extra client software has to be installed and the folder structure can be maintained while all benefits of the document management system are available to the CoLinK system.

To ensure intensive use of the system a major part of the knowledge collection takes place within the team members' task execution. The system, therefore, provides a "tasks" view where team members can not only see their assigned tasks but are also able to attach additional information like documents, contacts and annotations to it. The latter is intensively used for information/knowledge exchange between team members and can be seen as an integrated forum for each task allowing them for example to report problems and jointly find solutions for them. Next to annotating the task itself, a created link can be annotated as well, e. g. to explain the role of a company/person within a task.

Similarly to the "tasks" view, the "contacts" and "documents" view allows users to attach any of the earlier mentioned types of information to contacts/documents; however this paper focuses mainly on the functionality within the project context.

Information about projects as well as general project functionality like creating and editing projects is provided in the "projects" view, which lets users add project-members to the project, check project documents and model projects by creating and adding processes to the project.

Having this functionality in place, any information that was acquired during a project can later be evaluated and used for future projects gaining efficiency as well as providing quality assurance.

4.2. Interface design

The CoLinK interface design consists of several views that offer support for the different actions. In each view the screen is separated into frames that hold the panels, which provide a distinct part of the view's functionality. For example the "tasks" view shown in figure 1 contains the "tasks" and the "info" panel.

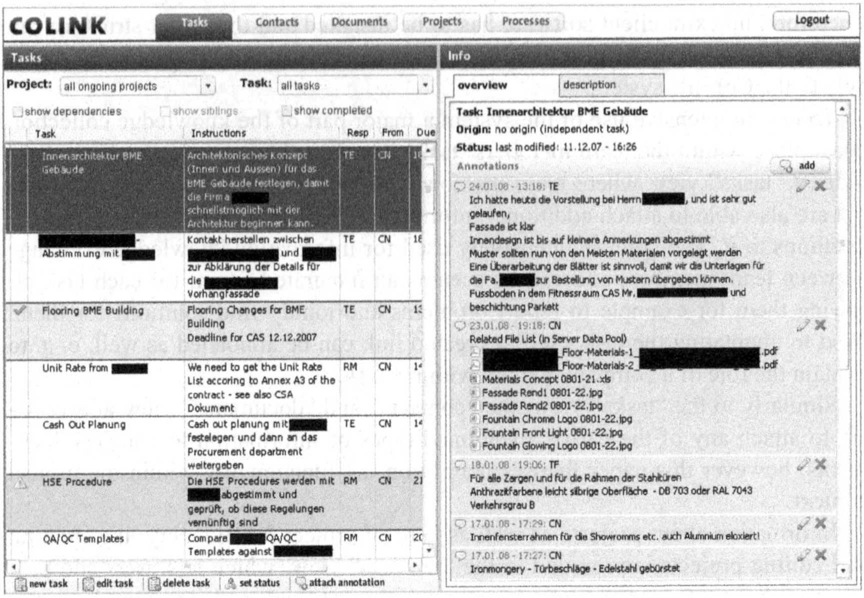

Figure 1. Tasks view with two panels

By clicking a task on the left side, detailed information is shown on the right side. This allows the user to browse through the tasks without losing the context. Similar to actual browser frames the frames in CoLinK can be resized, causing the embedded panels to adjust to the new size. This allows users with a higher resolution to benefit from the extra space. For many actions in CoLinK (e. g. "new annotation" or "create new project") popups are used to avoid switching to a new screen, which could distract users from their current "position" in the system.

4.3. *Processes vs. tasks*

A major requirement of our project partners was the possibility to create generic process descriptions for common actions within a project. These descriptions serve as guidelines and are especially useful for young engineers as they provide important knowledge about how the company works.

The description of the processes is comparable to Wiki articles; however, the CoLinK processes differ in a way that (just like explained earlier for the tasks) contacts, documents and annotations can be attached.

While these general processes can often be reused in several projects (see "modelling projects" in 4.4) the actual execution differs depending on the type of project. Therefore, the processes (i. e. the description and the additional information) have to be adapted to the individual project. To enable this, CoLinK implements a versioning system that keeps track of the processes being used in the different projects.

To connect the processes to the task management it is possible to assign a process to a user, which will make the process appear in the corresponding task list.

Since a complex project cannot be described only by generic processes CoLinK offers different types of processes within a project:

- ***Generic processes*** are created in the "processes" view and stored in the process library. They are added to projects from the library and can then be modified within the project.
- ***Project specific processes*** can be created independently from the library within the project modeler. They are especially useful for processes that are expected to be only used in one project or processes that are used for the first time and cannot yet be generically described.
- ***Tasks*** can be created directly within the "tasks" view and are expected to be less complex and not easily reusable in future project. They are, therefore, only shown in the task list and not in the project modeler.

While the initial idea for the process handling was to create generic processes and then adapt them to the project needs, results from the companies use of the system show that so far they almost only used project specific processes to model their projects. It is assumed that it is easier for them to first create a process for an actual project and derive generic processes afterwards.

4.4. Modelling projects

To exploit the similarity of projects and make use of information and knowledge that was created in former projects, it is necessary to set certain parameters for every new project. Since companies specify their projects differently, these parameters can be configured to fit the companies' needs (e. g. country, project type, facility type, etc.). In a next step processes are added to the new project frame, which can be either done from the process library or from existing projects. Due to the fact that processes in the engineering sector are usually complex it is possible to create sub processes which are displayed in a hierarchical list.

Since it is the aim of the CoLinK system to embed knowledge management in the everyday work as proposed by Hoffmann et al. [22] project managers can assign the project processes to users who can then add information to them during the actual tasks execution (see 4.5). The project management functionality is very limited (e. g. assigning due dates and setting task status) and is not supposed to replace existing project management systems. In further versions of CoLinK we may consider implementing an interface for integration of existing project management tools.

4.5. Contextual linking and annotation

The acquisition of project specific knowledge is done within the execution of tasks to minimize the required effort. Since engineers regularly use the CoLinK system to view, select and set the status of their tasks, any information can easily be added within the process context. By selecting a task, related information is shown, which includes the process description, related documents, contacts and hyperlinks. By integrating a document as well as contact management system, users can easily link any of the mentioned artefacts to the task. Unlike the generic process descriptions, which require a collaborative approval process, changing the description within a project can be done directly by the person who is currently working on the task.

A central part of the knowledge acquisition is the use of categorized annotations, which are attached to the task. These categories allow for example to report obstructions that require the help of other engineers. To encourage the collaborative finding of solutions, any task that is marked with an obstruction is visible to all other engineers, enabling them to reply to the reported obstruction.

With contextual links and annotations being the major means of knowledge management in the CoLinK system, we realized that in fact a combination of both enables interesting possibilities to foster knowledge acquisition, therefore.

- any annotation can include links to other artefacts and
- any link can be augmented with annotations

The application of the above mentioned cases can be illustrated with the following examples:

1. An obstruction within a task is reported with an annotation that includes a link to the corresponding document (e. g. problem within a drawing).
2. A contact is linked to a task with an annotation that explains the connection between the contact and the task.

To give users the chance to attach information in multiple steps, created links and annotations can be modified and enhanced with further information at any time.

5. Implementing the CoLinK system

The CoLinK system is designed to link different types of information within a project/process context. To enable the integration into existing infrastructure it aims at using enterprise content management (ECM) components and connecting them to the CoLinK core system. So far this is implemented for the open source document management system Alfresco, which is integrated via web services; however, the use of other systems is generally possible.

The CoLinK core system consists of a database driven process management that also takes care about the versioned linking of the various kinds of information. Processes can have an unlimited number of hierarchies and also store information about their origin. This enables the required traceability when processes are copied and modified within the same or between different projects. The database also holds tables for projects and the company specific configuration of project properties as well as tables for companies and persons with the corresponding relation. Furthermore tables for the versioned annotations exist. Linking is done in a very generic way, storing sourceType and sourceID as well as destinationType and destinationID, which allows any combination of linking between the different types of information. Similar to the processes, the origin is stored for the links as well to enable traceability for the linked information of project processes.

The CoLinK client is a web based system using Web 2.0 technology to provide a user experience that is otherwise only known from desktop applications. Currently the prototype is implemented in Adobe Flash, which allowed rapid prototyping due to many existing components. For client/server communication Flash Remoting is being used, which offers RPCs and great debugging functionality.

While the performance and general user experience with the Flash client has been received positively by our partners, several aspects let us consider changing to an AJAX implementation in the future. For example the following usability problems with the Flash client have been discovered: keyboard initiated copy and paste does not work properly with the Firefox Flash plug-in; browser search functionality does not work; browser plug-ins do not work (e. g. Skype plug-in for direct dialling from within the application); parallel use of Flash and HTML causes problems in some browsers. Especially the last point is an important factor as we plan to include existing HTML/JavaScript components (e. g. TinyMCE for editing process descriptions).

6. Conclusion and perspectives

Our approach of process oriented knowledge acquisition with contextual linking and annotation enables a simple and user friendly way of creating an organizational memory and provides engineers with the opportunity to benefit from the stored knowledge during their everyday tasks. The CoLinK system is being used successfully by our partner companies and continuous feedback is reported back to our research group.

The prototype already changed the organizational strategies in participating companies to an extent that distributed teams work together on tasks that used to be done only in a collocated manner. It has shown that connecting the system to the companies' existing infrastructure (e. g. contact management) was a critical success factor for introducing the system.

While the user interface in general has been adopted well, further improvements are necessary, especially drag and drop functionality will be a major aspect.

Even though several types of additional information can already be linked, observation of the system usage has shown that including email attachments for the annotations would be a great feature.

By introducing the CoLinK system not just in one company we have the opportunity to compare the evaluation results from different viewpoints which will give further input for the development. It is expected that the results will bring up aspects of customization to adjust the system to the specific needs of the companies. The next step could then be a generalization of the approach to apply our concept for process oriented knowledge management also to companies outside the engineering sector.

References

1. Beyer, H., Holtzblatt, K.: Contextual design: defining customer-centered systems. Morgan Kaufmann Publishers, San Francisco (1997)
2. Friedrich, J.: Participatory prototyping. In: Rauner, F., Maclean, R. (Eds.), Handbook of Vocational Education Research. Springer Publishers, Dordrecht (2007)
3. Kensing, F., Blomberg, J.: Participatory design: issues and concerns. Computer Supported Cooperative Work, Vol. 7, pp. 167-185 (1998)
4. Gärtner, J.: Participatory design in consulting. Computer Supported Cooperative Work – A Journal of Collaborative Computing, Vol. 7, pp. 273-289 (1998)
5. Polany, M.: The tacit dimension. Routledge and Keel Paul, London (1966)
6 Neale, D.C., Carroll, J.M., Rosson, M.B.: Evaluating computer-supported cooperative work: models and frameworks. In: CSCW '04, Vol. 6, Issue 3, pp. 112-121, ACM, New York (2004)
7 Ramage, M.: The learning way: Evaluating co-operative systems. Ph.D. Thesis, Lancaster University, Lancaster (1999)
8 Argyris, C.: On organizational learning. Blackwell Publishing, Oxford/Malden (1999)
9 Schwartz, D.G., Divitini, M., Brasethvik, T. (Eds.): Internet-based organizational memory and knowledge management. Idea Group Publishing, Hershey (2000)
10 Ramage, M., Reiff, F.: Links between organisational memory and cooperative awareness. http://www.comp.lancs.ac.uk/computing/research/cseg/projects/evaluation/OM_CA.html. Accessed 1 Feb 2008.
11. Bonifacio, M., Bouquet, P., Traverso, P.: Enabling distributed knowledge management: managerial and technological implications. Informatik/Informatique, no. 1, pp. 23-29 (2002)
12. Dreyfus, H. L., Dreyfus, S. E.: Mind over machine. Free Press, New York (1986)
13. Shankar, R., Singh, M. D., Gupta, A., Narain, R.: Strategic planning for knowledge management implementation in engineering firms. Work Study, Vol. 52, no. 4, pp. 190-200 (2003)
14. Edler, J.: Knowledge management in German industry. Fraunhofer Institute for Systems and Innovation Research (ISI), Karlsruhe (January 2003)
15. Simmie, J., Strambach, S.: The contribution of knowledge-intensive business services (KIBS) to innovation in cities: an evolutionary and institutional perspective. Journal of Knowledge Management, Vol. 10, no. 5, pp. 26-40 (2006)
16. Wenger, E.: Communities of practice. Learning, meaning and identity. Cambridge University Press, Cambridge (1998)

17 Twenty years of CSCW – what have we learned? Plenary panel. CSCW '06, ACM, New York (2006)
18 ACM (Ed.): GROUP '07. Proceedings of the 2007 International ACM Conference on Supporting Group Work. ACM, New York (2007)
19. Pipek, V., Wulf, V.: Pruning the Answer Garden: Knowledge Sharing in Maintenance Engineering. In: European Conference on CSCW, Kluwer, Amsterdam, pp. 1-20 (2003)
20 Ackerman, M.S., Malone, T. W.: Answer Garden: A Tool for Growing Organzational Memory. In: Proceedings of the ACM Conference on Office Information Systems, pp. 31-39, (1990)
21 Perry, M.J.: Distributed cognition and computer supported collaborative design: The organisation of work in construction engineering. Ph.D. Thesis, Brunel University, Uxbridge (1997)
22. Hoffmann, M., Loser, K., Walter, T., Herrmann, T.: A design process for embedding knowledge management in everyday work. In: Proceedings of the Conference on Groupware, ACM, pp. 296-305 (1999)

Conceptual Model of Activity as Tool for Developing a Dementia Care Support System

Helena Lindgren

Department of Computing Science, Umeå University, Sweden, helena@cs.umu.se

Abstract: The clinical domain of cognitive diseases and dementia is recognized by its highly complex knowledge domain, requiring expertise and experience in handling situations with a variety of symptoms and diseases, distributed over different levels in organizations and different professions. In this paper a case study is presented where the process of investigating suspected dementia in patient cases were analyzed. An early prototype of the decision-support system DMSS (Dementia Management and Support System) was integrated in the process. The main aim for the case study was to capture and model the complex target activity for the purpose of knowledge acquisition and formalization in the development of a decision-support system for the domain. The resulting model is general, in that it captures structures and required knowledge at different levels of care, however, specific enough to provide a perception of use context and semi-formal base for further development of the system for different use environments, with different local solutions to work division, etc. The results are fed into the development of DMSS and the general activity analysis framework is being developed.

Keywords: Activity theory, Work analysis, Knowledge-based systems, Decision support, Knowledge management, Dementia care

1. Introduction

The clinical decision-support system (CDSS) DMSS (Dementia Management Support System) is being developed for assisting medical personnel in the investigation of suspected cases of dementia [1]. The application domain is used to investigate a range of aspects concerning knowledge acquisition, knowledge formalization and representation, interaction design and methods for transforming informal clinical practice knowledge into usable support in a CDSS. The main purpose of the system is to function as an extension of the individual actor's cognitive ability and as a common ground for collaborative and distributed team

---

Please use the following format when citing this chapter:

Lindgren, H., 2008, in IFIP International Federation for Information Processing, Volume 270; *Knowledge Management in Action*; Mark Ackerman, Rose Dieng-Kuntz, Carla Simone, Volker Wulf; (Boston: Springer), pp. 97–109.

work. The system is designed to support higher-level cognitive functions as reasoning, decision-making and learning.

The clinical domain of cognitive diseases and dementia is recognized by its highly complex knowledge domain, requiring expertise and experience in handling the progressivity of the disease, and consequently, re-occurring situations with a variety of social, cognitive, psychological and behavioral complications [1]. In an organizational perspective, work can be done differently depending on the available resources, treatment protocols and priorities. In addition, the organization of work is also subject to evolvement and change. When focus is put on the clinical activity, issues such as the distinction between facts, judgments, qualities of evidence, what is normal vs. abnormal, levels of dysfunctions, distinction between acts of decision and acts of data collection, collaborative and/or distributed actions, sources of evidence, etc, become essential to clarify in order to formalize the knowledge correctly and create a design for interactive clinical reasoning. An analysis of the qualities of the medical domain knowledge expressed in clinical guidelines is needed as well as a thorough formative activity analysis of how the actual clinical work is performed and could be developed. By taking an activity-oriented stand, i.e., keeping the activity as the focus of analysis (with an early DMSS prototype integrated), an activity model was created for the purpose of serving as a tool for:

- transforming informal structures and knowledge into formal knowledge in a CDSS,
- identifying ambiguities and inconsistencies in domain knowledge and clinical practice, and integrating means to handle these in the interaction with the CDSS,
- distinguishing between formalizable knowledge and knowledge that is better integrated through the design of interactive clinical reasoning,
- identifying different types of processes in order to provide support for respective and their interactions,
- identifying local organizational factors posing constraints on the design and use of a CDSS, and distinguishing general/universal and transferable knowledge,
- future evaluations of the CDSS in different local clinical practices.

A secondary purpose of the study was to investigate to what extent activity theory, which commonly is described and applied in an informal and general manner, can be used as base for knowledge acquisition and formalization work [2, 3, 4, 5, 6].

The results presented in this paper of the case study, including the development and application of the activity model, are used as a bench-mark for further development of the theoretical foundations for knowledge structures to be implemented in the system, for the design of interactive clinical reasoning, and as a base-line for evaluation studies in clinical practice.

2. Methods, Materials and Procedure

A prototype of the system DMSS is developed, which contains support mainly for assessment of evidence in a clinical diagnostic reasoning process aimed at supporting physicians in their main tasks. In our case study the prototype was integrated as a prompting tool for discussions about content and design of the system. However, the main focus was the investigation process as a whole.

Five patient cases investigated for a suspected dementia disease were in focus for this work. The studies were conducted in the setting of an out-patient ward at a geriatric clinic which investigates patient cases with suspected cognitive diseases. The patients were selected by including all new cases who were willing to participate in the study and who was assigned a particular physician from a certain date. We use the term *investigation* to denote the sum of diagnostic actions, interventions and follow-up actions, executed at this particular clinic. The time period of investigation for each patient was in the range of 3-10 months.

The investigation process was documented in the electronic health record (EHR), and by observations of clinical encounters and interviews. An approach inspired by grounded theory was used as method for analysis in order to identify general purposes and structures of activity, however, combined with the theoretical framework of the cultural-historical activity theory for integrating an understanding of the characteristics of particular tools, conflict situations and reasons for changes in purposes and structures [2, 3, 5]. The semi-formal structure that emerged, was applied at later stages of analysis to patient data in order to investigate to what extent it fits the data, and the structure was modified as a result. With the activity model as base, a process of differentiation of knowledge is ongoing, with an emerging knowledge base and a design of UI as result. The model is used as a dynamic reflective conceptual artifact in terms of [7] in the process of developing the system, which can be understood both by medical personnel and system developers, thus, having the potential of bridging the problem of transferring knowledge between the different communities.

3. Results

The results are organized into three sections. The activity model, which frames the clinical investigation activity in focus for our case study, is described in Section 3.1. Knowledge-based structures evolved based on the activity model are introduced in Section 3.2. Implications for and a proposed design of the DMSS user interface (UI) are presented in Section 3.3.

3.1. Activity Model

We take as starting point, the view that the clinical activity of investigation essentially consists of two parts; the *clinical process* with its actions and sub-processes, and an *activity system* in terms of activity theory, which includes the object for activity, resources involved and their relations, and which imposes constraints on the execution of the investigation activity. The distinction is made for ontology and knowledge representation reasons, enabling a distinction between formal and informal described routines, treatment protocols and work divisions in the organization from what actually is implemented and applied in the execution of activity in a certain situation. A necessary property of the anticipated model is an ability to capture dynamic and changing situations and objects. We use the notion of *object* for data and phenomenon such as symptoms or diseases, when referring to what is in focus for each action.

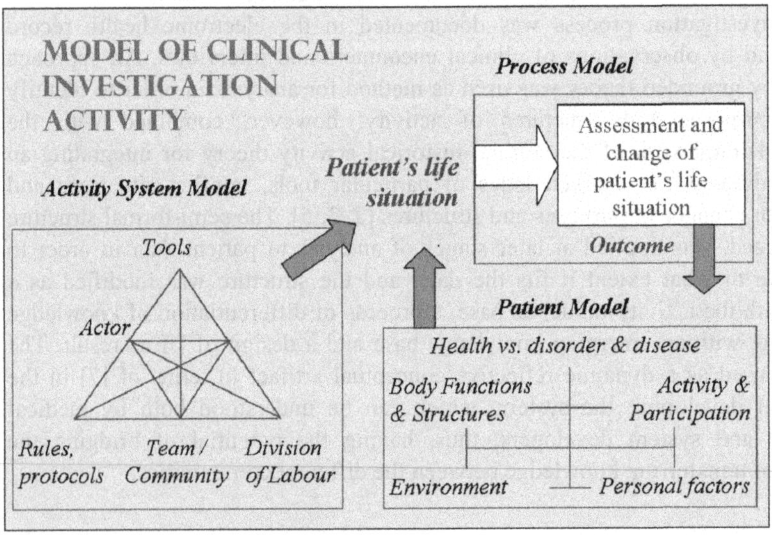

Figure 1. Activity model consisting of an activity system model based on [3], a patient model based primarily on [8], and a process model integrating the former two in the execution of an activity.

The model is based on cultural-historical activity theory (CHAT), which is a suitable framework for our purposes in that it integrates both systemic components such as resources and constraints, and emphasizes change and development of purposeful activities [3, 5]. The theory describes human activity as a dynamic system restricted by a set of conditions and inter-relations between the parts of the activity system and between systems. The theory defines an activity by the motive of the activity, driven by conscious or unconscious needs of a subject, or actor. The anticipated outcome of the whole clinical investigation process is identified as an optimal and satisfactory life situation for the patient, which can also be seen as the motive for and definition of this particular activity, and that guides the execution of the activity. It is important to take the patient-oriented view of the activity, since although it is the same type of activity in the investigation of two different patients, the execution will most likely differ, due to different needs of the patients, available resources and decisions made during the process. Therefore, we supplement the two analytic perspectives *activity system model* and *process model* with an elaborated object model, which in this domain is a model of the patient's life situation (*Patient Model* in Figure 1).

An overview of the activity model is provided in the following subsections, while a semi-formal description of components in the model and examples from patient cases can be found in [1].

3.1.1. Activity System Model and Patient Model

In terms of activity theory the activity system in focus includes the basic and original entities the subject, or *actor*, the *object* (here *patient's life situation*[1]) and *tools*, which are all entities with certain characteristic properties and roles in the activity system [5]. Their relations can be summarised by viewing the actor *changing* the patient's life situation (object and focus for activity) by *using* tools. The tools *mediate* the activity and should not be in focus for the activity.

For identifying the actor and the organisation he or she is representing, the activity system model viewed in Figure 1 can be used by defining the object as the main commission of the organisation [4]. For representation purposes it is convenient to distinguish the entities of an organisation, or *actor* in a wide interpretation, separated from the entities representing the patient's life situation (object). The patient model that is formed in the activity analysis presented in this work addresses terminology and ontological issues, issues of evidence identification, valuation, refinement, ambiguities, levels of granularity treated by different actors or professionals, the question of how to present the content to a user of a CDSS, etc. Therefore, in order to create a patient model that can function as a basis and instrument for formalisation of knowledge and outcomes of care activities, the patient model is based on nationally and internationally established classifications and terminologies created to structure knowledge concerning patients for different purposes. However, since the purposes differ, the resulting patient model is a synthesis of the WHO classification of functioning, ability and health (ICF) as base [8], supplemented with more elaborate and specific classifications of diseases and behavioural functions. Key components in the patient model are mechanisms for valuing the existence and amount of features,

---

[1] To be distinguished from the patient as an actor, participating in modifying his or her life situation.

and their change over time, for decision support purposes, for evaluating care outcomes and for medical research purposes.

3.1.2. Process Model and Typing of Actions

The activity system involved in the execution of a task can be defined for each sub-action in the investigation process, as well as for the whole activity. The outcome of each action is another piece of evidence, related to the patient. Consequently, typically each action concerns a *change* of the incomplete knowledge about the patient's situation, and capturing this *change* is crucial in the design process.

When the investigation process as performed in the case studies was analysed, different sorts of actions were distinguished by the purpose, or the goal of a particular action. Typically, the actions were aimed at either collecting raw data (CO); refine or interpret raw data or knowledge (RO); using the interpreted data for higher level of reasoning for the purpose of determine the existence of a phenomenon (DEO); determine the type of a phenomenon (i.e. increase level of granularity in the knowledge) (DTO); impose changes to the phenomenon in focus (CHO) and value the effects thereof (ECHO). The actions of higher complexity which aim at a holistic assessment and change of a phenomenon we denote *investigation* actions (IO), which typically integrate all the other purposes. In addition, actions were identified which aim at controlling and directing the process (DA). Examples of such actions are referrals for examinations, involving colleagues for consultations, assignment of team-members to tasks and team-meetings. There are also actions, which aim at providing the patient, relatives and home care with information. These actions are interventions, aimed at changing the knowledge in the patient and/or the relatives or home care personnel (actions of type CHO). Actions of the type CHO and ECHO typically belong to the intervention-part of the investigation activity.

Some of the sub-processes involved in the activity are viewed in Figure 2. The levels distinguished by lines in the figure indicate the different levels of complexity in the actions. As can be seen in the figure, the activities of analytic and decisive character are organised in the upper levels. The actions defined at these levels are typically defined as necessary for the main activity to be executed, according to the clinical guidelines and the domain knowledge. However, the level of necessity can differ depending on which guideline is used as tool for reasoning.

The object-creating actions, which are typically automated processes (i.e. operations) for the experienced actor, are organised at the bottom of the structure. Automated in the sense that the experienced actor does not have to put mental load or conscious thought on the execution, instead the actor can focus on the larger perspective and motive for the activity of which the action constitutes a part. These actions are typically administration of tools such as execute tests and examinations involving the patient. The actions defined at the lower levels in our analysis can very well be exchanged by other actions, which produce equivalent information necessary for accomplishing the decisive actions. Typically, this is the case when the routines and priorities at different workplaces direct the usage of different tools in the process, for instance, which radiology methods to use. Differences in which tools that are used may also due to different habits and values hold by individual actors.

The participation of patient and/or patient's family is necessary in the object-creating actions at the lowest level, however, not at the other levels. This gives suggestions on how a decision-support system should be designed and for what kind of clinical situations, depending on which kind of actions are to be supported. There may be less need of a support system in the clinical patient encounter situation for the experienced actor when the examinations for obtaining evidence are executed. However, at this level different clinically validated methods as well as ad-hoc methods can be used. The less experienced actor can be supported in the choice of methods and in the execution of these sub-actions as well as in the higher-level actions of diagnostic reasoning.

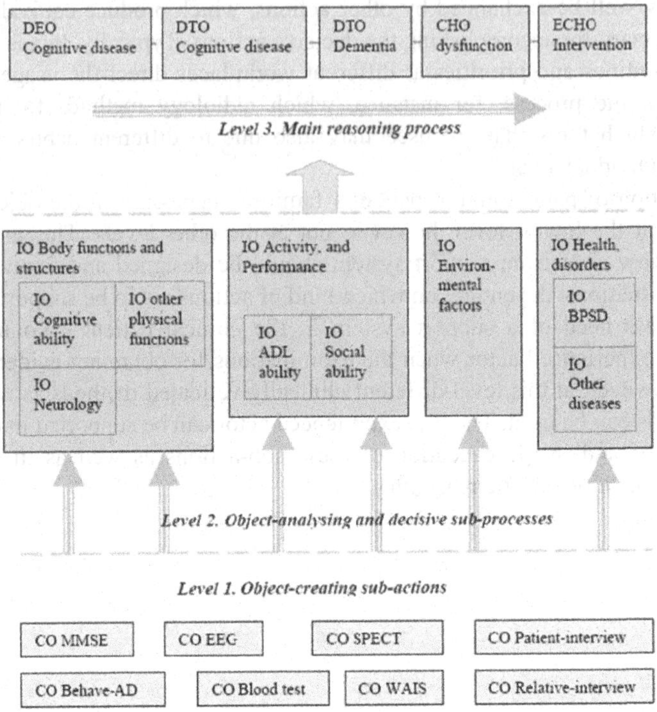

Figure 2. Different levels of complexity in the process of investigating cognitive diseases. BPSD is an abbreviation for Behavioral and psychological symptoms in dementia, and MMSE, EEG, WAIS, SPECT and Behave-AD are abbreviations for clinical examinations.

By distinguishing actions by their purposes a model is created, which identifies reasoning processes and logistic processes and their respective sub-actions, including their characteristics (e.g., complexity, dependencies, suitability for formalization, required resources and constraints for completion, etc.). Based on the model formal modules for decision support are created and supplemented with functionality provided through the interaction with a system.

3.1.3. Levels of Complexity

In our case study, three main dimensions of the process were distinguished, representing different levels of complexity. For practical reasons the two perspectives were distinguished from a logistic (or administrative) perspective, considering that the CDSS is primarily aimed at supporting higher-level reasoning. The logistic process became visible in the event-based documentation in the electronic health record (EHR) and in the scheduling of the patient's encounters with different personnel and for examinations. However, the quality of the information included in the EHR is typically raw data, which needs to be refined to be useful for reasoning, or summaries of coarse granularity, also not particularly useful for the level of reasoning that is needed for diagnosis. Therefore, the actions of higher complexity leading towards qualified decisions are focussed in our analysis, where raw data is being refined and interpreted within different frames of reference. Such actions are partly supported in the prototype system by production rules, based on clinical guidelines in the domain and formulated in knowledge-building sessions with domain experts. The basic actions of collecting raw data (CO) are supported by the system in that suggestions are given of which methods or clinical instruments to use, of which some are integrated in the system as basic data collecting frames. The logistic perspective was in the case study taken into consideration when conflicts between the perspectives occurred. Typically, conflicts were caused when the reasoning process had to be adjusted to the routines, time-scheduling constraints and bottlenecks in the organisation.

Two levels of reasoning processes from a physician's perspective can be identified in the activity. The main reasoning includes diagnostic reasoning and decision-making concerning interventions. Supportive reasoning processes involve investigations of specific domains in an individual, such as neurology, cognition, psychology, physiology, etc. (Figure 2). These domains correlate to the categorisation made in the patient model (Figure 1). The different purposes of these processes can be summarised by viewing the supportive processes as investigating dysfunction per se, while the main reasoning relates the dysfunctions in the perspective of a possible dementing disease. The three views of the process (logistic process, investigation of specific domains and the main reasoning process) are executed in parallel, they are cross-fertilizing and dependent on each other, and are partly overlapping depending on circumstances in the environment.

A similar structure is seen if viewing the contributions to the investigation process from other professional's perspective. The granularity of evidence differ between the different professional categories when they investigate the different domains of the patient model, which generates a richer synthesis through the different professional contributions than when an investigation is done by the physician alone, as is the case in some care environments. Therefore, the patient model needs to be elaborate enough to also capture evidence from other professional perspectives than the physician's, and consequently, the UI should integrate means to support all professional's work and reasoning processes that are involved in a patient case. By using ICF as basis for framing the patient's situation, different fields of expertise is covered at Level 2 (Figure 2).

3.2. Knowledge-Based Structures in DMSS

The model includes an analysis of the international domain knowledge based on evidence-based medicine (EBM), which represents a category of tools in the activity system model (Figures 1, 3). The knowledge is interpreted in clinical guidelines, treatment protocols, however, informally described, often ambiguous and incomplete [1, 9]. For knowledge representation purposes a distinction is made based on the activity model of which knowledge is suitable for formalization in a rule-based knowledge base and which knowledge needs to be mediated through the design of the UI. A goal of the design of the system is to present the domain knowledge including its limitations. This is done by providing the user the evidence in a patient's case visualized and interpreted within different and sometimes conflicting frames of interpretations. These frames represent clinical and internationally validated tools for categorization, terminology, and screening. The frames can also refer to different clinical domains of expertise. In order to support the reasoning process, this functionality also provides the user support for creating bases for, and valuating diagnostic hypotheses at different point in the process. This is accomplished by integrating a meta-level in the knowledge base, which handles the ambiguities, the process components, the local and individual preferences and, consequently, the interaction with the user. The meta-level knowledge structure uses formalized knowledge from different clinical guidelines, synthesizes and ranks these sources in interaction with the user, while leaving the final decisions to the user when the evidence in a patient case is ambiguous.

As a result of the activity analysis, a strong orientation to support for processes is included in current design process, since there are supplementary professions working towards the goal of achieving an optimal situation for a patient, each with their reasoning processes and frames of interpretations. A key issue is the structure, content and visualization of the patient model, which should function as a common tool for communication and cooperative work. Furthermore, the patient model also serves as a basis for data structures to be implemented in databases, serving purposes of follow-up of individual patients as well as evaluation of care provided by an organization. In a longer perspective, the information needs to be useful for evidence-based medical research, which puts additional quality requirements on the data structure in order to obtain sustainability.

The basic rulebase (based on international evidence-based knowledge and guidelines to the extent they can be formalized in a rigorous way), the meta-rulebase (containing and handling additional knowledge concerning differential diagnosis, ambiguities, local preferences) and the data structure based on the patient model (structured according to international classifications) need to be formalized using different formal techniques in order to fulfill their purposes. The activity analysis reveals at a semi-formal level their respective requirements and which knowledge items to be handled by the different knowledge structures. Ongoing research addresses the possibility to integrate these into a common formal framework based on general logics in a fundamental view of transformations between different logics [10, 11, 12, 13].

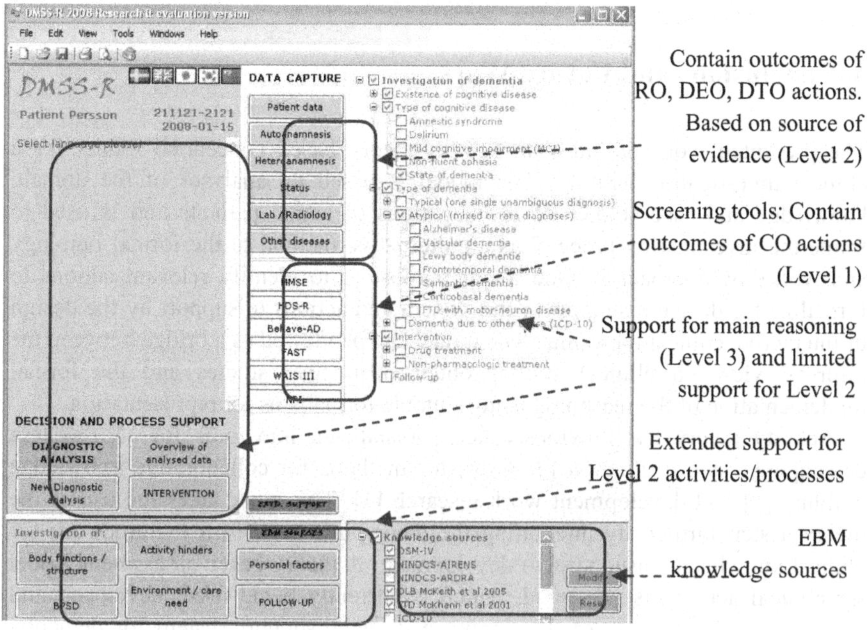

Figure 3. Design of the main frame of DMSS.

3.3. Activity-Oriented Interaction Design

We argue that the basic components of the activity model, i.e., process, tools, rules and regulations, cooperative aspects, patient model, etc., need to be reflected in the UI of a CDSS. The design of the DMSS UI is tightly intertwined with the meta-level of the knowledge base, which directs the use of the system and provides the support that is needed at different points in the process. This part of the system needs to be flexible, so that local and individual preferences can be met, such as which clinical guidelines and screening tools to use. In Figure 3 an initial re-design of the system is shown, in which the different categories of components correspond to different levels of activity in the investigation process. A major distinction is done between containers, or tools, for data capture and components for analysis and decision support. Further distinctions and categorizations of data capture functionality are made based on sources of evidence and validated screening tools, in order to obtain reliable data. The advanced support for reasoning is based on the main reasoning process (Level 3 in Figure 2) with a limited support for supportive reasoning processes (Level 2 in

Figure 2). This functionality is currently being supplemented with extended support modules for these processes, developed from a teamwork perspective.

4. Conclusions and Future Work

The presented work provides an activity-theory based conceptual model for a clinical investigation activity. The model is based on analyses of the domain knowledge and case studies of investigations of actual patients and is used to frame the investigation process, as an alternative method to the formal ontology and workflow approaches. One major purpose is to identify relevant actions to formalize for decision support in the system and actions to support by the design of interactive clinical reasoning. The model can be viewed as a bridge between the informal view on clinical actions obtained in field studies and the formal implementation of the reasoning using suitable formalisms for representation.

Activity theory has previously been crystallized into tools for e.g., system development and evaluation [2, 4, 6], for methods for collaborative knowledge building [7] and development work research [3]. This work takes the use of the theory a step further, by integrating the theory in a semi-formal framework for clinical knowledge-based system development. A theory-based assessment model for clinical activity is presented, which is currently being used, developed and evaluated in the process of developing a decision-support system for dementia care. The approach is activity-oriented and integrates support for processes as well as the creation of a shared understanding of, and a common ground for activity, i.e., the patient's health and well-being. The model frames the knowledge to be integrated in the system, in what way different knowledge structures is best mediated to the user and in what way the system can be used as a tool for development of knowledge and skills in an individual user or in a team, as well as develop collaboration in health care.

Furthermore, the need for methods that can bridge the gap between system developers and medical professionals in the development of clinical knowledge-based systems is addressed. The activity model (partly crystallized into prototypes in the process) constitutes a product of a collaborative knowledge building process, both for different health care professionals at different levels of care, but also for persons with different professional backgrounds in the development team.

Since the work presented in this paper is based on a limited amount of patients and focusing a specific domain, the activity model and implementations based on the model will be further evaluated and developed using additional patient cases. Furthermore, the framework will be used for developing knowledge systems in different domains. Ongoing work includes evaluations of DMSS in clinical settings concerning interactive support for hypothesis building, as well as evaluation of the basic knowledge base. The theoretical development of a framework for knowledge-based structures is continuing, in addition to the implementation of the patient model and extended support for teamwork.

Acknowledgments: We thank patients and physicians who have participated in evaluations. The DMSS-project is partly funded by Swedish Brain Power.

References

1. Lindgren, H.: Decision Support in Dementia Care – Developing Systems for Interactive Reasoning. (2007) http://urn.kb.se/resolve?urn=urn:nbn:se:umu:diva-1138. Accessed 4 Feb 2008.
2. Bødker, S.: A human activity approach to user interfaces. Human-Computer Interaction, Vol. 4, pp. 171-195 (1989).
3. Engeström, Y.: Learning by Expanding: An Activity-Theoretical Approach to Developmental Research. Helsinki, Orienta-Konsultit (1987).
4. Kaptelinin, V., Nardi, B., Macaulay, C.: The Activity Checklist: A tool for representing the "Space" of context. Interactions, July – August (1999).
5. Vygotsky, L.: Mind in Society: The Development of Higher Psychological Processes. Cambridge, Harvard University Press (1978).
6. Häkkinen, H., Korpela, M.: A participatory assessment of IS integration needs in maternity clinics using activity theory. Int. J. Med. Inf. Vol. 76, pp. 843-849 (2007).
7. Singh, G.: Investigating the support of reflective activities by collaborative technologies: an activity theory based research model. In: Proc. TT211C2006, pp. 49-58 (2006).
8. WHO.: International classification of functioning, ability and health: ICF. http://www3.who.int/icf/icftemplate.cfm. Accessed 4 Feb 2008.
9. Lindgren, H., Eklund, P.: Differential diagnosis of dementia in an argumentation framework. Journal of Intelligent & Fuzzy Systems Vol. 16, pp. 1-8 (2005).
10. Goguen, J.A., Burstall, R.: Institutions: Abstract model theory for specification and programming. Journal of the Association for Computing Machinery Vol. 39, pp. 95-146 (1992).
11. Meseguer, J.: General logics. In: Logic Colloquium '87, pp 275-329 Elsevier, North-Holland (1989).
12. Eklund, P., Helgesson, R., Lindgren, H.: Towards refining clinical evidence using general logics. To appear in: Proc. ICAIS (2008).
13. Eklund, P., Lindgren, H.: Towards dementia diagnosis logic. In: 11th Int. Conf. Information Processing and Management of Uncertainty in Knowledge-based Systems (IPMU'06), 1251-2257. Editions EDK, Paris (2006).

On Problems, Requirements and Solution Approaches when Supporting Knowledge Intensive Processes in Industry

Christian Lütke Entrup and Thomas Barth

Information Systems Institute, University of Siegen, Hölderlinstr. 3, Siegen, Germany, {luetke-entrup|barth}@fb5.uni-siegen.de

Abstract: Optimizing and hence reorganizing processes as well as increasing their flexibility and agility are constant challenges companies face in the presence of revolving markets. The term 'Business-Process-Reengineering' (BPR) describes the approach of organizing processes along the customer's requirements. Since those requirements are constantly rising in terms of a product's quality and complexity under simultaneously cost and time pressure, effective and efficient re-use of an organizations accumulated knowledge is seen as an important – if not the only – comparative advantage in developed countries where labor, energy, etc. is of substantially higher cost compared to others. As a consequence, importance as well as intensity of knowledge needed to fulfill an organization's most important processes has risen significantly. This article focuses on providing support of knowledge intensive processes by analyzing product data. Retrieving the relevant knowledge in the context of a given process needs tools and methods beyond the well-known approaches for data or document management or organizational knowledge management. The domain of automotive supplier industry as an example is analyzed with respect to dominant strategic challenges like short lifecycles, complex systems, and collaboration with competitors, to retrieve associated knowledge-related documents, and this way offering opportunities to manage those challenges.

Keywords: Knowledge intensive process, Knowledge management, Product data analysis, Similarity search

1. Introduction

The global and increasingly all sectors of industry concerning change from seller's to buyer's markets (Tietze 2003) in conjunction with worldwide simultaneously progressing severe competition confronts enterprises of the manufacturing sector,

---

Please use the following format when citing this chapter:

Entrup, C.L. and Barth, T., 2008, in IFIP International Federation for Information Processing, Volume 270; *Knowledge Management in Action*; Mark Ackerman, Rose Dieng-Kuntz, Carla Simone, Volker Wulf; (Boston: Springer), pp. 111–124.

especially contract manufacturers, with the problem of rising pressure in cost and competition, whilst seeing the necessity of designing and producing innovative and highly sophisticated products in steadily shortening development cycles. Customers and competitors use all possibilities, e.g. the internet, of gathering knowledge about products to get a quick, independent and comprehensive survey of the market. This way, competitors – even from emerging nations – are able to reduce the technological gap to technologically leading enterprises in less time and cost as some years ago. Customers use the ability of immediate comparison; therefore enterprises need to enhance customer retention by improving surplus values and services around their products. Overall, enterprises have to focus on their customers to fulfill their needs.

Since the 1990s these challenges are answered with the reorientation of the company's organization and culture (Hammer and Champy 2001). The keyword "Business-Process-Reengineering" (BPR) describes the approach of consequently organizing high-merit-processes along the customer's requirements. To meet these requirements, high capabilities of innovation as well as short reaction- and development-cycles are necessary. One important feature of innovation- and development-processes is the high intensity of knowledge (Remus 2002), whereby knowledge becomes the decisive factor in the markets (Jänig 2004). Therefore, knowledge management (KM) and explicit support of knowledge intensive processes can be regarded as crucial and essential for the company's positioning and even continuity in the market.

Common approaches of KM focus on the collection, representation, and distribution of a worker's knowledge. They rely on the ability and willingness of the knowledge owners to explain and share their skills in a certain field. To support the externalization of knowledge, IT-systems have been built that provide functionality for gathering, sorting, and representing one's knowledge in the way of document management. Although these systems evolved and became more powerful, the main problem still remains. The inherent weakness of these approaches is the human factor: Socio-cultural reasons cause cognitive and motivational barriers that interfere with the transfer of knowledge (Zelewski 2005). Furthermore, the already mentioned time pressure prevents knowledge workers from spending additional time on document management and even a motivated expert cannot always couch why precisely this way of doing leads to the desired result.

The approach of supporting knowledge intensive processes described in this article differs from this traditional 'organizational' KM as mentioned above in a way that it does not rely on the explicit externalization of knowledge by the owner, but instead relies on taking advantage of the documents and data generated regularly while working on the subject. The main assumption of this approach is the absence of knowledge in data. According to Riempp (2005), only data is stored in databases, the extraction and recombining to knowledge has to be done by a domain's expert. While working on a subject, the expert uses his expertise to produce a certain output that is highly dependent on his experience. E.g., engineers in the automotive sector use their specific knowledge and experience to design parts and components of a new car. The output of this process (besides others) is a 3D-CAD-model specifying the geometry of a part, which in turn can be used as input for requests to their suppliers having to produce it. If an expert of the domain who was not involved in the developing process examines the model he will understand e.g. why a part's geometry was designed in a certain way, a certain material was specified etc. because of his own domain knowledge.

Following the assumption that domain knowledge manifests in the documents and data generated in knowledge-intensive processes, a way has to be found to retrieve the adequate documents in a distinct situation and present it to the expert who has to recombine it to knowledge and hereby maybe reuses it independently from its originator. In order to support processes this way a search engine is needed, exceeding the text based search functions of conventional (product-)data management systems significantly. By applying a "fuzzy" search on product data, also to a certain degree similar and not necessarily identical objects can be found whose associated documents provide support in complex decision-making situations being the essential part of knowledge intensive processes.

In this paper, requirements for a framework comprising a general approach as well as methods to support knowledge-intensive processes are discussed. Efficient reuse of knowledge seamlessly within processes is identified as a generic method for support. As one approach to supporting knowledge intensive tasks – which already proved to be successful in industrial scenarios – a similarity analysis is discussed that retrieves "similar" (according to domain specific similarity metrics) documents in a company's data store on the basis of a source document. Beyond these search capabilities, extending the search towards considering more complex knowledge structures in distributed scenarios is also outlined.

The next chapter outlines the methodical approach we applied to conduct the research work utilizing interviews, modeling, prototype implementation/evaluation, and workshops. Chapter 3 describes the results of the performed domain analysis in automotive supplier industry, how it constitutes in the global competition and what kind of problems emerge from the new environment they act in. Subsequent sections show the solutions and approaches to handle these problems, as well as an example of an implementation supporting processes in research and development within an automotive suppliers R&D department.

2. Research Method

The approach applied within the project being the basis of this contribution consists mainly of the following components: Interviews, data and knowledge models, prototype implementations, reviews, and workshops.

The proposed process model for supporting knowledge-intensive processes (s. (Lütke Entrup et al. 2006)) was used as a guideline for the selection of interview partners and the topics for the interviews. Since the processes to be supported act as the guideline for the analyses of relevant knowledge and its data representation, interview partners from the involved organizational units were selected. Hence, two persons from conceptual planning, controlling, and R&D were interviewed and the requirements were compiled from their answers. All interviews were performed going collaboratively through real-life examples from the domain expert's daily work to get a detailed understanding of their approach to solve the sophisticated problems involved in their individual contribution to the overall decision-making process. This understanding was subsequently rendered to knowledge and data models as a basis for the design and implementation of adequate tools. Aspects covered by observing the expert's role and activities in the processes comprised the information they need access to (e.g. technical drawings, bills of material, transportation cost) and the technical data sources the information is provided from (e.g. CAD systems, ERP systems) as well. Prototypical implementations of this tool were frequently presented to all the interviewed process participants being with the future key users. The results of these reviews were integrated into the next-generation prototypes and the prototyping cycle was restarted. In concluding workshops the key users were trained at the system integrated to the company's IT infrastructure.

3. Domain Analysis in Automotive Supplier Industry

The domain of automotive suppliers experienced dramatic change during the last decades. The customer's rising requirements in matters of cost, quality, and configuration are passed from manufacturers to suppliers. This way, suppliers are forced to design, manufacture and deliver highly innovative, highly complex and high quality products in less time to market, while being confronted with increasing pressure in cost and by an increasing number of competitors in their market.

Automobile manufacturers are increasing the number of outsourced components reducing the number of suppliers at the same time. Hence, suppliers are becoming more and more providers for complete subsystems, thus changing from single-part-supplier to system-developers. These sub-systems or assemblies consist of up to some hundred parts, maybe from different engineering domains, e.g. from metal forming, electrics and electronics exceeding the competencies of most suppliers being typically experts in only one of these domains. This complexity fosters cross-organizational collaboration with competitors and/or subcontractors to complement own competencies to assure continuity in the market.

The major requirements that have to be addressed are therefore

- steady shortening development and production time
- rising complexity of products
- collaboration with competitors

These requirements affect the IT support of knowledge-intensive processes

- provision of methods to support efficient reuse of knowledge seamlessly within processes (identification of relevant processes, relevant knowledge and adequate models for both)
- provision of tools to support human experts in complex and knowledge-intensive processes (searching/finding/reusing documents and data sets representing relevant process-specific knowledge)
- support processes in distributed environments (decoupling between search/find/reuse and – maybe multiple – knowledge bases)

The aforementioned requirements for a framework to support knowledge-intensive processes comprises methodological as well as tool support to bridge the gap between the actual processes, the human process participants, their knowledge and the actual tools supporting them. To validate this approach, knowledge-intensive processes in automotive and automotive supplier industry were analyzed in the course of projects to design, implement and introduce software tools to support knowledge-intensive processes especially in the early phases of the product lifecycle. A qualitative analysis of the domain was done by interviews with domain- and IT-experts of an automotive supplier. It was derived from these interviews that the development time a new part can be reduced by up 90% if a template exists which structure is very similar to the one of the new part and that could be slightly modified to obtain the desired new structure. Fig. 1 shows typical questions arising during the work on a product in its lifecycle. The questions aim at the availability of similar previous products that can be included in the process as a template and can be used as a knowledge source. The interviews also elaborated the importance of documents associated with the template part to regain the knowledge used in that context.

The main problem is that there is currently no IT system available which is capable of searching, analyzing, and retrieving those templates on the basis of arbitrary input documents. Available IT systems (namely Product Data Management (PDM) and Product Lifecycle Management (PLM) systems) are almost solely focused on document management aspects like processing and transforming different CAD file formats, versioning of documents etc. The important aspect of managing the knowledge contained in these documents is not addressed by software vendors, at most providing search capabilities using regular expressions for analyzing mainly alphanumerical/text data and starting to offer search in CAD data mostly unrelated to the associated alphanumerical product data.

Hence, experts have to rely on their own or their colleague's commemoration to find a similar product by looking through technical drawings and typically browsing through various file systems containing CAD documents and other files. Having to work on lots of different projects during a year, the chance to remember the right product at the right time is quite low. In the case of a typical small to medium sized enterprise (SME) from automotive supplier industry, several hundred up to thousands of customer requests must be processed each year every one comprising large data sets in maybe many (in the worst case up to one hundred) versions created during one knowledge-intensive core business process.

The rising complexity of products is becoming a major problem for system developers. A new system has to be split in its single parts, every part has to be developed, its actual cost must be estimated, physically manufactured, and finally all parts have to be assembled and delivered. From the very beginning of the development to the final assembly, numerous change requests from the customer have to be regarded. A request as well as a change requests normally consists of a single CAD-file that has to be analyzed by experts from the company with respect to changes since the last version. Analyzing a CAD-file is a very tedious and error-prone process. In a system of about 100 parts a minor change in one of those parts can easily be missed. But the miss of a minor change can have major impact on the following processes: Tools do not fit anymore, parts do not match, etc. The adjustment of those misses is expensive and time consuming. Support can be offered through knowledge-related documents of previous projects that can be found by a similarity analysis on the basis of the part in question and its sub-parts. To analyze a complex product structure approaches of ontology and recursive structure analysis are taken into consideration.

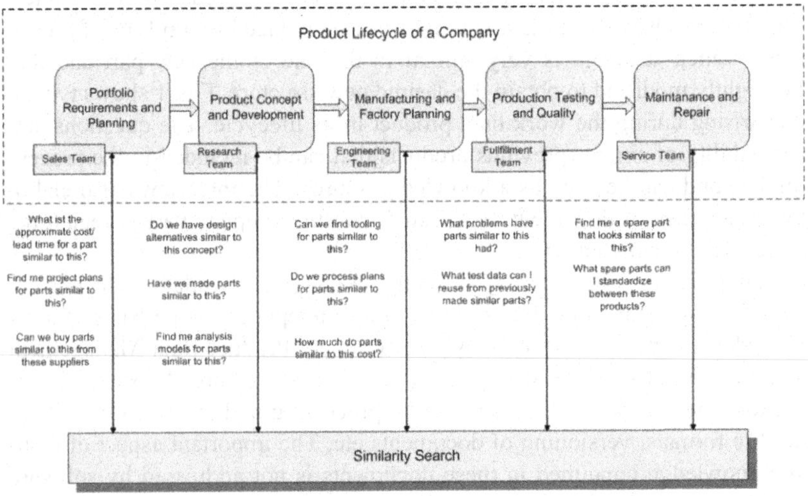

Fig. 1.: Knowledge-reuse across the Product Lifecycle (based on (Iyer 2005))

Collaboration with competitors is very ambivalent. On the one hand system developers cannot handle the entire product. Subcontractors need to be involved to take care of subparts, while the supply chain (or network) becomes larger and more complex. On the other hand there is the company's knowledge representing their most important advantage over their competitors, which has to be protected also in close collaborations with competitors.

Effective collaboration is only possible if the parties are integrated into one IT-system to exchange data sufficiently fast and secure. But the two or more parties may be still competitors on other markets, making it inevitable to separate the company's data from the data needed for the work on the mutual project, yet having the possibility of using supporting tools, e.g. a similarity analysis. Another perspective is the combination of the team member's data stores. The questions raised in fig. 1 are still valid, but in a multilateral collaboration there is a broader data pool available which has to be taken into account.

In the following sections the existing solutions and solution approaches will be presented, together with an implementation example of a similarity analysis in the research and development department of an automotive supplier company. This prototype with its underlying process, knowledge and data models was designed and built following the framework.

4. Reusing Knowledge Based on Similarity Analysis of Product Data

A similarity analysis of products with the intention of reusing the knowledge hidden in data and associated documents has major advantages. In the first place, the product structure can be reused and modified and this way the time-consuming process of creating the structure of the new product is significantly shortened. Another important aspect is the enhancement in (manufacturing) process reliability. Adapting the specifications from the previous product and avoiding its failures leads to less risk in actual production being extremely valuable for a company. Even "rules of thumb" can be applied when calculating, e.g., the cost-data of the template to estimate reliably approximated costs and present it to the customer in a short time.

The overall goal is the reuse of knowledge from existing documents. To find these documents, a search engine is needed that fulfills the following requirements:

- Diverse data types have to be taken into account, e.g. numerical, alphanumerical, and geometrical (CAD) data, to cover a search over all of the company's relevant documents.
- Search items should be allowed to be fuzzy to achieve first the aspired 'similarity' to exceed e.g. a text search with wildcards and additionally to be able to handle inexact data and information within the process (e.g. resulting from changes in the customer's request over time).
- Integration of the company's heterogeneous data stores into the search engine (e.g. ranging from flat files to ERP or PDM/PLM systems).
- User-, role-, and process-specific interfaces to the search engine (e.g. with context-sensitive selection of valid search items).

- Access to the search engine and resulting data across a network (via intra-/internet)
- Adequate visualization of input and output documents (e.g. 3D visualization of complex geometrical models).

These requirements were implemented as a web application and successfully tested in the research and development department of an automotive supplier. Analyses of the available data sources resulted in three different data types: numerical, alphanumerical, and geometrical (CAD) data. A fuzzy search on numerical data was realized with a threshold of ±S%, where S denotes the maximum percental difference to the search attribute.

The search on alphanumerical data was implemented with the Levenshtein-algorithm (Apostolico 2005), which is applied to determine the so-called "edit distance" between two text attributes. This algorithm computes the minimal number of edit operations necessary to transform one string into another. In relation to the number of characters in the longer string, a distance in the interval [0, 1] is generated, which is equivalent to the threshold value S of the numerical analysis.

Geometrical data in the form of a CAD file is analyzed as follows: The basis for the applied algorithm is not the CAD file itself, but a set of numerical "descriptors" that can be derived from the original file by extracting algorithm-specific properties. Taking into account the time-consuming procedure of building the properties, this is done offline for existing products, and the results are stored in a database. For the similarity analysis of a new CAD file, this file is analyzed online and compared to the already calculated descriptors of existing products. Fig. 2 (left) shows one example user interface of the search engine. In the upper area, the geometry in question is visible. Upload of a geometry file is sufficient for the start of a request. Dimension and position are extracted for orientation reproduced next to the parameter fields in the lower area. The range of the parameters can be widened by applying a threshold in form of a percental value next to the parameter fields. The search is done over all parameters filled with a value. Fig. 2 (right) shows the first two hits from the result list. All search hits are sorted by descending similarity and visualized with selected attributes. Overall, 867 similar parts were found in the data store. The user is now able to select an appropriate part; using the provided key attributes he can gain access to the relevant knowledge documents from the company's data stores. The geometry files in this example are taken from the free 'Engineering Shape Benchmark' of the Purdue University (Purdue 2008).

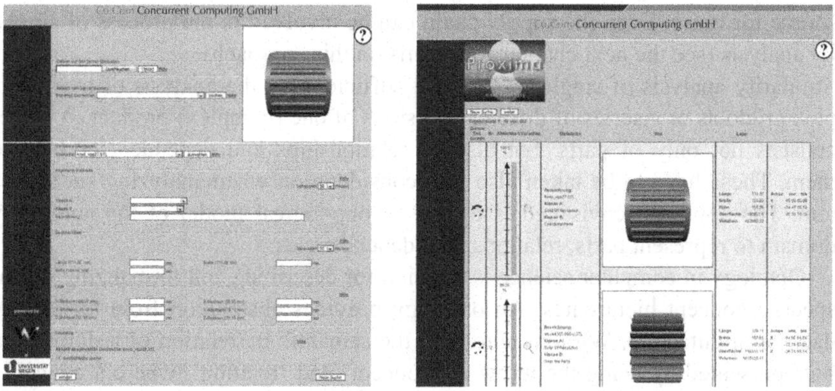

Fig. 2. (left): Example interface to the search engine supporting geometrical search items (uploaded CAD file in the upper right) and other (alpha-)numerical features, e.g. dimension and position. Fig. 2 (right): An example list of search results with similarity measure, file information, visualization of the geometry and additional information, e.g. dimension and position.

5. Process Support by Reusing Knowledge of Complex Systems

During the last decade, the global competition and customer's rising requirements forced automotive manufacturers to shorten the lifecycle of their products, thereby reducing the time-to-market while simultaneously being under increasing cost pressure. To reduce cost as well as time-to-market, efficiency not only in production but also in all the previous phase of the product lifecycle must be enhanced. This conflict of objectives is solved by outsourcing not only of the production but also of the design of complex systems to companies of the supplier industry. Complex systems (assemblies represented by hierarchical bills of material, BOM) of this kind consist of up to some hundred parts produced and assembled using various machinery in complex, multi-stage processes (represented by complex working plans) typically in various production sites of one or maybe more collaborating companies. The resulting need for knowledge vastly exceeds the knowledge required for producing rather simple parts. In addition to these problems when designing assemblies, one of the main problems of a system provider (tier-1-supplier) is to keep track of the change requests the manufacturer submits. A supply chain has to be created and the production and actual assembly must be pooled. For every change in one ore more parts of the assemblies, the tier-2-supplier and tool manufacturers have to be informed about the design change to keep all the interdependent documents (BOM, working plans, CAD files) synchronized.

The similarity analysis described so far can be used to determine changes in single parts of an assembly and to find similar parts as a template and knowledge

source for reuse. Even the supply chain can be involved in the process of similarity analysis (see the next chapter for details on this approach).
Similarity analysis of single parts is not sufficient for the analysis of more complex products or a series of different versions of one (complex) product. A system consists not only of parts, but also of relationships and dependencies between them. These have to be taken also into consideration when analyzing such a system. The approach envisaged is to use an ontological model of the automotive domain to represent parts, relations, and dependencies.

Ontology in computer science is a notion for describing and formalizing domain specific concept hierarchies. An ontology provides abstraction from technology, data, or architecture. With an ontology, the semantic correlation of a domain can be represented by using the terms of 'concept' and 'relation', where a concept is the formal representation of a real 'thing' like documents, parts, etc., and 'relation' defines the dependencies between concepts.

Hence, the next step in research is developing an ontological model on the basis of the semantic context of the automotive industry. A product ontology that describes the relationships between different parts in an assembly and all properties and dependencies of a product can be used to measure the similarity between different parts and to filter the search results. Parts that are unequal in main aspects of similarity can be excluded from the search process or deleted from the search results. If a search request is based on one complete product ontology and contains not only single parameters, the measuring process can determine the similarity between different relationships. Just as a complete geometry can be used to optimize the result set it seems promising that a search process that uses semantic data to render the results increases the efficiency of the search.

To be able to use ontology in the search process it is first necessary to design a data model that is able to store all data needed by the ontology and a similarity measure to decide if one product is similar to another. The major problem when using ontology is to gain the relevant data. In most cases the user is required to insert all information into a database or an ontology editor manually. The aim of this ontology-based approach is to develop a method that gains all required information from the existing product data like part lists, work schedules, or cost estimations. Using such a method enables companies to create the desired ontology for each part in the product database automatically.

Having a running prototype that is able to improve the manually search by using numerical, alphanumerical and geometrical data, the next step is to acquire all the information needed to develop a model for the ontology that describes the semantic context of the suppliers and replicates the way experts perceive similarity between complex product structures. Similar to the way the requirements for process support were developed up to now, this can only be achieved by close collaboration with domain experts using prototypical tools reflecting and supporting their usual course of action during the knowledge-intensive processes.

By analyzing the inner structure of a complex system, the dimensions of the parts like length, width, etc., can be extracted with tools of the similarity analysis, and can be put in relation to the company's available machine data. That way it is possible to generate an automatic manufacturability analysis. When integrated with a resource management system providing all the relevant technical specifications on the machinery the knowledge structure within an assembly's design and it's working plan (e.g. by matching the physical dimension of a part against the machines dimension) can be exploited to extend the notion of similarity between parts. This extension allows in this context e.g. searching for similarly manufactured products and – based on this – also the generation of valid templates for BOM and working plans according to a given request. This would further increase a process's efficiency for process participants.

In conjunction with the dependencies inside the system and the knowledge about the capabilities of contractors in the supply chain (see next section), support can be given concerning e.g. where to produce parts or subsystems.

6. Supporting Knowledge-intensive Processes within Collaborations

A single company cannot accomplish development and production of complex systems, because different parts and assemblies need to be processed in separate manner. I.e., to weld and finally paint a stamping and a rolling part, four competencies have to be involved (stamping, rolling, welding, and painting). A system developer normally does not have all required competencies available, and therefore has to fall back on the production facilities and competencies of competitors and suppliers.

A project-based collaboration is mostly done in the form of a 'virtual organization' (VO). A VO is a loosely coupled, temporary pool of companies that share resources and skills with the goal of realizing a common interest, e.g. a product or service. In contrast to other organizational forms of cooperation like joint ventures, in a VO there is no central management level and the parties stay legally independent (Picot et. al. 2003). Communication and coordination is done by the intensive use of IT systems.

If a company creates a supply chain for the development and production of a complex product, the core competencies, skills, knowledge, and resources of the involved participants need to be communicated. For that reason, in addition to the supply chain an 'information chain' has to be set up transferring all relevant data to the appropriate destinations in a two-way-fashion.

To manage these requirements, a 3-layer-model for distributed environments was developed. Fig. 3 shows the concept of the model and the integration of distributed data and knowledge sources. Over the product lifecycle, the knowledge intensive tasks that have to be supported must be identified. In layer 1, 'Process Integration', the similarity analysis is integrated at the appropriate step of the process, where knowledge about previous products is useful and necessary. The data sources for the analysis are scattered over the entire supply chain, therefore at layer 2, 'Service Integration', each member of the chain is at least host for one analysis type, geometrical, alphanumerical, or numerical, depending on the data types available. At layer 3, 'Resource Integration', the particular data stores of the hosts have to be integrated into the analysis functionality.

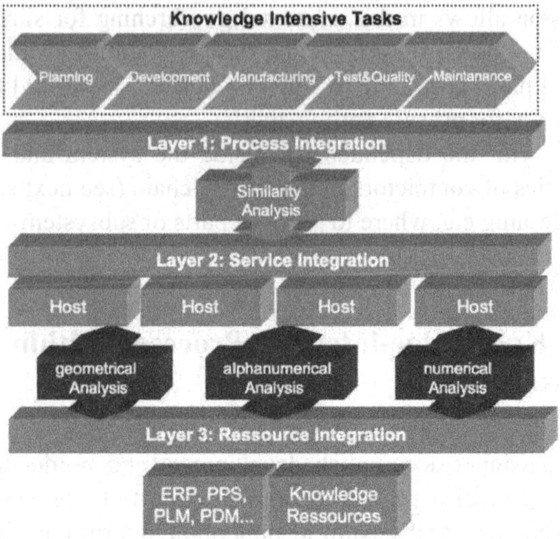

Fig. 3. A three-layer-model for distributed environments supporting knowledge intensive processes

If a participant of the supply chains needs, e.g., information about the producibility of a certain part, he can start the similarity analysis in his company, and feed it with the CAD-model of the part in question. The analysis tool looks up the integrated hosts in the service environment and sends the query to all embedded partners. Depending on the type of query, over the resource integration layer the corresponding database or file base is activated and the query is processed. Results are sent back to the initiator. Every participant has the option of activating or deactivating certain resources for distinct query initiators to handle security issues. Every chain member has to be informed about all other members, because two companies might be both suppliers for a third company, but they are still competitors and therefore might have a special interest of not sharing their skills and knowledge with each other.

Using this architecture, all members of the supply chain are able to look up core competencies, skills, knowledge, and resources of the other participants and speed up their production cycles.

7. Conclusions and Future Work

The subject of this article is to outline a framework for the support of knowledge intensive tasks in manufacturing industries by software tools. Providing the "right" tools requires an understanding of the commonalities between the knowledge-intensive processes to be supported and the process participants and their individual behavior within these processes. As a result, an efficient way of supporting the participants can be derived and adequate tool support conceptualized. In the context of automotive supplier industry, as it is the background of the work presented here, supplying these knowledge workers with documents reflecting the knowledge structure relevant to their reuse in processes was identified as the most promising approach. These documents are found in the data stores of the company on the basis of a similarity analysis. A framework comprising process, knowledge, and data analysis as well as a software architecture for the design and implementation of a similarity analysis tool for searching documents to be reused is validated.

The analysis tools itself was briefly introduced. The search on numerical, alphanumerical, and geometrical data, evaluation and implementation as a web application show the performance and potential benefits of such a search engine.

Beyond the current capabilities of the framework and the search engine, the problem of handling complex products (assemblies) was grasped and the usefulness of the search engine in conjunction with ontology models in this area was addressed. Collaborative environments as a major topic in automotive supplier industry were also introduced and a 3-layer-architecture for widening the search base of the analysis tool over the supply chain for mutual benefit was presented.

Next steps focus on the preparation of an ontology model for automotive supplier industry. Despite the fact that since many years ontology is a matter of academic research and not completely solved, there are promising approaches made in (Maier et al. 2003) especially for automotive supplier industry, that keep track of ontologies as a knowledge representation model. The 3-layer-architecture of the concept for distributed environments has to be implemented to validate the idea.

References

Apostolico, A. (2005): General Pattern Matching. In: Atallah, A. (ed.): Algorithms and Theory of Computation Handbook. CRC Press 1999, pp. 13-5 - 13-10

Hammer, M., Champy, J. (2001): Reengineering the Corporation. Brealy, London.

Iyer, N., Jayanti, S., Lou, K., Kalyanaraman, Y, Ramani, K. (2005): Shaped-based searching for product lifecycle applications. In: CAD 37.

Jänig, C. (2004): Wissensmanagement. Springer, Berlin.

Lütke Entrup, C, Barth, T., Schäfer, W. (2006): Towards a Process Model for Identifying Knowledge-Related Structures in Product Data. In: Reimer, U., Karagiannis, D. (eds.): Proc. Practical Aspects of Knowledge Management (PAKM 2006), LNAI 4333, pp. 189-200, Springer

Maier, A., Schnurr, H.P., Sure, Y. (2003): Ontology based Information Integration in the Automotive Industry. In: Proc. of the 2nd Int. Semantic Web Conference (ISWC2003), LNCS 2870, pp. 897-912. Springer.

Riempp, G. (2004): Integrierte Wissensmanagementsysteme. Springer, Berlin.

Purdue Research and Education Center for Information Sciences in Engineering (2008): PRECISE Engineering Shape Benchmark. http://shapelab.ecn.purdue.edu/, (10.01.2008.)

Picot A., Reichwald R., Wiegand R. T. (2003): Die grenzenlose Unternehmung: Information, Organisation und Management, Gabler, Wiesbaden

Remus, U. (2002): Prozessorientiertes Wissensmanagement. Dissertation. Universität Regensburg.

Tietze, Oliver (2003): Strategische Positionierung in der Automobilindustrie. Gabler.

Zelewski, Stephan (2005): Wissensmanagement in Dienstleistungsnetzwerken. Wissenstransfer fördern mit der Relationship Management Balanced Scorecard. DUV, Wiesbaden.

Third Generation Knowledge Management in Action: Relational Practices in Swiss Companies

Jens O. Meissner[1] **and Patricia Wolf**[2]

[1] Lucerne School of Business, Switzerland, jens.meissner@hslu.ch
[2] ETH Zurich, Switzerland, pwolf@ethz.ch

Abstract: This paper aims at answering the question: How do "third generation knowledge management concepts" help to understand relational practices in blended contexts of face-to-face interaction and virtual communication? In order to address this question, we firstly explain Scharmer's Concept of Self-transcending Knowledge and Snowden's Knowledge-Ecology-Approach 'Cynefin' to develop a heuristic for third generation knowledge management (KM). The heuristic highlights the critical role of relational practices for KM and will be applied to identify and discuss selected relational practices stemming from four Swiss organizations. We conclude by reflecting on the adequateness of third generation knowledge management concepts to explain these practices.

Keywords: Third generation knowledge management, Relational practices, Hybrid work settings

1. Introduction

The motivation of this paper results out of two basic trends that challenge today's organizational KM practices: The first is the pervasiveness of virtual communication which is enhanced by ubiquitous computerization and advanced networking technology (Dutta & Mia, 2007). The second is the ongoing unfolding of knowledge society that still seems to be in an early stage of its development (e.g. Castells, 2001).

It has been shown that cooperation and collaboration in organizations often have to be mastered in neither entirely co-located nor entirely distributed work settings. Instead, organization's members have to manage their actions in hybrid settings in which face-to-face interactions and virtual communications are blended together (Griffith, Sawyer & Neale, 2003). In this environment, all the involved

Please use the following format when citing this chapter:

Meissner, J.O. and Wolf, P., 2008, in IFIP International Federation for Information Processing, Volume 270; *Knowledge Management in Action*; Mark Ackerman, Rose Dieng-Kuntz, Carla Simone, Volker Wulf; (Boston: Springer), pp. 125–137.

actors work and communicate with a specific mix of communicative practices that consist of face-to-face and computer-mediated interaction (Zachry & Thralls, 2006). For being effective, KM approaches have to be aware of these rich situational conditions in organizations. The guiding question that we are going to answer in this paper is: How do "third generation knowledge management concepts" help to understand relational practices in blended organizational contexts of face-to-face interaction and virtual communication?

To answer this question, we firstly develop a third generation knowledge management heuristic which is based on two well-known concepts. We rely upon epistemological roots of Newer Sociological Systems Theory (Luhmann, 1995), knowledge sociology (Berger & Luckmann, 1966) and relational constructivism (Gergen, 2001). Our basic assumption is that organizations consist mainly of communicative routines. From this background, Weick´s concept of the "double interact" (Weick, 1995) plays a crucial integrating role between relationships and organizations. Secondly, we apply the heuristic to analyze selected relational practices we uncovered during our research in Swiss organizations.

2. Third Generation Knowledge Management

Third generation KM approaches were developed approximately ten years ago. While first-generation KM concepts treated knowledge as a thing, second-generation concepts understood knowledge as a process which is partially explicit and implicit (Nonaka & Takeuchi, 1995). The third generation KM approach focuses also on implicit knowledge but purposefully deals with the function of knowledge ecology, chaos and the sensing of opportunities-to-come. Knowledge in this approach is also tacit but it is 'not embodied yet' and has to be generated (Scharmer, 2001). From a knowledge management perspective, third generation concepts base on the assumption of knowledge as an "'ephemeral, active process of relating" (Stacey, 2001) thus highlighting the process of "knowing" instead of conceiving knowledge as an objective entity.

Third generation KM concepts highlight the relevance of chaos, complexity and paradox and frame them as critical KM resources. This can lead to a challenge for 'traditional' KM experts who are interested in an object-like understanding of knowledge and who usually try to make knowledge transferable, manageable and teachable. We will not contribute to this positivistic understanding of KM. Instead, we will develop a general "Third Generation KM Heuristic" and provide insights from an empirical set of qualitative data on relational practices in Swiss companies. For the development of the heuristic, two particular relevant approaches will be described in the next sections: Scharmer's Concept of Self-transcending Knowledge (2001) and Snowden's Knowledge-EcologyModel 'Cynefin' (2002).

2.1. Scharmer's Concept of Self-transcending Knowledge

Claus-Otto Scharmer refers to Polanyi's (1967) distinction between explicit and tacit-embodied knowledge and advances this understanding by adding a third type of knowledge that is "self-transcending" (Scharmer, 2001). This latter type of knowledge is characterized as knowledge that is "not-yet-embodied" which is a source for leaders to sense, actualize and engage in emerging business opportunities. The concept is tightly bound to personal awareness and psychological presence and thus can be found as a crucial resource for entrepreneurial thinking (Scharmer, 2007).

The three types of knowledge can be traced back to different epistemological assumptions (Scharmer, 2001:143ff). Explicit knowledge refers to know-how and to know-what. It's knowledge about things that can be found within an external reality. We can explore it, detect it, construct it, store it in databanks and IT systems and so on. Within this type of knowledge the separation between the knower and the known is constitutive. Implicit knowledge is a living process and can be understood as knowledge-in-use. As such, it is knowledge about doing things and can be experienced within action settings. This knowledge becomes very visible in master craftsmanship but also knowledge processing within communities of all kind. Self-transcending knowledge goes one step ahead to pre-sensing (Senge et al., 2005 call it "presencing") reality. It can be understood as reflection-in-action and knowing about thought-origins for doing things (Scharmer, 2001:143). The domain of self-transcending knowledge is the field of intuition, inspiration and imagination. Many entrepreneurs and leaders – especially those who are refered to as "charismatic" – are able to perform with virtuosity within this domain.

Obviously, the three types of knowledge are very different in character and each type requires a different type of knowledge environment and learning infrastructure. Crucial, from Scharmer's perspective, is the spiral of creating self-transcending knowledge within the interplay between the organizational commonalities 'shared praxis', 'shared reflection' and 'shared will': "The more distributed organizations and networks of collaboration become, the more critical [learning infrastructures for self-transcending knowledge] tend to be, because shared praxis, shared reflection, and formation of shared will are the glue that keeps distributed networks in synch and together." (Scharmer, 2001:147). Thus, the main KM challenge lies within the turning of distributed labour into shared experience, abstract discussions into shared reflection and negotiation of objectives into the formation of collective will (Scharmer, 2001:148).

Scharmer concludes that "requisite conversational complexity" will need different forms of conversation to sustain diverse forms of knowledge. The most relevant form (and infrastructure) to successfully handle self-transcending knowledge is 'generative dialogue'. Most KM systems fail in this because they fail in establishing the necessary conversational complexity for this form of dialogue. This failure has significant consequences: "Without the capacity for dialogue, for instance, teams are unable to express their tacit, taken-for-granted assumptions about how reality works“ (Scharmer, 2001:22).

For our purposes, Scharmer's concept enables us to ask some interesting questions concerning KM in organizations, for example: Where can we find modes and places of presencing? How and why is requisite conversational complexity created and accepted? And, which pre-conditions have to be fulfilled to enable generative dialogues (and to stay in them despite of the guaranteed upcoming impertinencies)?

2.2. Snowden's Knowledge-Ecology-Approach 'Cynefin'

The second third generation KM approach to be outlined here was developed by David Snowden (2002). His concept focuses on organizational knowledge ecology and became known as the "Cynefin"-model. It highlights the capacity of an organization to create just-in-time KM as well as disruptive innovation. It bases on the contextuality of knowledge in which the degree of abstraction and cultural dependence play a critical role in managing it: "In the third generation we grow beyond managing knowledge as a thing to also managing knowledge as a flow. To do this we will need to focus more on context and narrative, than on content" (Snowden, 2002:101).

Whereas Scharmer conceptualizes third generation knowledge beyond the process scope, Snowden stays within this category. But, Snowden emphasizes the contextuality of knowledge – and thus stays close to the idea of knowledge as a flow. Towards knowledge ecology, its context and its embeddedness into narratives have to be taken into account. Snowden states, that human knowledge is deeply contextual and triggered by circumstance: "In understanding what people know we have to recreate the context of their knowing if we are to ask a meaningful question or enable knowledge use. To ask someone what he or she knows is to ask a meaningless question in a meaningless context" (Snowden, 2002:102). Therefore, KM needs the clear distinction of content, context and narrative to be managed adequately – Cynefin focuses more on the latter two, less on the content.

The Cynefin model is segmented into four knowledge domains (see Figure 1): The domain of bureaucratic and structured knowledge is the formal organization consisting of policies, procedures and controls. The language within this domain is known and explicit. Within the professional and logical domain, a high abstraction level of knowledge is possible. Typical knowledge artefacts are e.g. textbooks which usually contain codified terminologies of specialists (Snowden, 2002:104). In the informal and independent domain, the trust in social networks plays an important role. Learning, shared values and beliefs, and the making of shared experiences belong. Last, the uncharted and innovative domain comprises temporary, often spontaneous communities for the generation of new knowledge and disruptive innovation. "Each of the domains contains a different model of community behaviour; each requires a different form of management and a different leadership style" (Snowden, 2002:106).

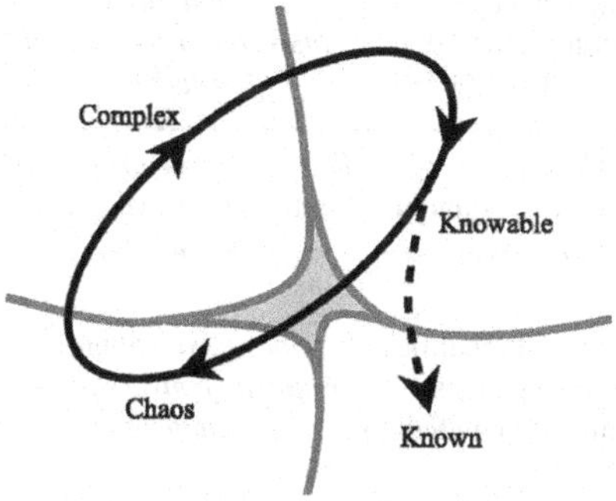

Figure 1. Cynefin: Knowledge flows (Snowden, 2001:108)

The Cynefin model signifies two critical knowledge transitions: Firstly, the shift from complex to knowable knowledge for sustaining "Just-in-time" knowledge. Secondly, knowledge that is trespassing from the knowable to the chaotic sphere to radically question existing knowledge and to achieve knowledge innovation.

For our purposes Snowden's concept provides us with some important questions, as there are: What kinds of contexts arise within hybrid work settings in organizations? What kinds of narratives are stipulated? And how do they affect relational practices?

2.3. *A Third Generation Knowledge Management Heuristic*

Theoretically informed by the both concepts, we can now define a guiding third generation KM heuristic. Scharmer's concept highlights the emergence of self-transcending knowledge and the need to presence it - i.e. to reflect on it (Scharmer, 2001). He states the requirement of a requisite conversational complexity for sustaining all types of knowledge. He proposes the generative dialogue as an adequate "technique" especially for maintaining and dealing with third generation knowledge. Snowden emphasises the capacity of an organization to create just-in-time knowledge as well as disruptive innovation. He argues an ecological understanding of knowledge and identifies four domains with different rationalities that serve as order criteria for knowledge. Snowden delineates two critical transitions to address the two main problems for knowledge transformation: From 'complex' to 'knowable' and from 'known' to 'chaotic'. Both transitions radically question the rationality and functionality of existing knowledge in organizations. The insights of both third generation KM models are shown in Table 1.

Table 1: Third Generation Knowledge Management Heuristic.

	Self-transcending Knowledge Model (Scharmer, 2001)	Knowledge Ecology Model (Snowden, 2002)	*Analytical question for relational practices*
Knowledge Source	Presencing (reflection-in-action)	Contextual (ecological, bound in narratives)	*Does it enable presencing and (re)contextualizing of knowledge?*
Knowledge Order	Requisite conversational complexity (heterogeneity)	Different rationalities and languages (domains of knowledge)	*Does it contribute to requisite conversational complexity?*
Knowledge Management Challenge	Generative dialogue (enabling mind shifts)	Critical transitions (Just-in-time, disruptive innovation)	*Does it foster the emergence of generative dialogue?*

To bring out the impacts for third generation KM, we can now subsume the results by asking: How is knowledge sourced, ordered and managed within relational practices? Focusing on relational practices we can ask three analytical questions: Does the respective practice

- enable presencing and (re)contextualizing of knowledge?
- contribute to requisite conversational complexity, opens up for different rationalities and languages, which is increasing the "knowledge variety"?
- foster the emergence of generative dialogue and of critical transitions, which we name as increasing "knowledge conversion"?

The three questions of the heuristic signify the three dimensions of third generation KM which subsequently serve the systematic assessment of the following selected relational practices in Swiss organisations.

3. Selected Knowledge Practices in Swiss Organizations

In this section we describe our research design as well as the relational practices that we were able to identify in Swiss organizations. The practices will be analyzed with the third generation KM heuristic.

3.1. Research Design

Our research followed a social constructionist rationale, which assumes that reality is a product stemming from social relationships (Gergen, 2001, Dachler & Hosking, 1995). This perspective on relationships implies that our research had to focus on relationships and topics that might be highlighted in stories about relationships. Thus we had to gather insights about knowledge processes by trying to "look through the eyes of the other" (Bryman, 1988).

We selected interviewees from four service and knowledge-intense companies in order to assure a certain degree of contextual diversity in the sample. The first company was a services department of a document imaging service provider that relies heavily on its project organization. As a second organization, the holding of a financial services company was chosen. The third organisation was the global headquater of a multi-national pharmaceutical company. As a fourth organization we selected the national branch of a multinational stategy expert consultancy with more than hundred employees in Switzerland and several thousands world-wide. All companies are located in the German-speaking part of Switzerland.

In each organization, four to seven interviews were conducted between late 2004 and April 2005. Interview partners were selected in cooperation with one "gatekeeper" who was appointed by leaders in upper or top management (leader of the staff division/assistant of the CEO/the site leader/managing partner). The selected interviewees had to fulfill two minimum requirements: Firstly, they should have access to a variety of five or more distinguishable communication technologies in their working context – for example phone, mail, webconferencing, videoconferencing, shared databases or platforms, mobile phone and/or mail, etc. Secondly, their everyday work life should be predominantly related to communication activities. Overall, the whole sample consists of 21 interviewees, working in aidee and management positions to the largest part.

We chose a problem-centered narrative interview approach (Witzel, 2000) to generate stories. While the pure narrative interview demands the researcher to reduce his own influences to a minimum, the problem-centered interview focuses on generating meaningful sequences. Each interview began with the question "When you reflect upon your daily communications, what comes into your mind?", took about one to one and a half hours and was transcribed verbatim.

Throughout the subsequent analysis all participating researchers were guided by the following questions: How does the narrator see relationships in his context and what qualities does this construction offer? The main advantage of this method (compared with other well-known content analysis techniques like those used by Glaser and Strauss (1967), for example) is that there is no pre-formulated coding scheme which could be used. The coding scheme emerged out of the issues and topics that were adressed by the narrator himself.

For the validation of the analysis we advanced in two steps: The first step was to compare our own analysis with that of another researcher, who also analyzed it.

During this step the interpreted topics and the landscape were critically discussed, reviewed and validated in multiple sessions (see Meissner, 2007 for a detailed description of this process). In a second step, the results were validated with the interviewee him or herself. In the end, the aggregation of topics from multiple organizational members enabled the researcher to identify typical common traits (communicative practices) of the organization. The analysis resulted in a list of topics and quotations from all interviews. Each interview was illustrated with a thematic map (the "landscape") which displayed the specific topics and their relations to each other. Also, a landscape over the whole sample was developed.

Overall we found eight typical relational practices. These can be subsumed under the categories "contextualization of the message content", "shaping relationships", "technological enabling of communication" and the "social construction of technology by human communication". These four categories stem from the "relational scaffolding model" provided by Meissner & Tuckermann (2007). As the section serves as illustration for the explanatory power of the third generation KM heuristic, only two of the categories are investigated in more depth. We focus on the categories "Contextualization of message content" and "Shaping Relationships", both comprising two typical relational practices.

3.2. Contextualization of Message Content

The practices *people placements* and awareness of social spheres can be seen as measures to enact a specific context for technologically mediated messages.

Especially in the second organization, *people placements* took care for an efficient and holistic information transfer between organization and client. This means, that within client projects at least one employee of the organization was located at the site of the customer to get in touch with the culture and the work atmosphere. That way it was possible to 'translate' the clients problems in the organizations' language. One project leader described a situation in which a project faced severe problems. Instantly, the project leader took the next flight to the customer's site. Originally, it was not his project and he was not involved – but somehow he was the only one at-hand. He remembers:

"For the customer this really had a calmative effect: 'Ah, someone else is coming to help us here to solve the problem. That's a new face... someone who is reliable.' This was an enormous help. You cannot get such an effect by video conferences or anything technical. By the way, in this sense there is no difference between web conferences and even telephone conferences. Conferencing just doesn't contribute to trust building. That's our experience at least."

By people placements, the organization adds a pre-existing relationship (between the core team of the organization and distributed members) to the otherwise solely message-centered information exchange. Organisations can build other relationships around the secured connection.

Awareness of social spheres directs towards the increased attention of the employees to maintain places and times for face-to-face meetings in which the social contact is consciously nurtured. Within these interaction spaces people appreciate the socially rich context. Especially the informal coffee breaks have a social value on their own which can become relevant for conducting business as it allows for personal relationships to build across the departmental "garden fences":

"We care for this interaction but they are not formal settings – they are informal talks. But we do care for business issues, too. Well, it's a platform where we meet once or twice a day. One comes along the floor [he is pointing on the open door] – 'Coffee!' and then we know now comes a phase of relaxation and to talk about things beyond the garden fence. We can deal with private issues – 'my cat's sickness' and such things. And I think, that is very important."

Employees use these interaction spaces as social contexts where they can validate or improve virtual messages which were sent afore. Thus, they can verify and improve the creation of shared meaning that was intended by prior virtual communication activities. To realize this practice, organizational members need to have niches of physical presence where conversation with a high degree of synchronicity is possible, e.g. coffee breaks and water cooler talks.

Both practices serve to backup virtual messages with relational information and to contextualize them in this way.

3.3. Shaping Relationships

Committing on ground rules and also *communication code of conduct* are two practices that serve the shaping of relationships. In both practices the norms of how to behave in virtual communication are explicitly discussed.

By generating *commitment to ground rules* of communication relational issues within virtual teamwork are acknowledged that would otherwise be ignored. A HR manager explained:

"[There are] simply certain physical limitations, how much you can realize the personal get-together. As a leader you have to possibilities: Either you pull all people together or you visit them at the site. For virutal work this means that other rules have to be defined. We named them "groundrules". For example, we imposed on us different groundrules depending on whether we work with video conferencing, NetMeeting or shareweb. Especially the rules have to be changed about how we deal with these issues in interpersonal communication."

The central challenge lies in the use of communication technology in a way that it's no barrier to efficient work. People have to try to discipline themselves in virtual communication but are not really successful in developing collective routines that foster this striving. The use of video conferencing is such a part of mutual disciplining in virtual communication because this type of communication cannot be that inflationary used like e-mails can.

A strongly shared *communication code of conduct* makes it easier to effectively communicate via communication media especially within an organizational setting consisting of project oriented teams. By knowing the explicitly concerted communication code of conduct, the project members can build expectations about each others' communication behaviour. In most companies there seems to exist a wide agreement upon the standard how reachable the project team members have to be. A project member states:

"A manager of us is actually reachable. He cannot say 'good bye' and go into vacation. Maybe reluctantly, but you'll reach him somehow. He will check his voice mail and reply. Whereas an a project associate: If he goes in vacation, he really will be in vacation. It's very seldom that someone calls him there or leaves him a voice mail message."

The communication code of conduct is a part of the organization's memory and contains a pre-understanding about the nature of the work, the importance of communication and the expectations regading the reachability within the company. The code of conduct reduces uncertainty and prevents circumstantial coordination (who is how when and why reachable). Without this mutual understanding, the coordination efforts for simple regular day-to-day collaborations would be prohibitive high.

These two practices in this category point towards the shaping of relationships by explicitly communicating the norms of how to behave in hybrid communication.

3.4. Applying the Third Generation KM Heuristic

We now can use the developed KM heuristic to analyze the relational practices regarding their implications for third generation KM (see Table 2).

Table 2: The Third Generation KM Heuristic and identified relational practices.

	Does it enable presencing and (re)contextualizing of knowledge?	*Does it contribute to requisite conversational complexity?*	*Does it foster the emergence of generative dialogue?*
People placements	Brings new people in the organization and creates a new context.	Brings new people in the organization and creates new knowledge.	Brings new people to lead a dialogue with.
Awareness of social spheres	Contributes to the emergence of new spaces for new contexts.	Contributes to the emergence of new spaces for new knowledge.	Contributes to the emergence of new spaces to lead a dialogue in.

Committing on ground rules	Contributes to a shared context to generate new knowledge.	Contributes to a shared context to make complex issues knowable.	Contributes to a shared context between the people involved.
Communication code of conduct	Contributes to a shared language to make complex issues discussable.	Contributes to a shared language to generate new knowledge.	Contributes to a shared language between the people involved.

As can be seen, the heuristic offers interesting contributions of the practices to characterize their effect regarding the three dimensions of third generation KM.

In a second step, it would now be possible to reflect more deeply on each field of the table. For example, the communication code of conduct contributes to a shared language to make complex issues discussable. Therefore, presencing is supported by the relational practice. At the same time, the code prevents this presencing because it goes hand in hand with a kind of standardization within the organization: When a code of conduct exists, the degree of mutual reachability is (more or less) expectable. For presencing (that is reflection-in-action, spoken with Scharmer), exactly the opposite could be a better choice.

As can be seen here, further inverstigations could be induced here. The heuristic's aim is to systematically raise such questions and entry-points for discussions. Thus, the value-added of the heuristic lies within its systematic and comprehensible approach to reflect upon existing communication practices.

4. Conclusion

At the beginning of this paper, the research question was: How do "third generation knowledge management concepts" help to understand relational practices in blended contexts of face-to-face interaction and virtual communication? We used third generation KM approaches as a focus lens to identify crucial aspects of KM in organizations. Then, we described relational practices in hybrid work settings and applied the third generation KM heuristic to identify the effect of the relational practices on third generation KM. The usefulness of the third generation KM heuristic became apparent when we used it as a helpful lens to analyze relational practices in the studied organizations. However, it was mentioned, that the heuristic is to be understood as a vehicle to reflect upon existing communication practices. Therefore, it is not a tool to assess whether a practice is good or bad per se.

The results show that analysis benefits from qualitative research heuristics like the one we elaborated here. Heuristics as conceptual frameworks are still hard to find although qualitative approaches of organizational studies clearly left infancy behind. Especially, theory has to encourage the study of situational rich contexts like hybrid work settings. Hybrid contexts become the normal case – but they are more difficult to be accessed and researched than experimental designs are.

For the overarching theory of organizational communication the findings indicate, that existing concepts base upon too linear and static models trying to satisfy quantitative pressure upon the discipline. We assume that it's the rationality of the organization that decides which modes of communication are acceptable and which composition of relational practices within hybrid work settings is adequate to serve the organization's aims. Against the background of this essay, organizational communication as an academic discipline would be well advised to invest some time in studying sociologically informed communication theory and to combine it with organizational perspective. The Newer Social Systems Theory (Baecker, 2007; Luhmann, 1995) would be a valuable resource for this.

Acknowledgements: The authors would like to acknowledge the support of the WWZ-Forum at the University of Basel (research project number "D-90: Social capital in digital context?"). The authors especially thank the interview participants for allowing us access to their work lives and personal perspectives. An earlier draft of this paper was presented at the 23nd EGOS colloquium 2007 in Vienna.

References

Baecker, D.: Communication With Computers, or How Next Society Calls for an Understanding of Form. Soziale Systeme, 13(1/2) (2007).

Berger, P. L. & Luckmann, T.: The Social Construction of Reality: A Treatise in the Sociology of Knowledge. Garden City, Doubleday, New York (1966).

Bleicher, J.: Contemporary Hermeneutics: Hermeneutics as Method, Philosophy and Critique. Routledge & Kegan Paul, London and Boston (1980).

Bryman, A.: Quantity and Quality in Social Research. Unwin Hyman, London (1988).

Castells, M.: The Internet Galaxy. Reflections on Internet, Business, and Society. Oxford University Press (2001).

Dachler, H. P. & Hosking, D.-M.: The Primacy of Relations in Socially Constructing Organizational Realities. In D.-M. Hosking, H. P. Dachler & K. J. Gergen (Eds.), Management and Organizations: Relational Alternatives to Individualism. Avebury, Aldershot, 1-28 (1995).

Dutta, S. & Mia, I.: Global Information Technology Report 2006-2007: Connecting to the Networked Economy. Palgrave Macmillan (2007).

Gergen, K. J.: Social Construction in Context. Thousand Oaks, CA. Sage (2001).

Glaser, B. G. & Strauss, A. L.: The discovery of grounded theory. Strategies for qualitative research. De Gruyter, New York: (1967).

Griffith, T. L., Sawyer, J. E. & Neale, M. A.: Virtualness and knowledge in teams: Managing the love triangle of organizations, individuals, and information technology. MIS Quarterly, 27(2). 265-287 (2003).

Luhmann, N.: Social systems. Stanford University Press, Stanford, CA (1995).

Meissner, J. O.: Multi-stage analysis for knowledge reflection. In: A. S. Kazi & P. Wolf (Eds.): Hands-On Knowledge Co-Creation and Sharing: Practical Methods and Techniques. Knowledge Board. 291-307 (2007).

Meissner, J. O. & Tuckermann, H.: A Relational Scaffolding Model of Hybrid Communication. In: C. Steinfield, B. Pentland, M. Ackerman & N. Contractor (Eds.): Proceedings of the Communities and Technologies 2007, Michigan State University. Springer, London, 479-508 (2007).

Nonaka, I. & Takeuchi, H.: The Knowledge-Creating Company. Oxford University Press, New York (1995).

Polanyi, M.: The Tacit Dimension. Routledge & Kegan, London (1967).

Scharmer, C.-O.: Self-transcending knowledge: Sensing and organizing around emerging opportunities. Journal of Knowledge Management, 5(2), 137-151 (2001).

Scharmer, C. O.: Theory U: Leading from the Future as it Emerges. Society for Organizational Learning (2007).

Senge, P., Scharmer, C. O., Jaworski, J. & Flowers, B. S.: Presence: An Exploration of Profound Change in People, Organizations, and Society. Currency, New York (2005).

Snowden, D.: Complex acts of knowing: paradox and descriptive self-awareness. Journal of Knowledge Management, 6(2), 100-111 (2002).

Stacey, R.: Complex Responsive Processes in Organizations: Learning and Knowledge Creation. Routledge, London. (2001).

Weick, K. E.: Sensemaking in organizations. Sage, Thousand Oaks, CA. (1995).

Witzel, A.: The Problem-Centered Interview. Forum: Qualitative Social Research, 1(1), (2000).

Zachry, M. & Thralls, C. (Eds.): Communicative Practices in Workplaces and the Professions: Cultural Perspectives on the Regulation of Discourse and Organizations. Baywood Publishing, Amityville, NY (2006).

Knowledge Management-in-action in an EUD-oriented Software Enterprise

Bernhard Nett[1,2], Johanna Meurer[1], and Gunnar Stevens[1]

[1] Fraunhofer-Institut für Angewandte Informationstechnik FIT, Schloss Birlinghoven, 53754 Sankt Augustin, Germany , Telefon: +49 (0) 2241/14-1598, Fax: +49 (0) 2241/14-2146 {bernhard.nett;johanna.meurer;gunnar.stevens}@fit.fraunhofer.de

[2] Wirtschaftsinformatik und Neue Medien, Universität Siegen, Hölderlinstrasse 3, 57068 Siegen, Germany

Abstract: End User Development (EUD) aims at the enabling of end users to adapt, modify or extend software and has become an important keyword for software designers. Discussing premises for the success of EUD, several authors have stated that processes of knowledge development and diffusion play an important role. Current research discusses such Knowledge-Management issues mostly in the client organization. But if we want to bring an End User perspective into design practice, we have to take into account how producers manage their costumer-related knowledge and bring it into action. Therefore, the study presented here describes the results of a related *Business Ethnography*, which was carried out in a small enterprise of the German software branch. The paper explains how this ethnographic action research helped to identify practices, potentials and problems in the enterprise to acquire, secure and use knowledge about the end users of its products. Preliminary findings demonstrate that EUD is not only a technical, but also a Knowledge-Management challenge for software enterprises.

1. Introduction

In software design, End User Development (EUD) has become an established conception aiming at the enabling of end users to adapt, modify or extend software artefacts (Lieberman et al. 2006). EUD has become the focus of an EU-funded Network-of-Excellence (EUD-Net) and a well-known keyword, for example, in IEEE - the same way as Knowledge Management (KM) had become before. Further than that, both concepts do not seem to have much in common at first glance. EUD generally is associated with software design, while Knowledge Management is associated with information systems and organizational development. But appearances may be deceiving, as there are important links between EUD and KM:

Please use the following format when citing this chapter:

Nett, B., Meurer, J. and Stevens, G., 2008, in IFIP International Federation for Information Processing, Volume 270; *Knowledge Management in Action*; Mark Ackerman, Rose Dieng-Kuntz, Carla Simone, Volker Wulf; (Boston: Springer), pp. 139–149.

information systems can be designed for EUD, and EUD-oriented software development may call for KM in the client organization (Mackay 1990; Nardi and Miller 1992; Kahler 2001; Pipek 2005). Thirdly, knowledge and its management can play a crucial role in the customer-producer relationship (Fischer and Giaccardi 2006; Stevens and Draxler 2006; Stevens et al. 2007).

Although "for most design problems, the knowledge to understand, frame, and solve problems is not given, but is constructed and evolves during the problem-solving process" (Fischer and Giaccardi 2006, p.428), this third perspective on EUD and KM has remained under-investigated. It relates to possible strategies of EUD-oriented software enterprises to acquire, evaluate and secure knowledge of users of the targeted markets within their everyday operation. As the producer-customer relationship is partly mediated by technology (cf. Stevens and Draxler 2006; Stevens et al. 2007), its relationship with opportunities for Knowledge Management-in-action is an important question.

The application of Business Ethnography (BE) (Nett & Stevens 2008) for research on this relationship in a supplier organization is the focus of this paper.

The paper is structured as follows: after an introduction into the fields of EUD and KM, the methodological background of our research is described and positioned as BE. Following, the application of BE is explained. Closing the paper, the role of organizational learning for practical success of KM and EUD are discussed, as well as BE as a resource to study it.

2. Knowledge Management and End User Development

KM evolved as a discourse in the context of emerging new information technology, partly envisioning related opportunities of the Knowledge Society. Davenport and Prusak (1998) concluded that KM could not prevail if it reduced knowledge right from the start, i.e., by applying a managerial, individual or merely technology-oriented perceptive, and hinted at the necessity to embed KM in organizations instead. From this point of view, KM is not only about technical information systems, but on the interplay of technology and knowledge practices in organizations.

Conceptions such as KM and EUD are often described as plausible models (of knowledge use on the one hand, of design conceptions on the other). However, real-world actors, i.e. enterprises, can benefit from such general conceptions only if they develop strategies to contextualize them.

In particular, small enterprises hesitate to invest into KM, which they regard as comprising expensive technology accessible only for large enterprises (Nett & Wulf 2005). Hence, it is important to study if and how small enterprises learn in the action of operation about their products and their importance for the users on the one hand, and how they can bring knowledge on user demands, user habits and user competences into action again, on the other.

Research on “in-action” perspectives of KM in small enterprises, therefore, is of major interest. The study described in this paper is part of a public funded project called CoEUD. In this project a group of small and medium-sized software firms collaborate to develop more EUD-oriented products. The SME character of the enterprises in the CoEUD project is not untypical for the German software branch, where the average size of the enterprises is very small (Friedewald et al. 2001).

EUD has become a new focus for software design: when Henderson & Kyng (1991) identified tailoring of artefacts as a different activity from normal use, a large transition gulf could be identified between using and tailoring and between superficial and deep tailoring (MacLean et al. 1990; Bentley & Dourish 1995), where the latter involves changes of the system architecture and functionality. The complexity of customization was identified as a problem for end users (Mørch 1997), and the reduction of system complexity as the necessary solution (Myers et al. 2003; Fischer et al. 2004).

Some EUD-researchers investigated into real-world problems of users. Their work has been based on qualitative research, mostly ethnographic studies (Dourish et al. 1999). This kind of research demonstrates that knowledge development and knowledge diffusion are important for EUD. Obstacles to the exploit of technological options within organizations were systematically examined by Mackay (1991), Gantt & Nardi (1992) and Wulf (1999), positive impacts of related networks by Mackay (1990). Possible productive roles for local "gurus" and developers were analyzed as a part of “tailoring cultures” and group tailorability (Kahler 2001; Pipek & Kahler 2005).

Pipek (2005) argues that EUD research falls short if it only concentrates on artefacts. In relation to other EUD research, his argument shows a shift in perspective: whereas “human factors” had been mostly studied as a source of problems hindering users to benefit from a (supposedly fully transparent) possible use of a given artefact, his perspective now was how to make the social embeddedness of technology a benefit for the user.

It is not necessarily the intention of its developer, which makes an artefact a KM system, but its functioning as support for an organizational context. This perspective allows (but also needs) to study technological infrastructures in their functioning, this is: “in action”.

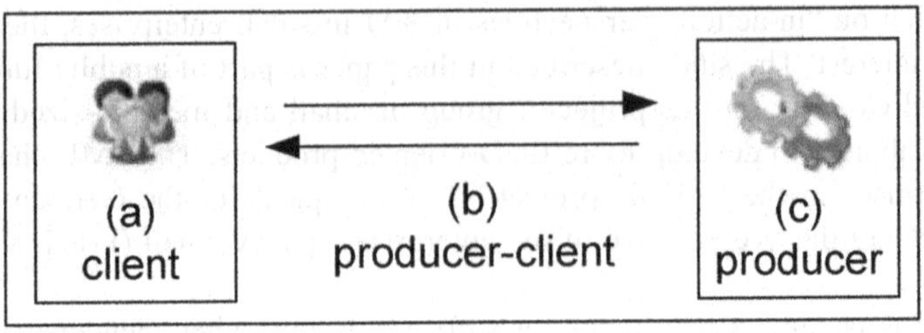

Fig. 1.. EUD related research on Knowledge Management-in-action

Reflecting on the relevant foci, research can be differentiated into three categories (cf. Figure 1):

(a) Research on EUD related knowledge processes on the client organization
(b) Research on EUD related inter-organisational KM infrastructure
(c) Research on EUD related knowledge processes the producer organization

The first category mainly focuses on Knowledge-Management systems in client organizations and covers most studies, in particular, the recent ethnographical ones. EUD-oriented KM systems like infrastructures for user communities (Pipek 2005) mainly target at the client side, too. Category b) addresses the aspect that EUD have to integrate inter-organisational Knowledge Management infrastructure. Fischer, for instance, drawing on his previous work on End-User Modification (Fischer & Girgensohn 1990), developed the concept of Meta-Design (cf.: Fischer & Giaccardi 2006). The general idea is that new products are not enough to establish sustainable EUD, but that it also needs production innovation. Fischer suggests an iterative model which he calls the Seeding – Growing – Reseeding (SER). This has consequences for the role of designers and users: "The SER model encourages designers to conceptualize their activity as meta-design, thereby supporting users as designers in their own right, rather than restricting them to being passive consumers." (Fischer & Giaccardi 2006, p.428).

The work of Stevens et al. (2007) addresses the question how to bridge production-related KM processes and appropriation-related practices, i.e. by the technical means of so-called "appropriation infrastructures". However, according to Fischer´s focus on iterative improvement on the basis of learning from practice, design of such products had to be guided by learning-by-doing, too. In this regard, they are as much a framework to organize costumer-producer interaction supporting EUD, as they open up problems for KM, setting questions on the agenda like:

- In how far does the communication and cooperation infrastructure between a software enterprise and its customers support the appropriation of the software products?

- How can an enterprise learn "in action" how to make the functioning of its communication and cooperation infrastructure with the customer more supporting for the appropriation of its products?

Research conceptions tackling these questions falling into category c), studying the EUD related knowledge processes in a producer organisation from the insider perspective. In particular such researches have to function in real-time operation, focus on learning processes, and cover on technology and organizational change, as well.

In the following section, Business Ethnography (BE) will be described as the related research design of our study.

3. Methodology

Business Ethnography (BE) was originally developed as the empirical part of the action-research oriented design conception of Integrated Organization and Technology Development (OTD) (Wulf et al. 1995, 1999). OTD is a process model to support a technology expert in his efforts to identify and tailor technology dedicated to help a client's self-organization instead of replacing it technologically. Related projects were based on a set of workshops, in which researchers and organization members took part to analyze and define requirements or to discuss design alternatives (cf. Rohde, 2006). BE, initially only the empirical part of OTD, informed the technical expert about the status quo in the given setting.
It is framed by the action research-oriented context of OTD. This implies that BE is conceptualized as a visible intervention into the field established by the cooperation of the project partners.

The qualitative research undertaken, therefore, originally was based more on interviews than on own field observations. This did not only help the ethnographers to understand the given situation and possible boundary objects (Bowker & Star 1999), but additionally helped them to establish Social Capital (Ackerman et al. 2004) between the actors in the project and supporting experts (Nett et al. 2006).

The goal of BE is to understand everyday work practices in a particular context. One oft the most important elements of BE is the central role of interviews with project partners on their cooperation practices, which form the basis of analyses. The interviews not only give insights into the distributed, sometimes even contradictory character of the organizational model(s) guiding the actors, but also uncover deviations from "normality", either perceived by the interviewees or deduced by the interviewer from analyses of the perspectives and experiences of different actors.

BE differentiates between formal organizations, on one hand, and practices and routines underlying them, on the other. It thus focuses on differentiations between routines, disturbances and normative aspects in everyday-work practices. BE aims at the actors´ perception of the situation in the field, but helps to produce a new picture, at the same time: an integral part of the BE is to confront the project partner with the analyses of the interviews with them, and ask them to comment.

The reason for that is two-folded. First this is a common method in action research to validate the analyses, which is adapted in BE. Secondly, this strategy is used to allow for self-organized learning processes: the feedback confronts the interviewees with a perception of their situation that has undergone a methodological interpretation by the ethnographers and thus is perceived by the interviewees as an expropriation of the experience that they expressed. This 'ex-propriation' allows the project to evaluate perceptions and expectations of the project partners on a related workshop from a distant position, and thus for their discursive 're-' and 'a-propriation'.

BE thus also offers data for analyses of learning processes. It is combined with common discussions of the interview partners about the validity of the interpretation, its impact for the understanding of the given situation and for the common project, as well.

This social process increases the distancing effect of the expropriation/ appropriation loop of BE in regard of the experiences of the interviewees fostering knowledge development. As a compound of action research and ethnography, BE has been applied in several projects, in which the ethnographer cooperated with the project partners to achieve common project aims. Organizing an expropriation/ re-appropriation loop of related knowledge with the project partners helps them to reflect on their local expertise and develop new strategies.

The application of BE in the case presented here shows two major differences compared to its role in an OTD process: first, in the given case, research had to be carried out not in a client organization with its specific technology demands, but in a producer organization, which had to address its market. Secondly, OTD normally searches for technological solutions, whereas in the presented case the task was to find organizational solutions to support a specific technological approach. Therefore, research could not apply OTD, but draw on BE. In the following, we present our process of conducting BE.

4. Proceeding

In order to study how small enterprises can gain und use their knowledge about end users to develop more EUD-oriented software projects, we contacted the CEO of a project partner. His enterprise works in the fields of learning products, CMS and e-Commerce and occupies seven employees with fix contracts and a network of free lancers. The study was conducted from September to December 2007, mainly based on 10 interviews of one hour of duration each. All were conducted on-site at the company, except for one, which consisted of a telephone interview with an employee in Brussels.

Interviews were recorded, transcribed, paraphrased and analyzed. In the study it was possible to interview all employees with a fix contract: the CEO of the enterprise, the CIO, one apprentice of IT-technology, two marketing employees, one additional technician and one designer. Additional interviews were conducted with one former marketing employee, as well as with one designer and one development freelancer, both of them with a long record of contracts with the company.

All interviews were based on a semi-structured guideline, which contained questions on the role, tasks and responsibility of the interviewees in the enterprise. Further questions were asked about processes and communication media in the context of possible knowledge on or contact to the clients. Interviews left room to answer according to an own relevance-system. Interviewees generally started answering according to formal processes and responsibilities.

Disturbances and specific work practices were seldom autonomously addressed by the interviewees themselves. But when asked about possible differences to normal product development processes, interviewees started to talk also about problems and extraordinary experiences within their daily work. Analyses were thus based on the differentiation between formal processes and informal practices. They started with the modelling of the formal organization of processes, which could be reconstructed by combining interviews. This could be made the basis to identify irregular situations. The results of the related analysis was presented and discussed with the interviewees on a workshop after analysis, allowing the correction of wrong interpretations by the interviewees themselves.

5. Preliminary Findings

A fundamental aspect of the EUD-oriented Meta-Design conception (Fischer, 1999) is that related KM should include the design of the customer-producer relationship. However, our preliminary findings indicate that for an SME, KM is difficult to be established. For example, the CEO, in the preliminary discussion preparing our study, explained how the enterprise lacked of customer feedback. In contrast, one of our surprising findings was that there was a lot of customer feedback, but obviously a fundamental problem to systematically make use of it. In opposition to the Fischer model, in most cases the first initiative for a user-designer communication was not coming from a designer but from a user. Alterations of the formal model and innovations were often only developed in reaction to such unanticipated user behaviour.

Although the producer did not offer the users "proper" feedback channels, users still responded to an astoundingly large extend by a creatively "mis-" using of the registration form. Users not only addressed problems to apply the product, but also made suggestions and proposals.

It is striking that some suggestions are used by the company as impulses for product development, but did not become organizationally aware, as there was no in-house discussion on user activities and their potential innovation. Based on this observation, we conclude that the main problem was not the lack of customer feed-back in general, but the problem of interpreting and managing it. In given cases, some reactions had been taken, but not systematically exploited. This shows that, if we want to bring EUD-oriented concepts like Meta Design into practice, we also have to develop EUD-oriented KM-in-action. Consequently, we have to study the situation in more detail. Our related findings yet remain only the first tentative ones.

Our interviews as well as the group discussion on the workshop showed that the CEO and the CIO very much dominated the discussion, indicating that even in this very small enterprise, there can be a strong hierarchy and a centralization of decision making. This obviously was partly in contrast to the de-central creation of knowledge during operation. The organization thus was neither a Tayloristic one, nor one of flat hierarchies.

This may explain why even the CEO was impressed by the approaches developed in his enterprise to benefit from unanticipated information about the customer, and how he could be astonished by the opportunities becoming apparent, when these approaches were connected to one whole picture in our presentation: *"this really shows a consistent philosophy to follow"*, he remarked after our presentation in obvious surprise. This is in line with the finding of Davenport & Prusak´s (1998), that it makes a difference to develop an innovative product and to develop an innovative development environment enabling the development of innovative products, and that the opportunities to share knowledge are the crucial prerequisite for the latter.

Discussing this point with the workshop members, a further workshop was decided upon to improve opportunities to exploit customer feedback by improving inner-organizational knowledge exchange. This workshop has not yet taken place, but we plan to further investigate into the opportunities and problems of this situated form of Knowledge Management-in-action.

6. Conclusion

Preliminary findings coming from using Business Ethnography to study Knowledge Management-in-action in a small enterprise demonstrate that EUD is not only a technical, but an organizational challenge, where Knowledge Management-in-action plays a critical role. This has often been ignored in literature on EUD, which has been interested in knowledge processes only at the client side. Generalizing our finding, there is too little awareness for client-oriented KM in producer organizations as a part of an EUD strategy. In our case, EUD was a motivation for the enterprise to participate in a related project and understood as a marketing argument, but had neither been reflected in the organization as a challenge nor as a basis for Knowledge Management-in-action.

This lasting lack of interest from both academia and industry could be seen as an argument against any importance of research or conceptions on the relationship between EUD and KM in producer organizations. However, our BE demonstrated that investigating into related opportunities made quite a handful of interesting approaches and related potential in the enterprise visible. However, these were neither reflected nor exploited systematically, due to a lack of knowledge sharing. This shows that BE, while requiring further elaboration as a conception for reflexive organizational learning to combine KM-in-action and EUD, can be of great benefit to orient software enterprises on sustainable EUD.

Acknowledgements: This work has been funded by the German Bundesministerium für Bildung und Forschung as part of the project "Component based End User Development" (CoEUD) No.: 01ISF01A-E.

References

Ackerman, M.; Huysman, M.; Carroll, J.M.; Wellman; B.; De Michelis, G.; Wulf, V. (2004): Communities and technologies: an approach to foster social capital? in: Proceedings of CSCW 2004, pp.406-408

Balka, E.; Wagner, I. (2006): Making things work: dimensions of configurability as appropriation work. Proceedings of CSCW'06, ACM Press

Bentley, R.; Dourish, P. (1995): „Medium versus Mechanism: Supporting Collaboration through Customisation". Proceedings of ECSCW95, Kluwer

Bowker, G.C.; Star, S.L. (1999): Sorting Things Out: Classification and Its Consequences. Cambridge, MA: MIT Press

Davenport, T.H.; Prusak, L. (1998): Working Knowledge: How organizations manage what they know, Boston: Harvard Business School Press

Dourish, P.; Lamping, J.; Rodden, T. (1999): Building bridges. Customization and mutual intelligibility in shared category management, Proceedings of the International ACM SIGGROUP Conference on Supporting Group Work; 1999 November 14-17th; Phoenix, AZ, pp.11-20

Dourish, P. (2003): "The appropriation of interactive technologies: Some lessons from placeless documents." Journal of CSCW 12(4), pp.465-49

Draxler, S.; Stevens, G. (2006): "Getting Out Of A Tailorability Dilemma". INFORMATIK 2006 Informatik für Menschen, GI-Edition-Lecture Notes, in: Informatics (LNI) P-93(1), pp.576 - 580

Fischer, G.; Giaccardi, E. (2006): Meta-Design: A Framework for the Future of End-User Development. End User Development, MIT Press

Fischer, G.; Girgensohn, A. (1990): End-user modifiability in design environments. Proc. of CHI90, ACM Press

Fischer, G. (1999): Symmetry of igorance, social creativity, and meta-design, in: Proceedings of the 3rd Conference on Creativity and Cognition.116-123

Fischer, G., Giaccardi, E., Ye, Y., Sutcliffe, A.G., Mehandjiev, N. (2004): "Meta-Design: A Manifesto for End-User Development." Communications of the ACM 47, no. 9 (2004), pp.33-37

Friedewald, M.; Rombach, H.D.; Stahl, P.; Broy, M.; Hartkopf, S.; Kimpeler, S.; Kohler, K.; Wucher, R.; Zoche, P. (2001): „Softwareentwicklung in Deutschland. Eine Bestandsaufnahme", in: Informatik Spektrum, Bd. 24, Nr. 2 (2001), pp.81-90

Gantt, M.; Nardi, B.A. (1992): "Gardeners and Gurus: Patterns of Cooperation among CAD Users". Proceedings of CHI92

Grudin, J. (1994): "CSCW: History and Focus". IEEE Computer 27(5), pp.19-26

Henderson, A.; Kyng, M. (1991): „There's no place like home: Continuing Design in Use. Design at work: Cooperative Design of Computer Systems". Lawrence Erlbaum, pp.219-240

Kahler, H. (2001): "More than WORDs -Collaborative Tailoring of a word processor". Journal of Universal Computer Science (7:9), pp.826-847

Kahler, H. (2001): Supporting Collaborative Tailoring. Department of Communication, Journalism and Computer Science, Dänemark, Roskilde University

Lieberman, H.; Paternó, F.; Klann, M.; Wulf, V. (Hg.) (2006): End-User Development: an Emerging Paradigm, in: Lieberman, H.; Paterno, F.; Wulf, V. (Hg.): End User Development, Springer Mackay, W.E. (1990): Users and customizable Software: A Co-Adaptive Phenomenon. Boston, MIT

Mackay, W.E. (1991): "Triggers and Barriers to Customizing Software". Proceedings of CHI91

MacLean, A.; Carter, K.; Lovstrand, L.; Moran, T.P. (1990): "User-Tailorable Systems: Pressing the Issues with Buttons". Proceedings of CHI90

Mørch, A. (1997): "Three Levels of End-user Tailoring: Customization, Integration, and Extension. Computers and Design in Context". MIT Press, pp.51-76

Myers, B.; Hudson, S.E.; Pausch, R. (2003): "Past, Present, and Future of User Interface Software Tools." TOCHI, ACM, New York

Nardi, B.A., Miller, J. (1992): "Twinkling lights and nested loops: Distributed problem solving and spreadsheet development." International Journal of Man Machine Studies 34, pp.161-184

Nett, B.; Dyrks, T.; Mueller, C., Durissini, M. (2006): Neither Essence nor Accident: Situated knowledge and its importance for the Community Broker, in: Ljungberg, J. (ed.): Proceedings of the 14th European Conference on Information Systems (ECIS 2006), Göteborg, Sweden 2006

Nett, Bernhard; Stevens, Gunnar (2008): Business Ethnography - Aktionsforschung als Beitrag zu einer reflexiven Technik¬gestaltung (Business Ethnography – Action research as a contribution to reflexive design), in: Becker, Jörg; Krcmar, Helmut; Niehaves, Björn (Hg.): Wissenschaftstheorie und gestaltungs¬orientierte Wirtschaftsinformatik (Science theory and design-oriented Information Science), Institut für Wirtschaftsinformatik, Westfälische Wilhelms-Universität Münster, Arbeitsberichte Nr. 120, pp.48-68

Nett, B.; Wulf, V. (2005): Wissensprozesse in der Softwarebranche. Kleine und mittelständische Unternehmen unter empirischer Perspektive (knowledge practices in the software branch, SME in an empirical perspective), in: Gendolla, P.; Schäfer, J. (eds.): Wissensprozesse in der Netzwerkgesellschaft (knowledge processes in the Network Society), Transcript, pp.147-168

Pipek, V.; Kahler H. (2005): "Tailoring together: A systematization and two cases". International Reports on Socio-Informatics 1(2), pp.1-48

Pipek, V. (2005): From Tailoring to Appropriation Support: Negotiating Groupware Usage, Department of Information Processing Science, Finland, University of Oulu

Pipek, V.; Kahler, H. (2006): "Supporting Collaborative Tailoring", in: Lieberman, H.; Paterno, F.; Wulf, V. (eds.): End-User Development, Springer

Rohde, M. (2006): Integrated Organization and Technology Development (OTD) and the Impact of Socio-Cultural Concepts -A CSCW Perspective, Disseration, Department of Communication, Business and Information Technologies, Roskilde University, Denmark, 2006

Stallman, R. (1981): EMACS: The Extensible, Customizable, Self-Documenting Display Editor. Proc. of the ACM SIGPLAN SIGOA

Stevens, G.; Draxler, S. (2006): Partizipation im Nutzungskontext. Proc. of Mensch & Computer 2006, Oldenbourgh

Stevens, G. et al. (2007): Infrastrukturen zur Aneignungsunterstützung. 8. Internationale Tagung Wirtschaftsinformatik, Karlsruhe, pp.823-840

Wulf, V. (1999): "Evolving Cooperation when Introducing Groupware-A Self-Organization Perspective". Cybernetics and Human Knowing 6(2), pp.55-75

Wulf, V.; Rohde, M. (1995): Towards an Integrated Organization and Technology Development, in: Ohlsen, G.; Shannan, S. (eds.) (1995): Proceedings of the Symposion on Designing Interactive Systems (DIS 1995). Processes, Practices, Methods and Techniques, ACM-Press, pp.55-65

Wulf, V.; Krings, M.; Stiemerling, O.; Iacucci, G.; Maidhof, M.; Peters, R.; Fuchs-Frohnhofen, P.; Nett, B.; Hinrichs, J. (1999): „Improving Inter-Organizational Processes with Integrated Organization and Technology Development", in: J.UCS, Vol. V, Issue 6, Graz, pp.339-365

Business Finder – A Tool for Regional Networking among Organizations

Tim Reichling, Benjamin Moos, and Volker Wulf

Institute of Information Systems, University of Siegen, Germany, {tim.reichling, benjamin.moos, volker.wulf}@uni-siegen.de

Abstract: Networks of organizations improve the competitiveness of its member companies. Computer applications can make the competencies of organizations more visible to encourage companies to find matching costumers, suppliers, or cooperation partners. Business Finder (BF) is a tool for improving mutual awareness among small and medium enterprises (SME) in regional networks. BF is based on text matching algorithms already applied among human actors within the field of knowledge management. Being integrated into the ordinary document management, BF allows creating updated, comprehensive, and detailed profiles of an organization's competencies and activities. Searching on profiles of other organizations enables identifying potential partners. The design of BF is based on an empirical study into networking needs among SME in the IT domain. The pre-study together with an early evaluation study was conducted in the German region of Siegen-Wittgenstein.

1. Introduction

Networks of geographically collocated companies are widely known to offer its members competitive advantages. Those advantages may be found in lower transportation costs, better knowledge spill-overs, more intense cooperation along the supply chain, or faster innovation cycles. According to Porter (1998), networks of highly interconnected and geographically proximate companies along a value chain, so called *clusters*, strongly encourage regional economy and create competitive advantage to its constituting companies. Popular examples to underpin this thesis are Silicon Valley for IT, Hollywood for movie production or the Ruhr Area in Germany for metal-work.

In this paper we focus on the role of IT to support transparency and mutual awareness in regional networks of companies. We do not focus on clusters exclusively since we also consider regional networks of companies which do not (yet) show the distinct properties of clusters. Creating and supporting networks of com-

Please use the following format when citing this chapter:

Reichling, T., Moos, B. and Wulf, V., 2008, in IFIP International Federation for Information Processing, Volume 270; *Knowledge Management in Action*; Mark Ackerman, Rose Dieng-Kuntz, Carla Simone, Volker Wulf; (Boston: Springer), pp. 151–163.

panies is often taken to be a central goal in regional economic intervention. However, technical approaches to support networks are rare.

With regard to the domain of knowledge management, expertise recommender systems have proved to be promising technologies to support networks of human actors within organizations (cf. Hinds and Pfeffer 2003, Huysman and Wulf 2006, Reichling et al. 2005, 2007). In this paper, we investigate whether these technologies can be successfully applied to support awareness and transparency in networks of regional companies.

The argument is structured as follows. First, we analysed requirements of SME with regard to mutual awareness. The study was conducted with the business development department of the Siegen-Wittgenstein region (Germany). Based on these findings, we designed the *Business Finder*, a keyword based search engine for regional SME. Business Finder is a synthesis of two existing technologies: an expertise recommender system designed for encouraging expertise sharing in large organizations (Reichling et al. 2007) and the database of regional companies (DRC) that is hosted by the business development department. DRC is a web based directory containing basic information about regional SME from media and IT sectors in the broadest sense. A first evaluation study focuses on the systems performance (compared to existing search engines like Google) and the actual value that it provides to potential users.

2. Related work

A variety of studies indicate that structures of regional proximity and interconnectedness to be important success factors for companies. While globalization and new media appear to outperform these seemingly antiquated assets, they seem to maintain their significance. Porter (1998) labels this phenomenon *The Location Paradox*. Lower costs for transportation or resources can not sufficiently explain why companies of a given sector appear to settle down in the same region.

Donhauser (2006) finds incentives for regional concentration in an increasing potential for innovation, productivity and growth by better preconditions for cooperation. These are a result of different circumstances: First, regional proximity leads to vivid informal communication among human actors even across companies resulting in a rapid diffusion of expertise and best practices. Second, the regional proximity often goes along with the creation of a highly specialized "Labour Pool" (Schiele 2003) from which regional companies can select their staff while saving time and costs for training. Third, another issue concerned with knowledge dissemination among actors of interconnected enterprises is trust (Porter 1998). Since trust is a property of social ties, *social capital* (SC) (cf. Bourdieu 1983) affects processes of knowledge dissemination (Huysman and Wulf 2004). Following Wolfe (2002) social capital is not transferable among human actors. It encourages the actors' (across companies) willingness to mutually support each other, initiate business cooperation and share knowledge.

Besides the aspect of an improved information exchange, clusters are also characterized by stronger competition as a result of a large number of enterprises in the same sector and improved transparency. According to Porter (1998) „*Companies can mitigate many input-cost disadvantages through global sourcing, rendering the old notion of comparative advantage less relevant. Instead, competitive advantage rests on making more productive use of inputs, which requires continual innovation.* [...] *Without vigorous competition a cluster will fail*". Porter realizes that cooperation and competition can coexist within a cluster and do not exclude each other. In fact both are required for successful clusters.

We now turn to the question of how IT can contribute to the development of regional networks which may lead to the formation of cluster structures. Krätke and Scheuplein (2001) suggest that IT systems could support cluster recognition and analysis to enable business development departments to better ground decisions on political interventions. They state that visualizing cluster boundaries as well as internal interconnections and offering comparisons of regional and super regional clusters are central requirements for this purpose.

IT systems that perform algorithmic matching of model based descriptions, recommender systems according to Resnick and Varian (1997), gain importance in different domains of information and communication technology (ICT) (cf. Balabanovic and Shoham 1997, Resnick 1994), especially knowledge management (cf. Hinds and Pfeffer 2003, Huysman and Wulf 2004, Reichling et al. 2005, 2007). With respect to cluster support, Porter (1998) suggests that IT systems could create awareness on other actors within a cluster. Similarly, Leuninger and Held (2003) – without specifying certain technological approaches – argue for an IS based address and communication platform.

Up to now, IT had little significance in dedicated cluster support and is treated neglectfully in the literature. Instead, existing technologies from other domains appear promising for network development among geographical proximate companies. As such, we can find common search engines like Google or Yahoo which cover websites in general. Their results can hardly be limited to regional companies. We also find directories of regional companies, hosted and maintained by local business development units that often suffer from out-dated and incomplete profiles or high efforts to keep them updated. We can further consider ontology-based approaches (Blomquist 2007). Omitting imprecise or ambiguous results, ontologies offer sophisticated search functionality for companies' competencies. However, meaningful ontologies need to be created and updated, which means a considerable effort. Hence, this kind of technology so far has not been applied for cluster support. Another aspect that can be found at many clusters is the existence of a common website representing the cluster as such (Sölvell et al. 2003). While it is unchallenged that representation towards the external market is highly important, it is remarkable that these sites in general do not contribute to foster connections between actors *within* clusters.

3. Business Finder: Approach and empirical study

Based on the findings above and promising results of recommender systems in several different domains, we decided to apply recommender technology to support transparency and awareness in regional networks. The BF approach goes beyond a simple address database which most likely does not improve transparency of a company's competencies and activities sufficiently. Our study covers requirements analysis, system design and a brief evaluation of the BFs performance.

3.1. Methods and field of application

The district Siegen-Wittgenstein has a population of 290,000 people. Siegen, as the regional centre, denotes the most populated town and hosts most of the SME in the region. As mentioned above, with respect to the media and IT sector, Siegen-Wittgenstein can hardly be denoted as cluster according to Porter (1998) since interconnections between companies can rarely be found. To a large extent business transactions are accomplished with external partners even though potential consumers, suppliers or cooperation partners exist within the region. Furthermore, no central database exists (or is widely accepted) that covers recent profiles of regional companies. The 'closest candidate' to such a database – from our point of view – is a public database that is hosted by the regional business development department which we refer to as the *database of regional companies* (DRC). DRC is a yellow page (YP) like directory that contains elementary data of selected regional companies (name, address, contact information, CEO, basic competencies etc.). The data is updated occasionally by employees of the business development, but no more often that twice a year on average. Details about a company's products, services, processes or methods are missing. DRC can be requested via a web front end.

We worked together with members of the regional business development who runs the DRC. They found their system to be rarely used by regional companies. Obviously, the contents of the database were recognized as out of date, poor and (in some cases) redundant to the companies' websites. Hence, basic objectives of our study were: Concept and design of an IS to create transparency of competencies and activities as well as mutual awareness of potential transaction partners within the region which may enable network structures to grow. The IS should be embedded into the existing DRC in order to improve its search results by offering data that is more comprehensive and up to date.

Our study followed basically an action research (AR) approach (Susman and Everd, 1978, Wulf and Rohde, 1995). We applied one AR cycle consisting of the five steps of *diagnosing*, *action planning*, *action taking*, *evaluation* and *specifying/learning* in a slightly adjusted way. Formally, the regional business development department can be referred to as our client. For the steps of analysing and evaluation, we relied on qualitative and ethnographical methods (Flick 2002) and conducted semi-structured and open-ended interviews with participants from representative companies (one participant per company). For the evaluation study further participants were asked to judge the results returned by the BF system.

For the requirements analysis (diagnosing) we conducted 16 semi-structured and open-ended interviews with participants of SME from different sectors: software development, web design / advertisement, trade, storage, hardware construction and training. Additionally, we had two participants from large scale enterprises. These and the participant from the training company were supposed to be 'consumers' of IT while the others were supposed to be 'suppliers'. In case of the IT suppliers, which were mainly rather small enterprises, most of the participants were founders and directors of their own companies. The participants of the two large enterprises were an IT manager of a regional brewery and a director of quality management of a switchboard manufacturer, respectively. In a later stage of the interview, interviewees were given a brief outline of our concept of network support by a dedicated search engine. The interviews were recorded by a tape recorder with the participants' agreement.

In a further step, we analyzed the interviews and generated requirements for the BF system. From that, we developed the basic concept of the BF, a central database containing rich keyword-based profiles of regional companies that can be requested via a web front-end (action planning). We implemented BF following the requirements and integrated it into the DRC system (action taking). To evaluate the BF system, we first compared its results to those of existing search engines – Google, Google Maps and the former DRC. As part of another interview session (evaluation), we presented BF to four potential users from regional companies of the media and IT sector. We finally interpreted and summarized the results (specifying / learning). The subsequent sections will describe the essential results of the steps 2, 3 and 4 in more detail.

3.2. Requirement for cluster support

While most of the business transactions, as mentioned above, are accomplished with partners from outside the region, the participants expressed their general willingness to transact with regional partners. However, especially for suppliers of immaterial, digital products (web designers or software developers who constitute a considerable part of our participants) it is easy to transfer their 'goods' over far distances, as interviewees stated. Hence, unlike other industry sectors, geographical proximity is no necessary precondition for cooperation. Besides this obvious argument concerned with the IT sector, other (more subtle) reasons for super regional cooperation were discussed. The companies were "too small and insignificant" to carry out large scale orders, as one participant stated. Similarly, another participant judged that regional companies were not likely to offer large scale orders which were the only orders they could profitably accept.

With regard to the selecting cooperation partners, participants stated that mutual trust between representatives was the main precondition for successful cooperation. In order to maintain the level of customer satisfaction, the actors value the cooperation partners' high quality demands that fit to their own demands. When former unknown partners shall be assessed, the actors rely heavily on oral recommendations given by trusted partners. As one interviewee states: “See, it works just about personal contacts or word-of-mouth recommendation, based on trust”.

We further asked the interviewees for their attitude on existing databases, search engines and yellow page directories. We found that all the companies that were covered by our inquiry had registered to numerous YP directories. However, from their experience participants were very sceptical about these this kind of systems: YP directories actually had little value measured against the effort of keeping the companies profiles up to date. At the same time the effort increases with the number of systems that companies were subscribed in. Merely two of the interviewees reported successful business transactions as a result of the system subscriptions. Hence, companies limit their efforts to a small number of well chosen systems.

Essential criteria of choosing YP directories that were given by participants are quality and up-to-dateness. Furthermore, the participants' impression of the operators in terms of maintenance and care is an important criterion. Again, trust towards the directories' operators appears to be a central factor. As one participant stated, he had lost trust in one directory after he discovered “…massive spelling mistakes in name or address […] such that you get the impression […] they try to make you update your profile”.

Controversy perspectives showed up concerned with the directories' focus. While some participants found highly specialized and sector specific directories useful, others demanded for comprehensiveness. In both cases completeness in terms of the covered companies and a critical mass of registered companies is required. At the same time, the actors worry about potential masses of advertisement (spam) that might go along with a large number of subscribers. Surprisingly with regard to their attitude towards existing databases (see above), all the interviewees expressed their interest and willingness to contribute to the BF after launching the first prototype.

The statements above illustrate that up-to-dateness and effort spent on maintaining it are central concerns to the participants. Hence, in order to minimize this effort, BF should be capable of automatically create and update profiles from existing data. This data, as interviewees stated, may consist of specific text documents related to the company like product specifications, advertisement, flyers, websites or newsletters. While some companies websites are updated rarely (one participant reported once in three years), newsletters – by definition – provide highly recent information about products, offers or services. Since many companies periodically send out newsletters, these appear to be a promising source of relevant and recent information about the company.

With regard to indicating sources of data, privacy concerns apparently had to be discussed as well. From the interviews we learned that product specifications, flyers, advertising material or newsletters did not collide with privacy concerns, since these are public by definition. On the other hand, internal documents which may contain highly relevant information should not be accessed, even though only basic information would be stored (see below). Some participants stated that careful selection of relevant (locally stored) documents with respect to privacy concerns was no significant reduction of effort but rather a "shift of effort".

3.3. Business Finder: concept and implementation

From the results of the empirical study we derived a set of requirements for the design of the BF system. BF, as a recommender system for regional enterprises of the media and IT sector, should provide recent and comprehensive profiles of companies while the effort for creating and maintaining them should be minimized by utilizing existing sources of data that do not collide with the users privacy concerns. For instance, documents like product descriptions, advertising material, newsletters etc. are adequate resources.

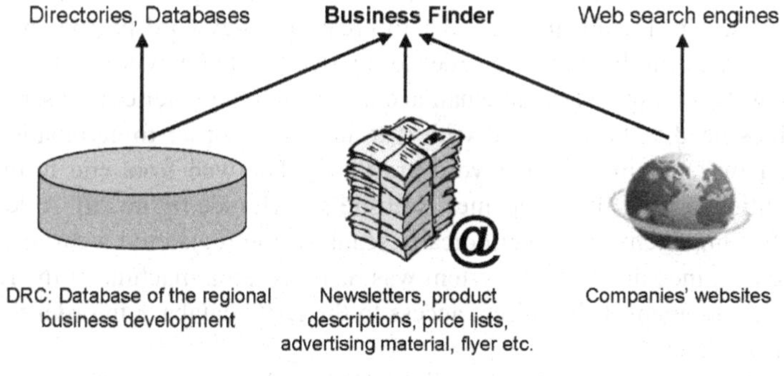

Figure 1. Basic concept of BF including three sources of data

Based on these requirements, we designed the BF system to meet the reqirements of the SME in the region of Siegen-Wittgenstein. BF can be regarded as a central database which stores keyword-based enterprise profiles and matches them against requests. Profiles consist of two types of data. First, *keyword profiles* (cf. Reichling et al. 2007) are an aggregate of the contents of arbitrary company specific documents and websites (see above). Second, *elementary data* is accessed which we obtain from the DRC. Hence, BF covers information from three sources of data: The DRC which is a traditional YP directory, Websites, which web search engines like Google or Yahoo use and arbitrary text documents chosen by responsible actors in the company. The latter two are regarded as analogue by their nature, so both are aggregated within the keyword profile. The concept of BF is shown in figure 1.

The implementation of BF is based on the *ExpertFinding* (EF) system (Reichling et al. 2007), an expertise recommender system for large or distributed enterprises. Its main purpose is creating awareness of activities, expertises and experiences of actors within an organization in order to foster transparency and collaboration of the staff. While EF is essentially knowledge management technology, from its purpose it is very similar to BF. The EF client system provides a software tool which allows users to easily select documents or folders from the local file system, specifying path, age, author and file format (typically doc, pdf, ppt, etc.). From these specifications EF creates keyword profiles which are an aggregate of the textual contents of all specified documents (cf. Reichling et al. 2007). For privacy concerns, all this takes place locally on the client machine. Users are given the opportunity to inspect and eventually correct their keyword profile before uploading it to the server.

As EF provides basic technology that can be used for BF as well, we decided to ground the BF on EF technology. Meanwhile, BF differs from EF in some elementary points: First, BF contains companies' profiles instead of user profiles (which is merely irrelevant from a technical point of view). Second, since arbitrary text documents, newsletters and websites are included, documents reach the server via manifold ways. 1) Via the web-based front-end (see figure 2a) users can select and upload single documents[1] in order to create the keyword profile. As in EF, keyword profiles can be edited in order to remove single keywords. 2) In order to receive newsletters, we set up an email account which the letter can be sent to – so mailing lists need to be extended with that address in order to automatically include the newsletter into the keyword profile. 3) The web front-end further provides facilities to enter the companies' website's URL (see figure 2a). A dedicated server side component of BF periodically scans all the registered websites, just as web search engines do. The BF system was installed on a machine at the regional business development. It has direct access to the DRC database in order to access its elementary data.

Figure 2b shows the searching facility of BFs web front-end. The way it works is analogous to web search engines and needs no further explanation. Exemplary, figure 2b shows the search results for the search term *Werbung* (*advertisement*). Multiple keywords can be entered as well. The semitransparent tooltip in figure 2b shows further details about the search results. Since rich data of the companies is stored, tooltips appeared to be a suitable way of visualizing.

---

[1] The BF prototype allows for uploading single documents. Eventual later version should support upload of entire folders as well

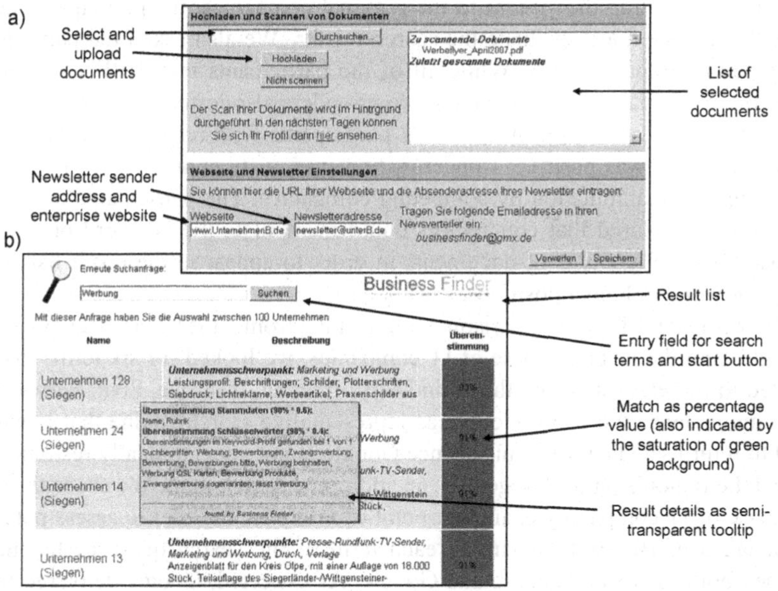

Figure 2. a) Uploading documents and specifying URL of the companies' websites and b) Result list of matching companies

3.4. Evaluation of the Business Finder

In March 2007, BF was presented to representatives of regional economy and launched shortly afterwards. We evaluated the design of BF on two levels. First, we presented the application to four different companies. Two of them were regional small-sized IT companies which offered software products and services. The other two companies, a large brewery and a producer of switching cabinets, both large scale enterprises which demand IT services on the regional market. In a second phase, we did a comparative analysis of search results created by BF and those of Google, Google Maps and two regional databases for IT companies[2]. It should be mentioned that at the time of the evaluation elementary data from the former DRC and websites were the only input to BF to create profiles from. No further documents like advertising materials or newsletters were used. Hence, the participating companies did not have any efforts to create their profiles (by means of selecting appropriate documents).

[2] The first database was given by DRC, the second database was the search engine hosted by the regional department of the Chamber of Industry and Commerce (*Industrie- und Handelskammer*, IHK)

When presenting the system to the regional companies, the participants could try out the system and evaluate the search results. We also asked the participants for potential improvements. While all of the participants tested BF's search engine, the participants from the IT service providers also tested the profile creation facilities. The overall judgement of the participants with respect to usability and profile creation was positive. Concerns, however, were expressed with regard to the danger of manipulation by competing companies. The participants of the two IT companies feared that competitors could manipulate the keyword profiles by uploading large amounts of documents in order to appear in the result lists more frequently and in higher positions.

To evaluate BF in comparison with results from other search engines, i.e. Google and the local database of IT companies, we looked for six terms that we judged to be relevant within the IT industry; Internet, database, PHP, Server, programming, Java. We chose Google as representative search engine that is widely said to return satisfactory results. Since Google is not geographically restricted we added the region's name "Siegen" as an additional search term. We chose the local database of IT companies as another point of reference in order to assess potential advantages of BF. With regard to each term of the search queries, BF outperformed both the local database and Google. As expected, Google delivered many results which were not hosted by companies.

Participants expressed some scepticism with regard to the choice of search terms. They found them too unspecific. Therefore, they were asked to enter arbitrary keywords they found relevant to find a specific local IT company – the IT companies' participants aimed at finding their own companies via BF and entered related keywords. In each case, this company was among the top five BF results. Google and the local database of IT companies performed worse. Looking for his own company, one participant of an IT company expressed satisfaction with BF's results, especially when considering that they did not have to input or update his profile: "…because you see, I was found even though I did not maintain any profile" (see above).

In a second evaluation phase, we carried out a comparative search analysis with regard to the findings recall and precision. We compared the search findings of Google, Google Maps and two local databases for IT companies using 10 IT relevant search terms. Again, we added the region's name as a search term in the cases of Google and Google-Maps. We took the 20 topmost results as representative for the search engines' results. Recall denotes the ratio of relevant results to the overall number of (potential) relevant results. Precision is defined as the ratio between the relevant results and the number of results. A result was judged to be of "relevance" in case the company was located in the Siegen-Wittgenstein region and fits the search term(s). Figure 3 gives an impression of the BF performance compared to the other four search engines.

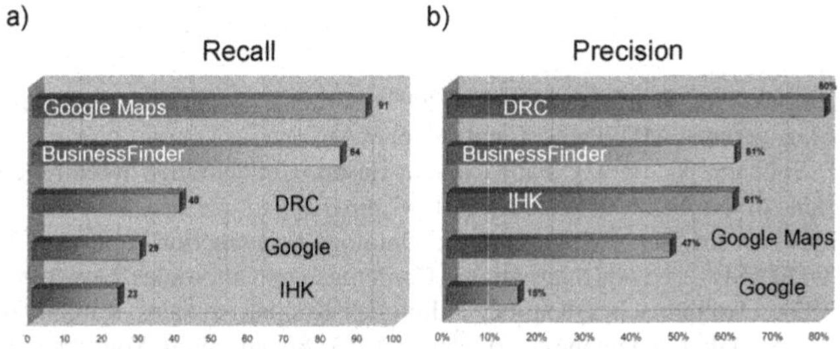

Figure 3. a) Recall and b) Precision of the search engines

With regard to both dimensions – recall and precision – BF is doing well, even though in each dimension it was outperformed by one competitor. While Google Maps appears to have the best recall (figure 3a) it does not perform well with regard to precision (figure 3b). Only 47% of its results were actually regional companies. One of the regional databases (DRC) does best with regard to precision, which is not too surprising since all of its entries are by definition from the Siegen-Wittgenstein region. However, it does not perform well with regard to recall since there are quite some companies which are not registered in the database. Combining the results for recall and precision, BF performs best.

The results of the evaluation further confirm the findings of the prestudy. The interviewees' already hinted to the fact that the existing databases of regional IT companies do not cover a sufficient amount of subscribed companies and hence do not offer a critical mass. Even if companies are registered, they may not be found due to the poor profiles kept in the database.

4. Conclusions

Our study in the IT sector of the Siegen-Wittgenstein region indicates that awareness among companies can foster regional networks. To offer awareness, BF created a company's profile from public, semi-public and private documents and data. An early evaluation shows pretty good precision and recall measured compared to existing web search engines (Google, Google Maps) and local databases (DRC and IHK). Given that the input to BF was restricted in this study to the companies' websites and DRC information, this is a quite remarkable result.

Future work will have to investigate into the use of BF in practise and its impact on interconnectedness and cooperation among regional companies. Our study indicates that cooperation is often hampered due to presumptions on regional companies' potential contract volume. BF may correct some of these presumptions.

References

Ackerman, M.; Pipek, V.; Wulf, V. (Hrsg.) (2003): Preface to Sharing Expertise: Beyond Knowledge Management, MIT-Press, Cambridge, MA.

Balabanovic, M, Shoham, Y. (1997): Fab: Content-Based, Collaborative Recommendation, in Communications of the ACM, vol. 40, no. 3, 1997, 66-72.

Blomqvist E. (2007): OntoCase - A Pattern-based Ontology Construction Approach. In: Proc. of OTM 2007: ODBASE - The 6th International Conference on Ontologies, November 25-30

Bourdieu, P (1983): Ökonomisches Kapital, kulturelles Kapital, soziales Kapital, in Kreckel, Reinhard (Hg.): Soziale Ungleichheiten, Opladen 1983 (Soziale Welt, Sonderband 2) S. 183-198.

Donhauser, S. (2006): Aktivierung von Wachstumspotenzialen durch Netzwerke - Clusterbildung in Baden-Württemberg. In: Statistisches Monatsheft Baden-Württemberg 4, S. 18-23.

Flick, U. (2002): Qualitative Sozialforschung : Eine Einführung, Rowohlt Taschenbuch Verlag, Hamburg.

Hinds, P. J. and Pfeffer, J. (2003): Why Organizations Don't "Know What They Know", in Sharing Expertise - Beyond Knowledge Management, MIT Press, Cambridge, 2003, pp. 3-26.

Huysman M., Wulf, V. (2004): Social Capital and Information Technology. MIT-Press, Cambridge, MA 2004.

Huysman, M.; Wulf, V. (2006): IT to Support Knowledge Sharing in Communities: Towards a Social Capital Analysis, Journal of Information Technology (JIT), Vol. 21, No. 1, pp. 40-51

Krätke, S.; Scheuplein, C. (2001): Produktionscluster in Ostdeutschland: Methoden der Identifizierung und Analyse -Kurzfassung- Eine Studie im Auftrag der Otto Brenner Stiftung. Berlin.

Leuninger, S; Held, H (2003): Kommunale Wirtschaftsförderung im Umbruch – Kundenmanagement in Bestandsentwicklung und im Standortmarketing praxisorientiert umsetzen. In: Standort – Zeitschrift für Angewandte Geographie (2003) 4, S. 161-166.

Porter, M. E. (1998): Clusters and the New Economics of Competition. In: Edward, Elgar (Eds.): Systems of Innovation: Growth, Competitiveness and Employment. MPG Books Ltd., Cornwall 2000, S. 309-322.

Porter, M. E. (2000): Locations, Clusters, and Company Strategy. In: Clark, G. L.; Feldman, M. P.; Gertler, M. S. (Eds.): Oxford Handbook of Economic Geography. Oxford University Press, New York, S. 253-274.

Reichling, T., Veith M. (2005): Expertise Sharing in a Heterogeneous Organizational Environment. In: Proc. of the 9th ECSCW. Springer, Dordrecht 2005, S. 325-345.

Reichling, T, Veith, M.. Wulf, V. (2007): Expert Recommender: Designing for a Network Organization, in: Computer Supported Cooperative Work: The Journal of Collaborative Computing (JCSCW), Vol. 16, No. 4 – 5, 2007

Resnick, P., Varian, H. R. (1997): Recommender systems. Communications of the ACM, special issue, vol. 40, 1997, 56-58

Schiele, H. (Hrsg.) (2003): Der Standort-Faktor. Wie Unternehmen durch regionale Cluster ihre Produktivität und Innovationskraft steigern. Wiley-VCH Verlag, Weinheim 2003.

Sölvell, Ö., Lindqvist, G., Ketels, C. (2003): The Cluster Initiative Greenbook. Bromma tryck AB, Stockholm 2003.

Susman, G., Evered, R. (1978): An assessment of the scientific merits of action research, Administrative Science Quarterly, 23, 582-603

Wolfe, D. A. (2002): Social Capital and Cluster Development in Learning Regions. In: Holbrook, J. Adam; Wolfe, David Alexander (Eds.): Knowledge, Clusters and Learning Regions. Queen's University, Kingston.

Wulf, V., Rohde, M. (1995): Towards an integrated organization and technology development, in Proc. of the conference on Designing interactive systems: processes, practices, methods, & techniques, 1995, ACM Press, New York, pp. 55-64.

Knowledge Management Capability Framework

Birinder Sandhawalia[1] **and Darren Dalcher**[2]

[1] School of Computing Science, Middlesex University, UK, b.sandhawalia@mdx.ac.uk
[2] School of Computing Science, Middlesex University, UK, d.dalcher@mdx.ac.uk

Abstract: This paper presents a Knowledge Management Capability framework based upon an empirical case study conducted at a CMM Level 5 software project organisation. The paper discusses the development of the organisation's knowledge management (KM) initiative from its initial state, to an organisational state where the KM practices are institutionalised and embedded within the daily activities and work methods of the organisation. The organisation's KM initiative is analysed through the development of two KM capabilities, namely infrastructure and processes, which were examined in depth while conducting the case study, and form the basis for the KM Capability Framework. The resulting framework helps organisations to analyse any imbalance that may exist in their KM initiative and needs to be addressed. In doing so, the framework benefits organisations in making corrections and restoring balance between their KM infrastructure and process capabilities, thereby improving the path of successful KM implementation towards a state of organisational KM capability.

Keywords: Knowledge, Knowledge management (KM), Knowledge management capabilities, Knowledge management infrastructure, Knowledge management processes, Knowledge Management Capability Framework

1. Introduction

Software project organisations need to leverage their existing knowledge and create new knowledge to be able to innovate and compete effectively. In order to achieve this, organisations must develop the ability to facilitate the flow of knowledge within the development processes of their software projects (Styhre 2003). This research conducted an in-depth case study of a CMM Level 5 software organisation, named XYZ, to identify and analyse the key knowledge management infrastructure and processes required to support and facilitate the flow of knowledge across projects within the organisation. A CMM Level 5 certification was considered important and relevant to ensure that the organisation practiced mature software development processes. Gold et al (2001) and Khalifa and Liu (2003) include leadership, top management support, knowledge culture, and IT

Please use the following format when citing this chapter:

Sandhawalia, B. and Dalcher, D., 2008, in IFIP International Federation for Information Processing, Volume 270; *Knowledge Management in Action*; Mark Ackerman, Rose Dieng-Kuntz, Carla Simone, Volker Wulf; (Boston: Springer), pp. 165–180.

capability in the form of repositories, asset libraries, intranet portal and collaborative technology as knowledge infrastructure. Alavi and Leidner (2001) list knowledge creation, storage, retrieval, transfer and application as knowledge processes. While conducting the case study, the researcher observed and examined how these knowledge processes manifested in the form of training, mentorship, interaction, feedback, collaboration and application while developing software at XYZ.

The knowledge management initiative at XYZ started as a concept and is now developing into a state where knowledge management practices are being increasingly institutionalised and embedded into the daily work practices and methods of the organisation. For a knowledge management initiative to achieve such an organisational state, the knowledge infrastructure and process capabilities also need to develop from an initial state of low availability, accessibility, usage and practice to a state of organisational capability of high availability, accessibility, usage and practice (Gold et al 2001, Khalifa and Liu 2003). This research adopts KM infrastructure and processes as two dimensions of KM capabilities, and the following sections explain the rationale for adopting them to analyse development of KM capabilities.

2. KM Infrastructure Capabilities

Gold et al (2001) identify information technology, organisational structure, and culture as infrastructure capabilities, and acquisition, conversion, application and protection as process capabilities. Khalifa and Liu (2003), while advancing Gold et al's (2001) proposition, establish leadership, culture and KM strategy as infrastructure required to develop a knowledge management initiative.

Information technology is an infrastructure capability as it facilitates knowledge flow and eliminates barriers to communication within an organisation. A flexible organisational structure encourages knowledge sharing and collaboration across boundaries within the organisation, while a rigid structure often has the unintended consequence of inhibiting such practices. Organisational structure capability for facilitating knowledge flow is also shaped by the organisation's policies, processes, and system of rewards and incentives, which determine the channels from which knowledge is accessed and how it flows (Leonard 1995). An organisation's culture is central to encourage interaction and collaboration between individuals that are important to facilitate knowledge flow, and also provides individuals the ability to self-organise their own knowledge and practice networks to facilitate solutions for problems and share knowledge (O'Dell and Grayson 1998). Organisational vision, mission and values embody the culture of the organisation and determine the types of knowledge that are desired and the types of knowledge related activities that are encouraged (Leonard 1995). Leadership sets the overall concept and implementation plan for the knowledge management initiative and obtains commitment from individuals to achieve the desired objectives and outcome. The KM leader helps create the appropriate culture to accomplish the knowledge vision and strategy of the organisation. The knowledge management strategy identifies the knowledge requirements and how they are to be fulfilled in congruence with the strategic goals of the organisation.

3. KM Process Capabilities

The knowledge management processes of an organisation are focused towards obtaining, sharing, storing, and using knowledge. Examples of these aspects of knowledge management processes within literature are: capture, transfer, and use (DeLong 1997); acquire, collaborate, integrate, experiment (Leonard-Barton 1995); create, transfer, assemble, integrate, and exploit (Teece 1998); create, transfer, use (Spender 1996, Skyrme and Amidon 1998); create, process (Ivers 1998); create, store; transfer and apply (Alavi and Leidner 2001); acquire, convert, apply, protect (Gold et al 2001). An examination of the characteristics of knowledge process capabilities enable them to be grouped into the four broad dimensions of knowledge creation, conversion, transfer and application.

Knowledge creation, as suggested by Nonaka and Takeuchi's (1995) SECI model, is enabled by the processes and activities of interaction, feedback, innovation, brainstorming, and benchmarking. Knowledge conversion (Nonaka and Takeuchi 1995) is made possible through the processes and activities of synthesising, refinement, integration, combination, coordination, distribution and restructuring of knowledge. Shared contexts and common representation are required for knowledge conversion, and mechanisms for facilitating the same are group problem solving and decision-making. Information technologies like email, repositories, intranet portal, teleconferencing, and the activities of mentoring, collaboration and training play a key role in transferring knowledge. Forums such as communities of practice (Wenger and Snyder 2000) and centres of excellence, and training provide a platform for the transfer of knowledge. Knowledge is effectively applied during the developmental processes of an organisation through rules and directives, routines and self-organised teams. Knowledge is applied to formulate and refine the standards, procedures and processes developed to execute tasks within the organisation.

4. Development of KM Capabilities at XYZ

The above knowledge processes are dynamic and highly interdependent and intertwined. At any point of time and in any part of an organisation, individuals and teams maybe engaged in several different aspects of these knowledge processes. The main focus of the knowledge processes is to facilitate the flow of knowledge between individuals, and consequently teams, and the major challenge for any knowledge management initiative is to facilitate these flows so that the maximum amount of transfer occurs. Styhre (2003) views knowledge as what emerges in the notion of knowing within a "processual perspective of knowledge that conceives of knowledge as both what is manifested in practices and simultaneously endowed within a conceptual framework." Styhre (2003) states that knowledge exists throughout an organisation and is not a clearly bounded and manageable resource that can be located in one single point in time and space. In other words, knowledge is fluid and emergent, and not fixed and stable, and being fluid and moving, it is embedded in social relationships, and emerges in practices and the use of concepts.

In order to make knowledge available throughout an organisation, knowledge management process capability needs be fully leveraged, and this is not possible without the presence of knowledge management infrastructure capability. Gold et al (2001) state that "the presence of both knowledge management process and infrastructural capabilities is critical to reach the intended knowledge management objectives." Appropriate knowledge management infrastructure needs to be implemented to routinise knowledge management processes and practice and to enhance knowledge application in daily business procedures, Grant (1996).

As organisations implement knowledge management initiatives, the knowledge management infrastructure and processes develop. One might expect the development of these knowledge management infrastructure and processes would progress smoothly and in congruence with each other, from an initial state to an organisational state where the KM capabilities are embedded in the daily activities and work practices of the organisation. The path of such an ideal development is represented in Figure 1 where KM infrastructure capability development is represented on the *y*-axis and KM process capability is represented along the *x*-axis of the graph and both capabilities progress from low to high along their respective axis. The ideal, congruent development of both capabilities is represented by arrow *q*, which depicts a smooth progress from an initial to an organisational state.

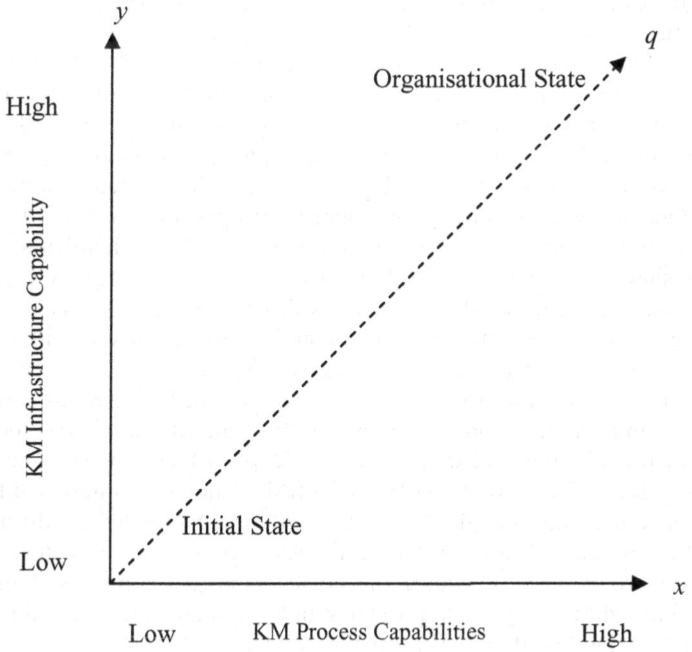

Figure 1. KM Capabilities

4.1. The Initial State

However, the research observed that in actual practice at XYZ the path taken during the development of KM capabilities was not smooth and ideal, as represented by arrow *q*. The KM initiative at XYZ evolved from the initial practice of documents stored in physical libraries. Individuals were, perhaps unknowingly, performing knowledge process activities while referring to these documents and past project data, and interacting with colleagues. While XYZ always possessed leadership, the organisational structure, culture, vision, and use of collaborative technology also evolved over a period of time. The creation of a central repository marked the beginning of a determined effort to harness the use of technology to improve the efficiency and productivity of existing and future projects. The realisation of the benefits of such efforts motivated senior management at XYZ to explore further possibilities and create a knowledge vision, thus signifying the initial state of development of KM infrastructure and process capabilities. During this stage XYZ defined what KM meant to it as an organisation, and made clear the concepts and objectives that it wanted to achieve by implementing a KM initiative. A KM strategy was developed ensuring that it was connected to other organisational needs and initiatives that already existed, and resources and infrastructure required to implement the initiative were identified.

Thereafter, XYZ started to develop the KM initiative, and consequently the infrastructure and process capabilities. The knowledge vision was translated into action by means of mission and value statements to encourage the growth of knowledge within the organisation. A knowledge culture of sharing was promoted and individuals encouraged to contribute, while project managers were expected to lead their teams in a learning environment of openness, trust and feedback. The introduction of collaborative technology was viewed as a significant step towards establishing the knowledge culture and to a certain extent a change in the organisational structure. The use of email, teleconferencing and bulletin boards were expected to promote collaboration and boundary crossing within department and development centres and hence reduce the silo effect of a previously more vertical structure. A central repository was developed to store process assets and process improvement proposals, while the intranet portal was developed to provide organisation wide dissemination of explicit knowledge (Polanyi 1967) and tools such as IPMS, EKMS, HRS, and CRM. Training was imparted to introduce and make individuals explicitly familiar with these knowledge infrastructure and capabilities. Knowledge sharing activities were made mandatory within the training programmes. However the emphasis on developing KM infrastructure capability while still providing training in knowledge process capability, resulted in high availability of this infrastructure to individuals within the organisation and is represented by arrow *i* in Figure 2 Arrow *i* depicts the actual progress of XYZ's KM initiative development, contrary to the expectation depicted in Figure 1, from a state of low infrastructure and process capability to a state where the emphasis on infrastructure capability development was greater than the practice of knowledge process capability. In other words, this state was characterised with a high availability and accessibility of infrastructure capability for individuals compared to the extent to which they were performing KM processes.

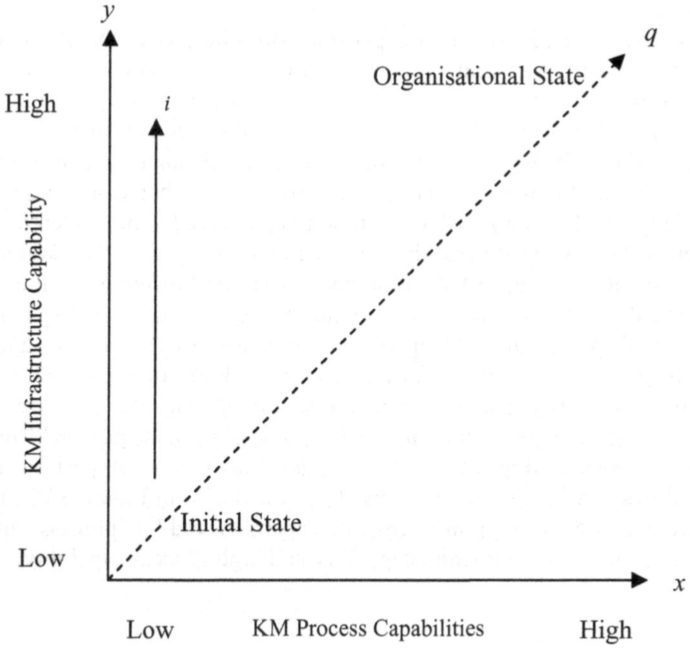

Figure 2. KM Infrastructure Development

4.2. The Deviation

When this researcher first visited and commenced research activities, the number of individuals employed by XYZ was 50,000. Thereafter, the researcher made numerous visits to XYZ over the course of the next two years by when the number of individuals employed by XYZ was 85,000. A senior Project Manager at XYZ stated that *"fifty percent of our new employees have been at XYZ for less than three years."* The rapid increase in the number of new employees was representative of XYZ's expansion strategy which was characterised with the acquisition and opening of development and delivery centres across the globe. This resulted in XYZ becoming a larger global organisation with employees from diverse background and cultures working in a more distributed environment. A small number of new employees were recruited as part of XYZ's strategy to employ *"bench strength that would provide a bigger talent pool."* The idea of employing 'bench strength' was that XYZ would provide individuals ongoing training and therefore have reserve skilled employee resources for job rotation, cover for absentees and starting new projects. However, the number of individuals employed as 'bench strength' was less that five percent of the total number of new employees.

The above mentioned rapid expansion had an effect on XYZ's KM initiative, and the infrastructure and process capabilities. New employees were provided with training to perform knowledge process capabilities as a part of their induction programme. However, when they were assigned to projects upon completing their training, the infrastructure capability proved inadequate and insufficient. There was a loss of knowledge richness due to the distributed and less face-to-face knowledge, and the knowledge assets were considered to be scattered. There was a perceived lack of 'teamness' that resulted in a coordination breakdown in project management activities. XYZ had to address cultural differences amongst globally distributed employees who had to adjust to new work practices. While the new employees' initial training helped overcome some of these issues and inculcated knowledge processes, the infrastructure capabilities of organisational structure, culture, information technology and KM strategy needed to be reassessed and improved upon. This resulted in XYZ's possessing inadequate KM infrastructure capability compared to the number of employees seeking to perform KM process capabilities. The progression to this state is depicted in Figure 3 by arrow *p* from the previous state of high infrastructure capability and low process capability, to a new state of low infrastructure capability and high process capability.

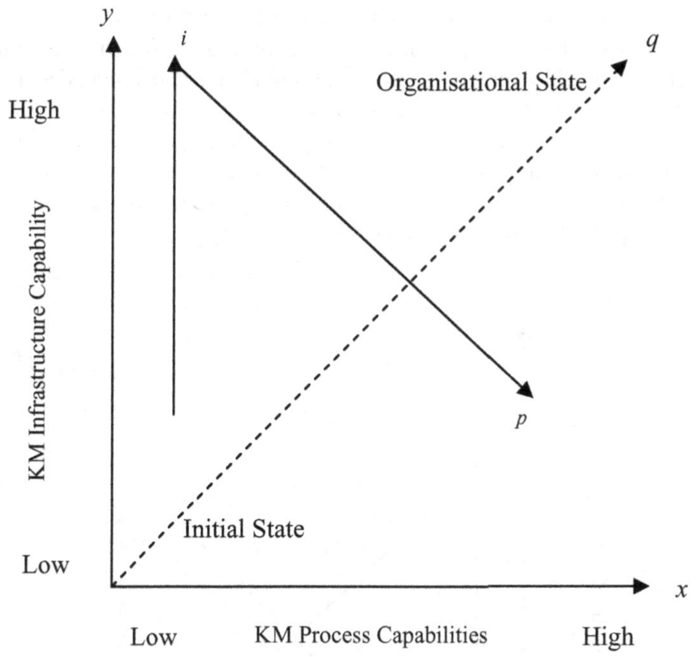

Figure 3. KM Process Capability Development

4.3. The Correction

Having recognised the problem, XYZ addressed the issues presented by the state of low infrastructure capability and high process capability by increasing site visits and travel of individuals amongst different development and delivery centres, having local, acculturated knowledge champions and interaction among them at the regional and corporate level, encouraging regional and virtual communities of practice, and also starting regional and corporate centres of excellence. XYZ attempted to create a combination of both "top-down and bottom-up knowledge culture." The knowledge champions were made responsible of ensuring that knowledge created at the global development and delivery centres, was made available to the local or regional centres and the overall knowledge owner at the corporate level. The existing EKMS was upgraded to a new knowledge management system (KMS) which as mentioned by a senior group lead during an interview, *"consolidated all scattered knowledge assets into one system that caters to the global needs of 85,000 diverse employees."* The people knowledge map was introduced as an integral part of the upgraded KMS to help identify experts and individuals with experience for projects with specific characteristics. The upgraded KMS was implemented, and along with the other measures mentioned above, was expected to be a catalyst that drives knowledge flow, and progresses XYZ to an organisational state of high infrastructure and process capability, where KM practices are institutionalised and embedded in the daily activities and processes of the organisation. This progress of XYZ's KM initiative from a state of low infrastructure capability and high process capability to a state high infrastructure and process capability is depicted by arrow *e* in Figure 4 completing the N-shaped journey to a higher organisational state in contract with the initial expectation of smooth transition.

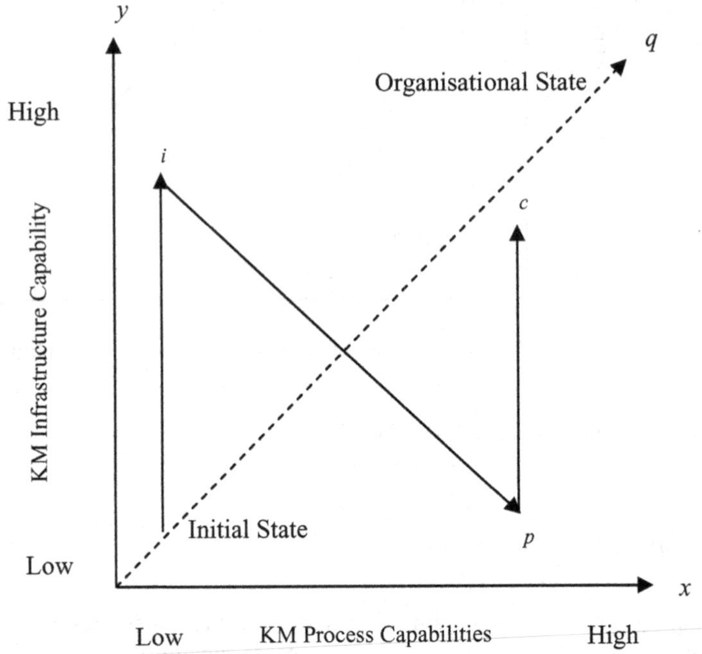

Figure 4. Towards an Organisational State of KM Capability Development

4.4. *Case Study Summary*

The implementation of the KM initiative at XYZ provides an example of how organisations need to balance the growth and development of KM processes and infrastructure while developing their KM programmes. Organisations expect a smooth path from conceptualising a KM initiative to its successful implementation. XYZ's experience highlights two stages within the implementation of its KM initiative when an imbalance existed between the KM infrastructure and process capabilities. When XYZ was developing the concept of the KM initiative after its initial conceptual stage, the organisation put an emphasis on developing the infrastructure. This resulted in greater availability of KM infrastructure capability than KM processes being practiced, even though training was introduced for these processes thereby representing a state of higher KM infrastructure capability and lesser KM process capability. Thereafter, with the addition of a number of employees and their training at induction, the KM infrastructure capability was inadequate to support the KM processes practiced by the individuals. This represented a state of greater KM processes being practiced and lesser KM infrastructure capability being available. XYZ started progressing towards a state of organisational KM capability after it addressed these imbalances.

5. KM Capability Framework

The above discussion highlights the issues faced by XYZ while developing a knowledge management initiative in order to mobilise and utilise its knowledge resources. While the findings pertain to a single organisation, they may also reflect the view of Eskerod and Skriver (2007) who studied the literature on knowledge transfer and identified persistent issues that impact such efforts suggesting a more general trend. Eskerod and Skriver (2007) state that "however…..many companies experience serious problems when trying to make knowledge transfer work." In the case of XYZ, the organisation struggled to make knowledge resources available to all individuals when it inducted a significant number of new employees. This problem is made apparent by the downward arrow *p* in Figures 3 and 4 when the KM infrastructure was found inadequate to support the knowledge needs of a larger number of organisational individuals. Thus Eskerod and Skriver's (2007) view helps understand the phenomenon observed at XYZ.

The discussion in Section 4 confirms that if an organisation conceptualises its KM programme in an initial state and intends to achieve an organisational state where the KM capabilities are institutionalised and embedded within the organisation's daily procedures, processes and practices, two other intermediate and distinct capability states also exist. One state is of higher KM infrastructure capability availability and lesser KM process being practiced, while the other state is of greater KM processes being practiced and lesser KM infrastructure capability being available. The four states are represented in Figure 5. Also represented in the figure is the ideal path an organisation would expect to progress along when launching a KM programme, and indirectly the possible paths along which their KM programme might progress during implementation. The path to implementing a KM programme does not progress directly and smoothly from the initial to organisational state as envisaged by XYZ, but might instead progress through either of the two intermediate states, or as in XYZ's case through both intermediate states. If an organisation initially lays more emphasis on developing its KM infrastructure capability it will progress to the state of higher KM infrastructure capability and lesser process capability before it can progress to an organisational state. On the other hand, if the organisation was to initially lay more emphasis on practicing KM processes it will progress to the state of greater process capability and lesser infrastructure capability and before being able to progress towards the organisational state. However, as XYZ's experience depicted, a large organisation could progress from one intermediate state to another before progressing towards the organisational state of KM capability. This is a very important observation because many organisations tend to launch knowledge management programmes without due consideration of the organisation's capabilities to guarantee any measure of success of implementation (Davenport et al 1998, Leonard 1995). As the case study evidence revealed, even one of the largest software project organisation with CMM Level 5 accreditation needs to coordinate its KM capability development to achieve a state of organisational knowledge management.

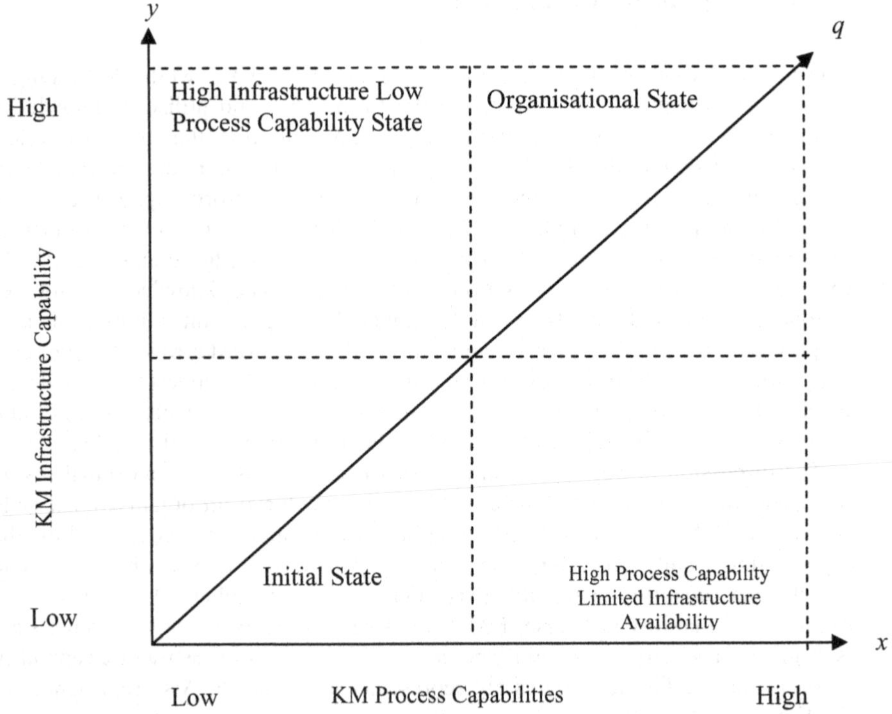

Figure 5. KM Capability Framework

The framework presented in Figure 5 depicts the possible states organisations may progress along while implementing their KM programmes. Organisations can benefit by referring to the framework to determine the progress of their KM programmes. The characteristics of each state described below will help organisations identify the current state of their knowledge management programmes.

5.1. Initial State

An organisation's KM programme can be considered to be in the initial state when the organisation is creating a knowledge vision and relating this vision to its strategic needs and other initiatives that already exist. During this state the organisation explores all possibilities related to the KM initiative and also the opportunities present. The organisation identifies the infrastructure required to support the initiative and the KM processes to be practiced. Financial support for the programme and other resources required to implement the programme are also identified and budgeted. An important activity or feature of this state is the top management's commitment to the KM initiative and development of a cross-functional team responsible to implement the programme. Within this state, management needs to communicate its knowledge vision across the organisation, and make individuals aware to the KM programme and its expected benefits.

5.2. High KM Infrastructure Capability

The KM programme is in the state of high infrastructure capability when there is an emphasis on developing the infrastructure. During this stage the knowledge vision is translated into action by means of mission and value statements to encourage the growth of knowledge within the organisation. A knowledge culture of sharing and learning is promoted with individuals encouraged to participate and contribute. The organisation reviews its policies and processes, and implements systems of rewards and incentives to motivate and reward knowledge sharing behaviour. During this state information technology support is developed in the form repositories and collaborative technologies. Through the linkage provided by collaborative technologies the organisation attempts to integrate previously fragmented flows of knowledge, Teece (1998). Collaboration technologies are developed to allow individuals within the organisation to collaborate, thereby eliminating the structural and geographical impediments that may have previously prevented such interaction. Knowledge discovery technologies are developed to allow the organisation to find new knowledge that is either internal or external to the firm. Knowledge mapping and application technologies are developed to enable the firm to effectively track sources of knowledge, creating a catalogue of internal organisational knowledge, and apply its existing knowledge. An organisation's KM programme could be considered to be in this state when individuals have access to the above mentioned infrastructure but do not avail themselves of its complete potential or capability, due to the lack of practicing knowledge processes.

5.3. High KM Process Capability

The KM programme can be considered to be in the state of high KM process capability when there is an emphasis on practicing knowledge processes. Openness and trust characterise the organisation's work environment and support knowledge sharing behaviours, which are included as an integral part of the training programmes. Communities of practice (Wenger and Snyder 2000) and centres of excellence evolve and individuals are encouraged to join and participate. Activities that establish an organisation's KM programme in a state of high knowledge process capability include identifying lessons learnt, best practices, benchmarking, brainstorming, group problem solving, mentoring and collaboration. The daily work processes support decision-making, feedback and interaction, which are made apparent in the team commitment. Knowledge champions from distributed centres meet regularly and knowledge flows across boundaries and development centres. Therefore an organisation would be in a state of high knowledge process capability and low infrastructure capability when the above mentioned knowledge processes are practiced but do not receive adequate support in the form of infrastructure support.

5.4. Organisational State of KM

An organisation will be in a state of organisational KM infrastructure and process capability when it achieves high availability of infrastructure capability to support frequent and regular practice of knowledge processes. In other words, knowledge processes are embedded in the daily routines, procedures and practices of the organisation which posses the knowledge infrastructure to support them. This state is characterised by a vibrant mix of vision, strategy, leadership, organisational structure, culture, technology infrastructure, and knowledge processes of creation, storage, retrieval, transfer, application and sharing. Forums such as communities of practice evolve and the organisational structure, culture, and technology support them. Lessons learnt are captured regularly and made available across the organisation, while best practices are implemented. Knowledge sharing and learning permeate the organisational environment of role models, mentoring, leadership, motivation, commitment, and training, where collaboration, feedback and interaction drive knowledge flow between individuals and teams. Acculturated knowledge champions and collaborative information technology support ensure that knowledge flows are not inhibited by organisational structures and distributed geographical locations, but instead flow across social networks and boundaries of the organisation. The knowledge flows ensure that the knowledge available within the organisation is current, integrated, usable, and applied. The organisation adopts a consistent approach to KM and it becomes a way of working within standardised work methods. Thus when KM is institutionalised within the organisation, the programme can be stated to be in the organisational state.

6. Conclusion

This paper presents a KM Capability Framework based upon a case study that identified the knowledge management infrastructure and process capabilities required to support and facilitate knowledge management practices within a software project organisation. The paper analyses the development of these KM infrastructure and process capabilities from an initial state to an organisational state. The analysis established that two other intermediate states exist, and identified the possible paths an organisation's KM capabilities development might progress along, and discusses the activities and characteristics of each state through which the implementation of organisational KM programmes could possibly progress. By assessing and focusing on the KM infrastructure and process capabilities and their characteristics that are being developed and practiced, organisations can determine the current state of their KM programme implementation. Not all organisations will manage to progress to the organisational state of KM in one smooth journey, as observed in the XYZ case study. The framework presented in this paper enables organisations to analyse if their KM programme is more focused towards developing KM infrastructure capability rather than KM process capability, or whether limited KM infrastructure is available for the KM processes being practiced. The framework helps organisations to better understand the issues related to developing a KM initiative, as suggested by Eskerod and Skriver (2007), and analyse any imbalance that may exist and needs to be addressed. In doing so, the framework benefits organisations interested in making corrections and restoring the balance between KM infrastructure and process capability, thereby smoothening the path of successful KM implementation towards a state of organisational KM capability.

References

Alavi, M and Leidner, D.E, 'Knowledge Management and Knowledge Management Systems: Conceptual Foundations and Research Issues,' MIS Quarterly Vol 25 No 1, pp 107-136, March 2001.

Davenport, T.H and Prusak, L, 'Working Knowledge,' Harvard Business School Press, Boston, 1998.

DeLong, D, 'Building the Knowledge Based Organization: how Culture Drives Knowledge Behaviours,' Working Paper, Ernst & Young's Centre for Business Innovation, Boston, 1997.

Eskerod, P and Skriver, H.J, 'Organizational Culture Restraining In-house Knowledge Transfer Between Project Managers-A Case Study,' Project Management Journal, vol. 38, no. 1, pp. 110-122, March 2007.

Gold, A.H, Malhotra, A, and Segars, A.H, 'Knowledge Management: An Organizational Capabilities Perspective,' Journal of Management Information Systems, Vol18, No 1, pp 185-214, Summer 2001.

Grant, R.M, 'Prospering in Dynamically-Competitive Environments: Organizational Capability as Knowledge Integration,' Organization Science Vol7 No 4, pp 375-387, July-August, 1996.

Ivers, J, 'Bringing Out Brilliance: Enabling Knowledge Creation in the Notes/Domino Environment, Enterprise Solutions, pp 24-27, November/December 1998.

Khalifa, M, and Liu, V, Determinants of Successful Knowledge Management Programs, Electronic Journal on Knowledge Management, Vol 1, No 2, pp 103-112, 2003.

Leonard-Barton, D, 'Wellsprings of Knowledge: Building and Sustaining the Source of Innovation,' Harvard Business School Press, Boston, 1995.

Nonaka, I and Takeuchi, H, 'The Knowledge Creating Company: How Japanese Companies Create the Dynamics of Innovation,' Oxford University Press, New York, 1995.

O'Dell, C. and Grayson, C, "If only we knew what we know: Identification and transfer of internal best practices," California Management Review Vol. 40, No. 3, pp. 154-174, 1998.

Polanyi, M, 'The Tacit Dimension,' Routledge and Keon Paul, London, 1967.

Skyrme, D, and Amidon, D, 'New Measures of Success,' Journal of Business Strategy, pp 20-24, January/February 1998.

Spender, J.C, 'Making Knowledge the Basis of a Dynamic Theory of the Firm,' Strategic Management Journal Vol 17, pp 45-62, Special Issue 1996.

Styhre, A, 'Knowledge Management beyond codification: knowing as practice/concept,' Journal of Knowledge Management, Vol 7 No 5, pp 32-40, 2003.

Teece, D, 'Capturing Value from Knowledge Assets: the New Economy, Markets for Know-How and Intangible Assets,' California Management Review, Vol 40, No 3, pp 55-79, 1998.

Wenger, E, and Snyder, W, 'Communities of Practice: The Organizational Frontier,' Harvard Business Review, Vol 78, No 1, pp 139-145, 2000.

DYONIPOS: Proactive Support of Knowledge Processes

Silke Weiß[1], Josef Makolm[2], and Doris Reisinger[3]

[1] Federal Ministry of Finance, Austria, silke.weiss@bmf.gv.at
[2] Federal Ministry of Finance, Austria, josef.makolm@bmf.gv.at
[3] m2n consulting and development gmbh, Austria, reisinger@m2n.at

Abstract: The success of knowledge-intensive organizations depends significantly on the degree of knowledge availability, knowledge transparency, knowledge structuring, and knowledge up-to-dateness. The research project DYONIPOS (DYnamic Ontology based Integrated Process OptimiSation) meets these challenges: DYONIPOS sets up a context sensitive, intelligent and agile assistant based on the development of semantic and generic knowledge discovery technologies [6]. The assistant supports the knowledge workers just in time and automatically with the currently needed knowledge, without additional work and violation of knowledge workers privacy. Furthermore an individual and a global process- and knowledge base is built-on.

This article is structured as follows: Section 1 addresses the relation between the applied approach and the challenge in e-Government, summarizes the aims of the research project DYONIPOS and emphasizes the motivation. In Section 2 the semantic and knowledge discovery technologies used are presented. The article concludes with the presentation of the use-case project, showing current results of the project.

Keywords: Knowledge management, Knowledge work support, Semantic technologies, Research project DYONIPOS, Use-case, Public administration

Please use the following format when citing this chapter:

Weiβ, S., Makolm, J. and Reisinger, D., 2008, in IFIP International Federation for Information Processing, Volume 270; *Knowledge Management in Action*; Mark Ackerman, Rose Dieng-Kuntz, Carla Simone, Volker Wulf; (Boston: Springer), pp. 181–193.

1. The Research Project DYONIPOS

E-Government means not only the use of information technology to improve the exchange of service and information with citizens or businesses. E-Government also means the use of information technologies to improve internal information, data and service quality. Public administration work is knowledge work par excellence, because information of governmental organizations is widely scattered and civil servants are confronted with an overload of information. An improvement can be generated e.g. through regulation and support of knowledge processes, which ensures the supply of administration processes with knowledge. The knowledge of an organization can be classified into three kinds of information: public domain knowledge, partly available knowledge and tacit knowledge. These three kinds of knowledge are mostly produced or at least organized by the knowledge workers and are required to carry out their processes. The present knowledge is often unstructured, intransparent and far-scattered, e.g. public domain knowledge is available for all knowledge workers. This knowledge is often stored online on the intra-or internet and accessible through search engines or knowledge databases. Partly available knowledge is only accessible for individual or specific groups of knowledge workers. This kind of knowledge is often stored on the employee's PC or the organization's server. The third kind of knowledge – tacit knowledge – is in the minds of employees and therefore only available to the owner of the knowledge. For a knowledge worker it is very difficult and time-consuming to find the adequate knowledge in the existing overload of information, which supports the achievement of his work steps. Furthermore if tacit knowledge is needed, the receipt of required resources depends on chance. The research project DYONIPOS meets these challenges. Its aim is to provide personal, agile and proactive support for the knowledge worker by means of proactive, context-sensitive knowledge delivery on the one hand and by suggestion of next process steps on the other hand. Furthermore DYONIPOS creates and continuously updates an individual as well as an organizational knowledge base. This knowledge base makes the organization's growing knowledge available. DYONIPOS provides all kinds of knowledge that has been released for the organizational knowledge database, assumed that the user has the right to access this knowledge. Knowledge not released to the organizational knowledge base is just available in a knowledge workers individual knowledge base. This knowledge is still only available for his owner. Furthermore DYONIPOS identifies tacit knowledge; the identified knowledge will be supplied through transfer of the name of the information owner. For ensuring data protection only the name of persons which are stored in a "whitelist" will be supplied. Only DYONIPOS users are stored in the "whitelist". Another aim is to support the process engineer through information about the recorded ad hoc processes, e.g. visualization of the workflow and process, landscape visualization of similar tasks and sub processes. A task is part of a set of actions which accomplish a job, problem or assignment. The process engineer can use this information for improving standard processes or compiling statistics [6]. The DYONIPOS research project started on January, 2, 2006, and it will be completed by the end of the first quarter of 2008. The DYONIPOS research consortium consists of m2n consulting and development gmbh[1], Know-Center Graz[2], the Institute for Information Systems and Computer Media (IICM) of the Graz University of Technology[3] as well as HP Austria[4]. Together they are developing the prototype DYONIPOS. The DYONIPOS research project is financed by the "semantic systems" program within FIT-IT, an Austrian research program provided by the Federal Ministry of Transport, Innovation and Technology (BMVIT)[5]. The proposal of the DYONIPOS project was awarded as the best proposal of the regarding call. In order to ensure the applicability of DYONIPOS, a parallel use-case project is carried out by the Austrian Federal Ministry of Finance (BMF).

2. Knowledge Discovery and Semantic Technologies

DYONIPOS is based on automatic and semiautomatic knowledge management methods and technologies e.g. knowledge discovery, semantic systems, knowledge flow analysis, and process visualization. The semantic technologies qualify as enabling technology to handle structured as well as unstructured parts and data of knowledge intensive processes [5]. DYONIPOS begins with the recording of all interactions between the user and his computer; these are the so called "events", e.g. mouse clicks or key strokes. Several events belonging to a logical unit are grouped together into event-blocks by using predefined rules. Similar event blocks form semantic sets are assigned to knowledge worker`s tasks. The assignment initially has to be done by the user, but after the training phase in which DYONIPOS learns the classification features, a task will automatically be detected. The events, event-blocks and tasks are represented and stored with semantic technologies (RDF) [2].

2.1. Functionality of DYONIPOS

The discovery of work patterns and the delivery of relevant information just in time are the major functions of DYONIPOS [10]. To provide these functions

---

1 http://www.m2n.at

2 http://en.know-center.at/

3 http://www.iicm.tu-graz.ac.at/rootcollection?timestamp=1188552118992

4 http://welcome.hp.com/country/uk/en/welcome.html

5 http://www.bmvit.gv.at/en/index.htm

DYONIPOS captures the knowledge work, discovers the tasks and processes and supports the knowledge worker with information.

The first challenge is the observation of knowledge worker`s interactions with- and reactions to the system and existing application data. This data is the so called low level sensor data on application and operating system level [5]. The second challenge is to develop adequate techniques to discover the work patterns and to support the users automatically with the information they need. The third challenge is to detect how knowledge workers can be effectively supported [5].

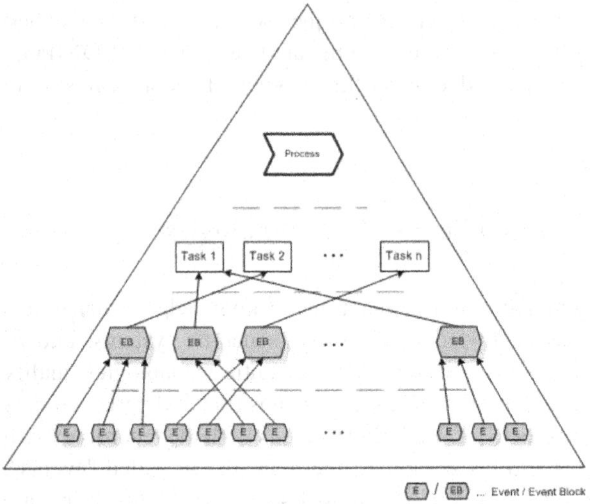

Fig 1: The semantic pyramid of DYONIPOS: all activities e.g. events, event blocks, tasks and process are modelled semantically and stored by RDF.

The semantic pyramid mapped in figure 1 displays the four different layers of the semantically modelled and stored data. The first layer is the event layer, the second layer is the event block layer, the third is the task layer and the layer at the top of the pyramid is the so called process layer. Only one single user executes an event while in the execution of processes different users can be involved. Each layer of the pyramid provides a different representation of the data regarding the semantic quality [5]. The semantic quality is a measure of accordance of the information document in the model with the mapped domain.

Below the specific steps required to capture the workers patterns are described. For capturing the workers patterns a java tool called DYONIPOS Task Recognizer has been implemented [5].

From user and system interactions to events…

DYONIPOS starts with the recording of all events. Different sensors of the context observer module observe all interactions of the user with the desktop environment. DYONIPOS uses a key logger program to record and log all recognized events [2]. The observed events e.g. keystrokes, mouse inputs or system events are stored in the so called event log. This monitored data are the base for discovering the work patterns.

...from events to event blocks...

The next step is to reduce the immense quantity of data and to assign events to event blocks by filtering and by relation analysis. Through filtering analysis it is possible to select the irrelevant data – e.g. mouse movements – from the relevant data. Mapping of a set of events to an event block is possible by relation analysis. Currently generic based rules, application based rules and web browser based rules are applied for mapping events to event blocks [5]. Generic rules are based on windows title, process, and application name. A reason for assignment of events to the same event block is the same windows title, process and application name. Application dependent events like reading and forwarding of an e-mail result in the same event block through appliance of the application based rules. Identification of similarity between URL`s is a sign for combination of the relevant events to event blocks. The implementation of further rules for mapping events to event blocks is easily extensible. An example for an event block is e.g. "start a file".

...from event blocks to tasks...

The utilized methods to learn task assignments are k-nearest neighbor classification, Support Vector Machines based on graph kernels (compare to 2.3) and the possibility of the classifier to learn task assignments from the user. Methods of extracting tasks are clustering based on similarity among content and structural features and the scatter/gather approach.

...from tasks to processes

The transition from tasks to processes emerges by combination of individual tasks which were conducted by a number of different knowledge workers. Similar methods as described in the part above will be used to learn the assignment from tasks to processes. To extract processes the application of the ProM Framework will be utilized (compare [5]).

2.2. Architecture of the DYONIPOS Task Recognizer

The DYONIPOS Task Recognizer consists of the context observer module, the task-recognizer module and the KnowMiner framework, which uses Apache Lucene, an open source java library. This tool supports the KnowMiner Framework by creation of the resource index. The context observer module is a C# program [7] and consists of different sensors. These sensors are able to send the observed low level operation system and application events based on XML in a specific event stream format to the context observer module. The server transfers the event streams to the task recognizer module. This module has the following purpose:

- Identification of tasks
- Revelation of information needs

- Discovery of used resources.

The KnowMiner Framework supports the mechanism of the task identification by classification and clustering algorithms. In addition the KnowMiner Framework is responsible for the resource indexing. The discovered information needs and resources, the observed events and identified event blocks, tasks and processes are semantically modelled, related and stored in the personal knowledge base, by RDF triple store (compare to [5]).

2.3. Classification of Task Instances via Graph Kernels

The objective of this chapter is to explain which techniques are applied for categorization of task instances to predefined task models and process instances to process models. The utilized techniques are Support Vector Machines. This technique allows the definition of the algorithm`s view in data by selecting the kernel [7]. Starting with the event blocks which consist of a sum of events stored in a RDF repository represented as a graph. Classification of event blocks to tasks is possible through determination of similarity based on common content, but this method is not enough to combine related task instances to task models. For example a user is writing a document which includes knowledge about two different scientific fields. Content information is not enough to classify the corresponding task instances into the same task, because the content of the task instances is different. Additional structural information is required. Structural information is information about the type of an event block e.g. which resources have been used or which person is involved. The type of different entity blocks provides valuable information for data mining [7]. The similarity of event blocks is determined by using graph kernels [1] and kernel methods for graphs [9] which allow processing of content and structure [7]. The assignment of event blocks to a knowledge worker task is performed by applying Support Vector Machines [13].

2.4. The Semantic Technology

DYONIPOS is a modern information system which supports the users by proactive delivery of contextual information (resources) while the knowledge workers are doing their daily work. The application of ontologies is useful in such a system, because they ensure interoperability and the development of "new" knowledge. Furthermore, ontologies can be used for the unambiguous description of information resources. As a consequence, RDF is a key technology of DYONIPOS. Resource Description Framework (RDF) is an ontology language, a formal language used to encode ontologies. An ontology represented in RDF language consists of:

- classes of entities (concepts) within a domain,
- properties of classes (relationships between the concepts),
- individuals belonging to classes and
- constraints on classes and properties [14].

An RDF-Statement or RDF-Triple is based on:

- the subject (resources),
- the predicate (property), and
- the object (value).

The subject identifies the described object, the predicate defines the data in the object, and the object represents the actual value [14]. All events, event-blocks and tasks described in section 2.1 are represented and stored by RDF-Triples [3]. This means all data extracted from metadata (e.g. from integrated applications), documents, presentations, e-mails etc. will be saved in a structured manner. For example, the DYONIPOS ontology consists of the concepts "Person", "Organization", "Document" and "Topic". An example for a concrete "Person" may be the employee John Q. Public. John Q. Public works at the Federal Ministry of Finance and has written some articles about semantic technologies. The circumstance described above results in the following concrete classifications: John Q. Public is an object of the concept "Person", the Federal Ministry of Finance is an object of the concept "Organization", all written articles are objects of the concept "Document", and the identified "Topic" is semantic technology. The following relationships exist between the objects: John Q. Public is employed by the Federal Ministry of Finance, John Q. Public is the author of some articles; John Q. Public deals with the topic of semantic technology. Further conclusions drawn are the following: John Q. Public is an expert in the topic of semantic technology and the Federal Ministry of Finance deals with the topic of semantic technologies. The newly learned knowledge – e.g. that John Q. Public is an expert in the topic of semantic technology – is a recognized resource of DYONIPOS. It should be mentioned that for privacy reasons only knowledge concerning persons who are registered DYONIPOS participants will be stored and supplied.

3. Use-Case Project

Parallel to the research project DYONIPOS the use-case project DYONIPOS is implemented in the Directorate General for Information Technology (DG-IT) of the Federal Ministry of Finance, Austria. Administration work is knowledge work par excellence, because the flood of information is immense and the existing knowledge is widely scattered. The knowledge workers of the administration need the following additional know-how to tackle the daily work:

- Where is the relevant information stored
- How can this information be found
- How relevant is the delivered information

The challenge is to provide the administrative employees automatically with the information they need. Consequently the above mentioned additional know-how is made available by DYONIPOS. The relevant information is stored in the internet and intranet, the server of the organisation or the fixed disc of each knowledge worker. DYONIPOS finds the information through detection of mouse clicks and key-board inputs. DYONIPOS assigns this information to a proper task and delivers the needed knowledge automatically in terms of documents, internet sites or DYONIPOS links the knowledge worker directly to the documents of the applications (ELAK). DYONIPOS delivers the information ordered by relevance.

Other objectives are to support the employees of the DG-IT without creation of additional work by means of knowledge management and to ensure the privacy of the knowledge workers. DYONIPOS supports this challenge. Due to this fact DYONIPOS will be used for efficiently and effectively supporting the daily work of the individual employees in the DG-IT. The DYONIPOS task recognizer supports the employees with the necessary knowledge which is produced by semantic cross-linking of the relevant information from the existing repositories and processes. Additionally, DYONIPOS independently develops new relations between the sources of knowledge. This explains, for example, that the DYONIPOS task recognizer at the one hand supports the user by visualization of existing documents, files or websites etc. and displays the new generated information such as the name of the person who has the specific know-how. The ministry respectively fifteen employees support the research consortium. Together they work on the realization of the research results and they ensure the transformation of current scientific results to an easily useable software solution. The staff of the ministry shares its domain specific know-how with the research consortium, by supporting the development of DYONIPOS base technologies.

Initial interviews with employees have been carried out to obtain an impression of the kind of work and how this work is done. The results of these interviews provide the information which sensors should be developed and which events the sensors should observe. The researchers found out that the employees work especially with the following standard applications: Microsoft Office tools, Internet Explorer and the e-mail system Novell GroupWise. That is why a first research step was to develop sensors to observe events of these applications. In addition to the observation of these standard applications the final DYONIPOS prototype should record all electronic artifacts from the electronic record management system (ELAK), the file-system on the servers, the mail-system as well as the specific application KOMPASS, a system to administrate persons, resources and authorizations.

The implementation of the use-case is structured in three evaluation phases. These tests serve as basis to support the improvement of the functions of DYONIPOS e.g. by a continuous refinement of the rules to assign events to event blocks. In the first test phase of the pilot software ten key-users took part to support the work of the researchers. The test occurred over a period of five weeks from April to May 2007. Main objective of the first test was to gather detailed information on the key users. The preliminary data collection has been included the user input and the work content. Further objectives are to test and evaluate the recording and analysis module of the DYONIPOS proactive assistant. In addition to the test and the evaluation key users had also the possibility to express concrete requests concerning the functionality and graphical user interface of DYONIPOS. Therefore the key users had the chance to take part actively in the design process of the system. At this stage the prototype DYONIPOS was stored and implemented on the local hard disc of each personal computer of the participating key users. A central storage on the server has not been carried out. The employees were introduced in the software handling and to do a manual assignment of event blocks to tasks. The collected information will serve as training basis for the DYONIPOS Task recognizer. Furthermore the key users had the possibility to evaluate the functions and to document suggestions for improvement. The results of this first test was stored in log files and documented in test protocols and questionnaires.

3.1. The Application DYONIPOS

Figure 2 shows the graphical user interface of the DYONIPOS task recognizer window. Different flags allow the navigation between the different supplied resources and functionalities. At the screenshot the flag "Übersicht" is opened. At this flag all recorded events (e.g. mouse clicks and movements as well as keyboard input and system interactions) and event blocks are displayed at the top. Central the so called "InformationNeeds" are mapped. Only after detecting of events DYONIPOS starts with the identification of information needs and suggests next tasks, resources and experts. All identified resources were displayed in the bottom field. These are resources of the individual as well as of the organizational knowledge base. Furthermore the key user has the possibility to search actively for information in the iteratively generated resource repository by using the search field. This search field is displayed in the screenshot at the bottom next to the magnifying glass. At the flag "Experte" the name of the experts can be displayed or the specific topic, which the organization deals with. At other flags the adjustment of the DYONIPOS functionalities can be carried out, e.g. the deletion of knowledge, which is stored at the organizational knowledge base.

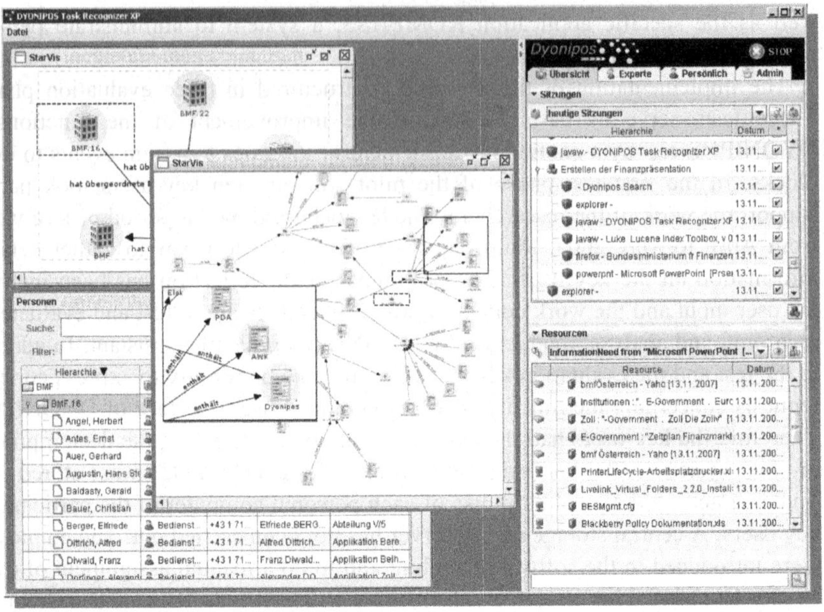

Fig. 2: Screenshot of the DYONIPOS Task Recognizer

3.2. The Results of the First Test Phase

Through evaluation of the logfiles, questionnaires and the test protocols it was possible to derive the following information and operating figures about the key user and about the DYONIPOS Task Recognizer: Typical activities which a key user implements are: project work, description and modelling of process, writing of protocols, compiling of statistics, participation in discussions, executive functions, searching in the Internet, providing of presentations, etc.

- A key-user performs the following activities without PC support: mental work, meetings, telephone calls and face to face discussions with other employees.
- A key-user uses the following tools to do the daily work: text processing tools, spreadsheet programs, presentation programs, web browsers and file explorer, e-mail and calendar, the electronic records management system (ELAK), different SAP systems, specific application programs, database and data mining tools, different information retrieval systems (Google or other special search applications) and occasionally image editing tools.

- A key-user often interrupts its activities because of: telephone calls, e-mails, individual spontaneous requests of other employees but also planned meetings.
- A key-user usually uses the following information sources: the Internet (basically Google), the documents stored on the hard disc on his own PC, the server-side data collection, the existing documents on the mailbox, paper based documents, meetings as well as vocational and private social networks.
- A key-user uses the following programs and IT applications to search for information: Internet search machines (Google and Wikipedia), SQL navigator, Windows search on PC and server, as well as the search function of the e-mail system.
- A key-user implements approximately 50% up to 90% of his/hers complete work by computer support (mean value: 74.4%).
- A key-user executes 25% to 90% of his/hers communication via computer (mean value: 60.6%).
- A key-user executes at least one task and maximal 15 tasks per day by computer (mean value: 7.8%).
- A key-user works parallel at least at 2 tasks up to 8 tasks (mean value: 5)
- A key-user daily spends between 2.1% and 60% of his/hers working time by accessing information (mean value: 16.1%).

A basic result of the evaluation is that key-users always work on several tasks at the same time. This information represents a challenge for DYONIPOS, because it is an objective of DYONIPOS to provide just-in-time information based on the context. Furthermore we found out that a key-user use different searching tools and search in very heterogeneous sources. An objective of DYONIPOS is to support the work of the user by proactive and context-sensitive information delivery. DYONIPOS searches for information in different repositories to support the user. DYONIPOS implements the function of a searching tool and creates cross-links between the context of different repositories to deliver existing information and new generated information. Using DYONIPOS the knowledge workers receive transparency over the existing sources of information. DYONIPOS gives additionally references about the relevance of the found search results, which includes all currently available information. The parallel implementation of the funded research project and the use-case project makes it possible to exchange ideas between research and practice constantly; this is useful for both projects. Furthermore the inclusion of all stakeholders [8] such as researchers, users, IT experts and also the staff council in the development process assures that the results of the research project DYONIPOS can and will be transformed optimally and in real-time into a practical application.

3.3. The Second Test Phase

The second test phase was started in Februar 2008. A fundamentally improved version of the prototype DYONIPOS which establishes an organizational knowledge base, with new functionalities and which also includes artifacts stored on server as well as electronic records is proved now. In the second test the former manual assignment of event blocks to tasks work automatically. The key-user just observes this assignment, by doing corrections of wrongly assigned event blocks and by confirmations of correctly assigned event blocks.

The second test has shown the assurance that it is not necessary to identify processes. It is enough to know on which task a knowledge worker works. Furthermore the agility of the system needs to be adequate. If the system is too agile, too much information will be found. This costs time and processing power. But if the system is too less agile, DYONIPOS finds too less ressources. The tuning of the system is a necessity.

3.4. Next Steps

Finally the third test phase starts approximately in April 2008. In this testing phase key-users will test the whole functionalities of DYONIPOS. This test will take 75 days. This third test will be closed with an evaluation and documentation of the use-case results in a final project report.

In 2008 the whole DG-IT or rather all 180 employees will take part on a final test of the prototype DYONIPOS. A Final evaluation will be done after one year of practical experience. Documentation and evaluation of this final test provides the basis for the decision whether DYONIPOS will be used in the DG-IT further on. In the same way the decision will be made whether DYONIPOS should be advanced to commercial tool or not.

References

1. Gärtner, T. A survey of kernels for structural data. SIKGKDD Explor. Newsl., ACM Press, 5, 49/58, 2003.
2. Kröll, M., Rath, A., Granitzer, M., Lindstaedt, S., Tochtermann, K. (2006). Contextual Retrieval in Knowledge Intensive Business Environments. GI-Workshop Information Retrieval 2006.
3. Kröll, M., Rath A., Weber, N., Lindstaedt, S., Granizer, M. (2007). Task Instance Classification via Graph Kernels, Mining and Learning with Graphs (MLG 07). Florenz, Italy.
4. Maier, R. (2005). Modeling Knowledge Work for the Design of Knowledge Infrastructures. Journal of Universal Computer Science 4, 11, 429-451.

5. Rath, A. (2007). A Low-Level Based Task And Process Support Approach for Knowledge-Intensive Business Environments. In Proceedings of the 5th International Conference on Enterprise Information System Doctoral Consortium (DCEIS 2007), 35-42. Madeira, Portugal.
6. Rath, A., Kröll, M., Andrews, K., Lindstaedt, S., Granitzer, M., Tochtermann, K. (2006). Synergizing Standard and Ad-Hoc Processes. Proceedings of 6th International Conference on Practical Aspects of Knowledge Management, LNCS Springer, Vienna (Austria).
7. Rath A., Kröll, M., Lindstaedt, S., Granitzer, M. (2007). Low-Level Event Relationship Discovery for Knowledge Work Support. 4th Conference on Professional Knowledge Management, ProKW2007 Productive Knowledge Work: Management and Technological Challenges. Potsdam, Germany, GITO-Verlag, Berlin.
8. Makolm, J., Orthofer, G. (2007). Holistic Approach, Stakeholder Integration and Trans-organizational Processes: Success Factors of FinanzOnline. In: E-Taxation: State & Perspectives, E-Government in the Field of Taxation: Scientific Basis, Implementation Strategies, Good Practice Examples, p.389-402, ISBN 978-3-85499-191-5, Schriftenreihe Informatik 21.
9. Schölkopf, B., Smola, A.J. (2000). Learning with Kernels Support Vector Machines, Regularization, Optimization, and Beyond. MIT Media Laboratory.
10. Tochtermann, K., Reisinger, D., Granitzer, M., Lindstaedt, S. (2006). Integrating Ad Hoc Processes and Standard Processes in Public Administrations. Knowledge transfer across Europe: 4th Eastern European eGov Days and 5th eGov Days. OCG Schriftenreihe Band 203, Wien.
11. Van der Aalst, Wil. M. P., De Michelis, G., Ellis, C.A. (1998). Workflow management: Net-based concepts, models, techniques and tools (wfm`98). In Computing Science Report 98/7.
12. Van der Aalst, Wil. M. P., Weske, M., Grünbauer, D. Case handling: a new paradigm for business process support. Data Knowl. Eng. 53(2), page 129-162, 2005.
13. Vapnik, V.N. (1995). The nature if statistical learning theory. Springer Verlag New York, Inc.
14. W3C webpage: http://www.w3.org/TR/owl-ref/#acknowledge, Accessed 28 January 2008.

A Community of Knowledge Management Practitioners: Mirroring Power across Social Worlds

Hiroko Wilensky, Norman Makoto Su, David Redmiles, and Gloria Mark

University of California, Irvine, USA, {hwilensk, normsu, redmiles, gmark}@uci.edu

Abstract: In our previous study, we focused on two spaces: a community of knowledge management (KM) practitioners and their respective work organizations. We found that the "community" largely existed to *legitimize* KM practices, rather than to *learn* KM practices. Our current study builds upon this work by uncovering how in fact power relationships in work organizations are transferred and mirrored into the community. Consequently, these relationships shape and define the community's processes: they set up boundaries of the community, reinforce the knowledge sharing practices among the members, and institutionalize community members' beliefs of KM. We have adopted Strauss's social world perspective to better understand how the actions and interactions outside of the community impact and mold the community.

Keywords: Knowledge management, Social worlds, Community of practice, Power, Aerospace industry

1. Introduction

For the past three years, we have been conducting an ethnographic investigation into a forum for knowledge management practitioners (KMPs) from the aerospace industry. According to their official website, this forum is a locale where "*leaders in knowledge management in industry (with a focus on aerospace industry) and academia come together to share, collaborate, and discuss.*" Coming from five different aerospace organizations, these KMPs participate in a quarterly face-to-face meeting called the "Mid West Aerospace Industry KM Exchange Community of Practice[1]" (hereafter abbreviated as the KM Exchange).

Our previous study (Su et al., 2007) revealed that a community (one labeled as a "community of practice") can have motivations that stem beyond the cultivation of an environment for mutual and reciprocal learning and supporting. Instead, the

[1] All names and locations in this paper have been anonymized.

Please use the following format when citing this chapter:

Wilensky, H., Su, N.M., Redmiles, D. and Mark, G., 2008, in IFIP International Federation for Information Processing, Volume 270; *Knowledge Management in Action*; Mark Ackerman, Rose Dieng-Kuntz, Carla Simone, Volker Wulf; (Boston: Springer), pp. 195–207.

KM Exchange was found to be a crucial legitimizing and affirming conduit for practitioners' KM practices in their respective work organizations. The KM Exchange served as a pulpit of sorts for its senior members to expound the worthiness of KM as a discipline of priority.

In this paper, we further explore the relationships among the members; in particular, we examine the role that *power* plays. We question how power relationships have influenced the boundaries of the community, knowledge sharing among community members and institutionalized beliefs of KM. We argue that power relations which exist in one's respective communities can be *transferred* and *mirrored* in new cross-organizational communities. In our analysis, we turn to the notion of social worlds explicated by Strauss (1978) as a way to understand how this community, despite its mantra of equalizing or flattening traditional hierarchical structures, is nevertheless influenced by the activities and experiences of the members in their work organizations as well as other interactions outside of the community, such as attending conferences and collaborating on KM projects.

Although members of the KM Exchange often call their forum a "community," their community has qualities distinctively different from well-known models of communities. Lave & Wenger's (1991a) communities of practice (CoP) is an immensely popular conceptual model of community among KM practitioners. This CoP theory posits that the mentor-pupil model is outmoded and stresses instead that learning occurs among peers and cohorts in a participant's periphery. Through *legitimate peripheral participation*, new members are able to move towards the core of a community, becoming experts or old-timers. KM practitioners view CoP as an ideal model to emulate in their organization. Countless books provide step-by-step instructions on "creating" CoP (e.g., Rumizen, 2002; Wenger, 2002).

It is our contention that KM practitioners tend to view a community as an isolated space for learning, knowledge sharing, and networking among its members (Dalkir, 2005). Brown & Duguid (2000), for example, describe CoP as tight-knit groups of people who work together directly. Lave & Wenger (1991) touch upon the need to expand the analysis of learning beyond the immediate context, but much of their work has focused squarely on one space and its social dimensions. For example, the analysis of meat cutters and an alcoholic support group primarily focus on the ongoing interactions of a single space.

We instead propose to see the KM Exchange as one of intertwined social worlds in which the members are involved. A social world (Strauss, 1978) is a collective unit of individuals with shared commitments who gather to perform a primary activity. Socials worlds are a highly fluid social structure, which constantly changes due to processes such as conflict, competition, negotiation, and exchange. Importantly, social worlds can intersect with other social worlds under a variety of conditions. Although anyone in a social world is associated with its actions, some members carry the power to decide which members are more "authentic" (see Section 3.2) via which social mechanism. Our analysis has shown that individuals who have the power to determine authenticity in work organizations have the power in the KM Exchange. These individuals play a crucial role as spokespersons: Latour (2005) notes that spokespersons "*speak for the group existence...all [groups] need some people defining who they are, what they should be, what they have been...justifying the groups' existence.*" We are attempting to uncover the processes by which spokespersons of organizations can become spokespersons of other organizations, thus reaffirming their appropriate role across multiple social worlds.

In this paper we first describe our field site setting and methodology. We then briefly describe the aerospace industry, followed by a recap of our previous study (Su et al., 2007) on the "rhetoric" of aerospace KMPs in the KM Exchange and in their respective workplaces. The next sections detail our new analysis incorporating the social world perspective. This mindset allows us to unravel the power relations that permeate from the work organizations into the KM Exchange community. Our central idea is that power structures emanating from multiple social worlds can reassemble themselves in new social worlds (or communities), dramatically defining the community's trajectory. This can transpire despite a community's mantra of equal sharing.

2. Methodology

Our data collection and analytical methods are steeped in the grounded theory (Strauss, 1998) practice of thematic generation. We carried out both participant observations and one-on-one interviews with members of the Midwest KM Exchange. It is a physical forum where aerospace employees interested in KM meet on a quarterly basis. Other members include people from universities and power companies. The meetings' physical location was rotated among the participants' organizations. The meetings usually lasted at least half a day (4.5 hours on average) and had a standard schedule of: 1) networking, 2) presentations about KM, 3) lunch plus networking, and 4) splitting up into small (roughly 5-10 people) break-out discussion groups concentrating on specific KM topics of interest. Interviewees were recruited at the KM Exchange and through snowball sampling.

This paper builds upon our previous dataset (Su et al., 2007), bringing it up to a total of eight meetings, three conferences, and 23 semi-structured interviews over three years. In this paper, we refer to the four founders of the KM Exchange as the *core* members. We call senior members who are designated as the representative of their company in the community the *focal* members. All the core members are also focal members.

3. Background: The Aerospace Industry

Compared to other businesses, the aerospace industry manufactures highly specialized technical components such as satellites, aircraft, and guided missiles. Only a few large companies have the technical competence and resources to create such products. Aerospace companies must seek out a uniquely skilled work force of scientists, engineers, and manufacturing workers. For security purposes, the export of aerospace goods is regulated by government agencies. An increase of global collaborations in the aerospace industry has led to new challenges in data sharing with government oversight (Lorell et al., 2002). As a result, aerospace companies have a culture of secretiveness and protectiveness of their intellectual property. Finally, there is a workforce "crisis" in the aerospace industry due to the loss of jobs from reduced defense budgets after the Cold War. According to the 2006 Aerospace Industries Association of America CEO's statement, the average age of manufacturing employees was 51 and 54 for engineers, with an estimated 27% of workers becoming eligible in 2008 (AIA, 2006).

3.1. Knowledge Management Practitioners in Aerospace

We now briefly summarize our findings about KM practitioners in the aerospace industry (Su et al., 2007). Our study examined the "rhetoric" of KMPs in their organizations and their community (the KM Exchange). By critically looking at how people talk and legitimize KM as a viable discipline in and out of their professional circles, we can describe how KMPs define KM and its usefulness. KMPs emphasize that KM is a way to *efficiently* manage knowledge: finding "lost" knowledge and eliminating "redundant" knowledge. The aerospace industry's special attributes make KM even more imperative; for example, the aerospace industry often hires people with rare talents (e.g., experts on Martian terrain). Losing such an employee is equated to losing knowledge. KM tools such as expert locators and KM practices such as CoP are regarded as *progressive* tools that are capable of solving knowledge issues. At the same time, KMPs are careful to set themselves apart from information technology (IT) personnel and tools (e.g., databases), noting that knowledge is not information and that knowledge is a far more complex and subtle entity (e.g., by delineating tacit and explicit knowledge). Moreover, KMP are personally equipped to understand the social nature of knowledge, having experience in social and organizational behavior (e.g., noting that software tools cannot be deployed without proper evaluation of a workplace's culture). Finally, KMPs argue that KM is even more appropriate for the aerospace industry in order to combat its secretive, counter-productive culture. KM is seen as a way to overcome a company environment where employees are mindful of sharing data, even among their peers, hence increasing company effectiveness.

We also observed KMPs "talking shop" in the KM Exchange. Despite the KM Exchange's own label as a community of practice, we found the community to be less about learning KM skills from peers and elders via legitimate peripheral participation, and more about learning how to "spread" the gospel of KM. In particular, we found the majority of discussions on and off-line to be about KM's legitimacy: people sharing their pains in getting the proper constituents to understand KM's value, how to embed KM throughout work processes at the organization, and how to establish KM as a reputable discipline. While disciplinary legitimacy was the usual topic at hand, we found that newbies[2] felt the community was stagnating—they were not learning enough about KM itself. The focal members, the oldies, wanted to promote, while newbies wanted to learn.

This disparity of motivations between the oldies and newbies leads us to the main focus of this paper. CoP are by far the most popular approach for fostering cross organizational sharing in the KM field. Books on cultivating or implementing CoP abound (Denning, 2005; Hasanali et al., 2002; Rumizen, 2002; Saint-Onge & Wallace, 2003; Wenger, 2002). At its heart, KM views CoP as a way to bring disparate groups together to foster sharing, thus, efficiently using knowledge and leading to increased company productivity. While the literature acknowledges that CoP require time and effort to implement, we feel that it often ignores the social structure inherent in the groups that CoP seek to bring together. Our previous study revealed that attributes from these groups can make so-called CoP very much different from Wenger's ideal. We now draw upon Strauss's social world model to allow us to explicate the community that the KM Exchange represents.

3.2. The Social World Perspective

According to Strauss (1978), social worlds have a primary activity and sites where these activities occur. Notably, Strauss describes a social world as a fluid and dynamic entity, often intersecting with other social worlds. Actions and interactions in one social world may significantly impact other social worlds. For example, Mark & Poltrock (2003) note that technology adoption can transfer from one social world to another: they describe how a virtual meeting system was adopted across different social worlds, changing in its usage (e.g., from being a teaching tool to a document sharing application) and its acceptance (e.g., rejection or acceptance by gatekeepers in social worlds). In discussing the analytical practicality of this theory, Strauss describes several focal points of interests that arise when using a social world's perspective. However, in this paper, we focus on *authenticity*. Authenticity pertains "*to the quality of action, as well as to judgments of which acts are more essential.*" Intertwined with authenticity is the

[2] Newcomers and focal members are used interchangeably with newbies and oldies, respectively.

issue of power. Those who wield power in the social world can decide which members are authentic. Moreover, those in power decide how newcomers are initiated into the social world. Strauss also stresses the importance of a social world's history. He admonishes those that "*focus on contemporary life while either avoiding history or using it as a backdrop for the analysis of ongoing organizations and processes*." Indeed, as we will discuss, a social world's history can have dramatic effects on future social worlds. Analogously, a social world's history of power can elucidate current power structures.

We argue that, sometimes, what one ends up doing by combining or bringing together multiple social groups is a sort of mirroring or replication of power structures. In other words, power structures inherent in the social worlds end up being transferred over and reestablished/reinforced in new social worlds.

4. A Social World Perspective into Power in the KM Exchange

Building upon our previous work, we now focus our analysis on how *power features* of social worlds have shaped the KM Exchange. In particular, we see how power relations in social worlds have played a role in 1) the founders, 2) the newcomers, 3) disparity of motivations between "oldies" and "newbies," and 4) delineating KM for members, resulting in the institutionalization of beliefs on KM within the community. The KM Exchange's power is largely concentrated in the core members who authenticate (via social mechanisms) the activities in the KM Exchange.

Social worlds can be in countless discernible forms: temporary or long-lived; small or large; local or international; emergent or established; virtual or physical; and with tight boundaries or permeable boundaries. Through the analysis of our field data, we identified these key social worlds surrounding the KM Exchange: the established aerospace corporations, the local universities, the master's degree KM program which one of the core members helped found, various KM conferences, KM project collaborations among some focal and senior members, and the tight-knit circle of the core members.

4.1. Founders across the Work Organization & the KM Exchange

The core members cemented their power in the KM Exchange by being the progenitors of the community. This establishment of power and leadership in KM in fact is a reflection of their own initiatives in the social worlds of their workplaces. All the core members were responsible for starting the KM team/department or were appointed as the head of KM efforts in their respective work organizations. Two core members brought up their pet knowledge-based projects to their upper management and these projects eventually morphed into a larger KM initiative, whereas others were hired by the corporation specifically to spearhead a new KM effort. One core member explained about his company's search for someone who could lead KM: "*The committee had certain level of effectiveness and tried to move initiative forward, but there was no single individual who was accountable…um...that could really lead the group and lead the broad group, not so much built an empire of knowledge management, but really coordinate across the company, great diversity of different organizations of the company to get everybody to kind of get move into the same direction effectively.*" Thus, these core members represented *the* leadership for establishing and encouraging KM in their organizations.

A number of small, short-lived social worlds existed prior to the formation of the KM Exchange, and these temporary social worlds eventually led to a tight-knit social world of the core members. The core members founded the KM Exchange after several small encounters at KM-styled conferences and subsequent lunch gatherings. Through these informal get-togethers, the core members formed a tight-knit, if not exclusive, group of KM leaders. Throughout our interviews, the core members described a special bond that existed between them: "*It's the four of us <laugh> who constantly bug each other…I think there's a closer connection. Like, I mean, Sam asked [me a KM question] at ten o'clock at night, and I didn't even hesitate to respond.*"

Despite the short existence of the KM Exchange, when we interviewed our informants, many of them could not accurately recall how the KM Exchange had initially started. Indeed, our informants provided us a number of curious variations on how the KM Exchange came into existence. The interpretations ranged from the simple, assertive answers of "*I created it*" and "*I founded the community*" by two core members, to the answer that it was a spin off from a preexisting KM forum in a particular aerospace company in which another core member was in charge of the KM team. These contradictory stories are indicative of the importance the creators of the KM Exchange place on holding power not only in their own organizations, but also in their discipline's cross-organizational community. As forerunners of KM in their own social worlds, the core members seek to reestablish their priority and repute in the KM Exchange as well.

4.2. Newbie Initiation into the Community

As we mentioned, the core members seek to establish a new community that nevertheless mirrors their place in the power hierarchy in their respective home organizations. They can continue to assert their power by creating a population of newcomers in the KM Exchange primarily from their own subordinates. Newcomers join the KM Exchange by being invited by the focal members or senior members. The majority of the newcomers usually work for the focal members, with the rest being students who are attending a KM master's degree program at a local university (which one of the core members helped establish;

this core member is also a newly appointed adjunct faculty in this university). A newcomer explained to us that becoming a KM Exchange member is really an informal job requirement: "*Um…when I joined the group, they said, 'Hey, there is a meeting and you are going.' <laughs>.*" Other newcomers told us that they were invited to attend the KM Exchange by the focal members: "*I was pretty much asked to go and do it back in 2000*"; "*The KM staff are invited, but it is optional.*" Because the focal members are authoritative figures in their work organizations, recruiting the new KM Exchange members was relatively easy for them. Moreover, because these newcomers were subordinates, they often felt obligated to go.

Although we had initially expected the KM Exchange to foster dynamic and frequent interactions as well as help the members establish a vibrant social network, we were surprised to learn that the majority of newcomers and some senior members had little or no interactions with other members once a meeting concluded. One newcomer noted that off-line communication (i.e., not during meetings) among peers was done only *through* core members: "*Because I talked to several people at the meeting and I would like to be able to contact them again…and I normally have to go through someone like Thomas or Ken [core members] to get information.*" One senior member noted that networking is the focal member's job: "*I don't have the time to be out there building relationships. Ken who is the higher level, that's his responsibility. That's his task to be building the relationships, making the connections, providing that for us. The rest of us—I personally don't do that because I don't have the time I just have too much on my mind.*" In contrast to the oldies, newbies had little connection with each other. While we observed a very tight-knit social world of the core members, we did not similarly observe a social world of newbies emerging from the KM Exchange: certainly, we observed interactions of newbies at meetings occurring between members of the same work organization, but little between newbies of different organizations. One might conjecture that hobnobbing with the boss carries the same subtle power dynamics as hobnobbing with the boss's own cohorts/peer. The social worlds and their hierarchical structure from which the newbies and oldies come from thus in some sense get replicated into the KM Exchange, possibly hindering legitimate peripheral participation among newbies.

4.3. Disparity Between the Newbies and Oldies: Stagnation

While in its nascent stages, membership boundaries of the KM Exchange were a concern: who could become members? During the meetings, boundary issues were often debated upon. Members asked about inviting the local KM master's degree program students which included some international students and KM practitioners from non-aerospace industries—this raised security issues. The debates would always end when some senior members voiced their opinion that the community should remain only within the aerospace industry. One senior member said, "*Our identity is 'aerospace' KM. Better to focus on 'aerospace.'*" All the core members seemed content with the boundaries of the community: "*I'd like to keep it an aerospace focus.*"

On the other hand, our interviews revealed that newcomers and some senior members had different ideas about the boundaries. Newbies sometimes remarked on the domineering personalities of the core members: "*Sometimes, the meetings are dominated by strong characters,*" or "*I worry that we're going to hear from the same people over and over again.*" These power relations played out in disappointing meeting content for many newbies. One junior KM staff member explained why she didn't attend recent meetings: "*Because a lot of them are really repetitive. That was good for the first maybe three or four [meetings] and after a while people just started talking about the same things over and over again. And then…so I was kind of losing interest <laughs> because I'm not learning anything new at these things.*" Another newbie gave a lukewarm answer about the meeting's usefulness: "*I mean, I don't find any meeting extremely helpful. They are all somewhat useful. I haven't found any of them to…if I hadn't attended, you know, my outlook on knowledge management and what I do would be not much different.*" One senior member informed us: "*My opinion is [the KM Exchange is] a little stagnated. You know, we can share so much for so long. I think we need to do…we might venture out and include more people.*" This sense of stagnation in the community reveals a disparity between those whose desire is to learn KM and those who need to legitimize KM practices to stay alive. In other words, the focal members have dictated the KM Exchange's content, which seems to serve a purpose contradictory to the CoP's supposed benefits.

At the second quarterly meeting in 2007, the focal members announced that they would make one of the quarterly meetings a conference open to other industries. This idea was already mentioned by one of the core members in September 2006 at our interview; therefore, it is not evident whether this core member reshaped the boundaries of the KM Exchange on his own cognizance or stagnation led to this decision. Nevertheless, the expansion of the KM Exchange serves to strength the core members' place in a reciprocal manner. One focal member commented on the expansion: "*They want to grow the group. There are a couple pressures that make them want to grow the group…the general theme for growing the group is that they want knowledge management to be the idea to spread. And at least for the term to be recognized [in their work organizations] more, what I would call legitimizing it.*" In other words, expansion of the group's boundaries allows the KM Exchange to become more reputable and therefore further legitimize KM in their own organizations.

One core member invited a professor from a local university whom he met at a conference. Because of this professor's enthusiastic and assertive nature and the prestigious nature of his social world (academia), he quickly moved to the center of the KM Exchange. He hosted a quarterly meeting and a conference sponsored by the KM Exchange that featured presenters and participants from other industries (e.g., construction engineering and high-tech) at his university.

4.4. The Delineation of KM by the Focal Members

Although the KM Exchange proclaims that it is a locale for its members to share their knowledge on KM, we found knowledge sharing practices were actually largely shaped by the focal members.

The majority of the members in KM Exchange work for or their work is associated with the focal members. Knowledge of KM was passed down from the focal members to their associates and subordinates at their work places. The focal members would impart a variety of KM tools and techniques via lists of books to read and types of conferences to attend. For instance, one newcomer explained with admiration on how her boss is knowledgeable of KM: *"Sam has a library of wonderful knowledge, lots of knowledge, all kind of books…he got, he basically gives us all copies of different books from that, wherever he quoted <laugh> wherever he quoted, anything he finds, anything good books on KM practices, he makes sure we all get that."* Another newcomer described how she learned KM at her workplace: *"Just listening to Thomas. Every time, he would pull together like an impromptu meeting—I used to go [to] all [of them]—every time he gave a briefing to someone explaining knowledge management and what the knowledge management office is going to do, what do they project for the future, I would attend those…Book[s], he gave me lots of, lots of books to read <laughs>. Yeah, there was a lot of that."* The focal members essentially defined KM for their subordinates in their organizations.

The focal members also prescribed which KM conferences their members were to attend. For example, the East Coast Knowledge Forum was a conference mentioned by some of the core members in our interviews. Many members also attend APQC conferences. One member described his experience at one of the conferences: *"I met people like Larry Prusak and Hubert Saint-Onge at different events. Sam [my boss] had me three months into my knowledge management <laughs> career, sent me to East Coast Knowledge Forum in [city] to represent our company. I was really kind of blown away, but I got to meet the who's who in knowledge management at that particular conference and it was very enlightening."*

Not only is the "curriculum" outlined by the focal members in the workplaces, but also in the KM Exchange. The community's meetings are planned exclusively by the focal members. At each meeting, either during lunch or breakout discussions, the focal members gather at a separate exclusive table to discuss future meetings and the future direction of the KM Exchange. In between the quarterly meetings, the focal members also exchange emails with each other in order to determine the schedule and content of the presentation topics. Members were often allowed to vote upon a set of topics they wished to discuss in the final break-out discussions sections closing the KM Exchange sessions.

Accordingly, we observed some beliefs on KM have become institutionalized within the community. It became difficult for newbies to oppose these prevailing beliefs. Often, newbies accept these beliefs without questioning. Two of the most common beliefs on KM we heard from our informants and at the quarterly meetings were: 1) the aging workforce issues *will* cause a serious knowledge drain and 2) the aerospace culture *needs* to be changed to a sharing culture. From our data, the informants' discussions on these two issues seemed too uniform and scripted for us, leading us to wonder whether this may be the result of the focal members' delineation of the KM Exchange. For example, statements from our data set like *"people are retiring left and right…that's going to cause a big hole"* by one newbie are typical with regards to the first belief. Contrary to such prevailing accounts, we found varied opinions in other arenas. For instance, AARP (formerly American Association for Retired Persons) recently reported that people often plan to work beyond their retirement age due to various reasons (Brown, 2003). Moreover, at a conference sponsored by the KM Exchange, one presenter from a high-tech company dismissed the aging workforce crisis by questioning the actual value of the technological knowledge that retiring workers have, given the rapidly changing nature of the engineering fields: *"Today's technology is different from yesterday's technology."* We are not attempting to prove that the focal members' KM beliefs are incorrect here; rather, we believe these counterarguments show that such KM views are contestable, and the little variety in opinions among the KM Exchange members on these views are indicative of the institutionalization of KM beliefs by those in power.

KM "knowledge" and techniques are passed down from the focal members to their associates and subordinates at their work places. In turn, the KM Exchange played a role in reinforcing the power the focal members have in defining and delineating KM for its members and subordinates. This control over the authenticity—the judgment of the *quality* of actions—is a key shaper and force for institutionalizing the KM Exchange's content.

5. Conclusion

In our previous study, we learned that the KM Exchange exists largely for legitimization rather than for learning. Legitimization of KM practices was crucial for the KM practitioners' survival in their respective work organizations. In our current study, we extended our analysis to focus on the power relationships within the KM Exchange and the social worlds surrounding this forum. We adopted Strauss's notion of social worlds to better understand these power alliances. We analyzed how power has impacted the boundaries of the KM exchange, its knowledge sharing practices, and finally the members' beliefs on KM.

Following Strauss's (1978) call for a historical perspective on social phenomenon, we found it imperative for us to examine the narrative of how past events intersecting multiple social worlds has lead to the formation of the KM Exchange and its current power characteristics. What we found was that the power structures extant in the social worlds of some members become mirrored into new social worlds. Being leaders in their own respective work organizations, these same leadership characteristics helped the core members form the KM Exchange. As authoritative figure in their organizations, the focal members brought their subordinates into the KM Exchange, thus reinforcing their authority in the community. Subjected to predefined "courses" of study, new members learned KM primarily from their focal member at their workplaces. This learning practice is then reinstated at the KM Exchange whose content is again largely shaped by the focal members. While new members often look up to the focal members with reverence and admiration (viewing them as authorities, just as they view their own boss as one), they also soon notice that the forum is becoming stagnated, leading to little learning of new KM techniques or skills. We also observed newbies accept without question the beliefs on KM passed down from the focal members. Some beliefs on KM are nearly without variation among the members and quickly become institutionalized within the community. This makes these beliefs difficult for newbies to contest. These events shaped and defined the KM Exchange into its current form, a *reflection* of discipline spokespersons' power within work organizations.

The hierarchical structure of the KM Exchange is distinctively different from the community of practice model. KM typically view CoP as a closed, isolated space for learning, knowledge sharing, and networking. KMPs often see CoP as a democratizing entity, leveling out chains of command. Yet, we ascertained that power relationships in and out of the KM Exchange dramatically shaped the community itself and its members' beliefs on KM. We argue that to truly understand a community, one needs to examine the actions and interactions in the social worlds beyond the community and how these social worlds intersect. In particular, when "implementing" CoP, one may end up merely transferring and mirroring extant social worlds, leading to little legitimate peripheral learning, but the strengthening of already existing power relations.

References

AIA: Statement by Mr. John W. Douglass President & Chief Executive Officer Aerospace Industries Association of America (2006). Available via www.aia-aerospace.org/aianews/speeches/2006/statement_douglass_061306.pdf. Accessed 28 Mar 2008.

Brown, J.S., and Duguid, P.: The social life of information. Harvard Business School Press, Boston (2003).

Brown, K.: Staying ahead of the curve 2003: The AARP in retirement study (2003). Available via www.aarp.org/research. Accessed 4 Feb 2008.

Dalkir, K.: Knowledge management in theory and practice. Butterworth-Heinemann, Burlington, MA (2005).

Denning, S.: The leader's guide to storytelling: Mastering the art and discipline of business narrative. Jossey-Bass, San Francisco (2005).

Hasanali, F., Hubert, C., Newhouse, B., O'Dell, C., Westal, W., et al.: Communities of practice: A guide for your journey to knowledge management best practice. American Productivity & Quality Center, Houston (2002).

Latour, B.: Reassembling the social: An introduction to actor-network-theory. Oxford University Press, New York (2005).

Lave, L. and Wenger, E.: Practice, person, social world. In H. Daniels (Ed.), An introduction to Vygotsky, pp.143- 150. Routledge, New York (1991).

Lave, L. and Wenger, E.: Situated learning: Legitimate peripheral participation. Cambridge University Press, Cambridge, UK (1991a).

Lorell, M.A., Lowell, J., Moore, R.M., Greenfield, V.,Vlachos, K., et al.: Going global? U.S. government policy and the defense aerospace industry. RAND Corporation, Washington D.C. (2002).

Mark, G., and Poltrock, S.: Shaping technology across social worlds: groupware adoption in a distributed organization. Proc. ACM Conf. Supporting Group Work GROUP'03, 284-293 (2003).

Rumizen, M. C.: The complete idiot's guide to knowledge management. Alpha Books, Indianapolis, IN (2002).

Saint-Onge, H., and Wallace, D.: Leveraging communities of practice for strategic advantage. Butterworth-Heinemann, Burlington: MA (2003).

Strauss, A.: A social world perspective. Studies in symbolic interactions, 1(1), 119-128 (1978).

Strauss, A., and Corbin, J.: Basics of qualitative research: techniques and procedures for developing grounded theory. SAGE Publications, Thousand Oaks: CA (1998).

Su, N., Wilensky, H., Redmiles, D., and Mark, G.: The gospel of knowledge management in and out of a professional community. Proc. ACM Conf. Supporting Group Work GROUP' 07, 196-207 (2007).

Wenger, E., McDermott, R., and Snyder, W. M.: Cultivating communities of practice. Harvard Business School Press, Boston (2002).

Author Index